Social History in Per...

General Editor: Jerem...

Social History in Perspective is a series of in-depth studies of the many topics in social, cultural and religious history for students. They also give the student clear surveys of the subject and present the most recent research in an accessible way.

PUBLISHED

John Belchem   *Popular Radicalism in Nineteenth-Century Britain*
Sue Bruley   *Women in Britain since 1900*
Simon Dentith   *Society and Cultural Forms in Nineteenth-Century England*
Harry Goulbourne   *Race Relations in Britain since 1945*
Tim Hitchcock   *English Sexualities, 1700–1800*
Sybil M. Jack   *Towns in Tudor and Stuart Britain*
Helen M. Jewell   *Education in Early Modern England*
Alan Kidd   *State, Society and the Poor in Nineteenth-Century England*
Hugh McLeod   *Religion and Society in England, 1850–1914*
Donald M. MacRaild   *Irish Migrants in Modern Britain, 1750–1922*
Christopher Marsh   *Popular Religion in the Sixteenth Century*
Michael A. Mullett   *Catholics in Britain and Ireland, 1558–1829*
R. Malcolm Smuts   *Culture and Power in England, 1585–1685*
John Spurr   *English Puritanism, 1603–1689*
W. B. Stephens   *Education in Britain, 1750–1914*
Heather Swanson   *Medieval British Towns*
David Taylor   *Crime, Policing and Punishment in England, 1750–1914*
N. L. Tranter   *British Population in the Twentieth Century*
Ian D. Whyte   *Scotland's Society and Economy in Transition, c.1500–c.1760*

FORTHCOMING

Eric Acheson   *Late Medieval Economy and Society*
Ian Archer   *Rebellion and Riot in England, 1360–1660*
Jonathan Barry   *Religion and Society in England, 1603–1760*
A. L. Beier   *Early Modern London*
Andrew Charlesworth   *Popular Protest in Britain and Ireland, 1650–1870*
Richard Connors   *The Growth of Welfare in Hanoverian England,
1723–1793*
Geoffrey Crossick   *A History of London from 1800 to 1939*
Alistair Davies   *Culture and Society, 1900–1995*
Martin Durham   *The Permissive Society*
Peter Fleming   *Medieval Family and Household England*
David Fowler   *Youth Culture in the Twentieth Century*
Malcolm Gaskill   *Witchcraft in England, 1560–1760*
Peter Gosden   *Education in the Twentieth Century*
S. J. D. Green   *Religion and the Decline of Christianity in Modern Britain,
1880–1980*
Paul Griffiths   *English Social Structure and the Social Order, 1500–1750*

Titles continued overleaf

List continued from previous page

Anne Hardy   *Health and Medicine since 1860*
Steve Hindle   *The Poorer Sort of People in Seventeenth-Century England*
David Hirst   *Welfare and Society, 1832–1939*
Anne Kettle   *Social Structure in the Middle Ages*
Peter Kirby and S. A. King   *British Living Standards, 1700–1870*
Arthur J. McIvor   *Working in Britain 1880–1950*
Anthony Milton   *Church and Religion in England, 1603–1642*
Christine Peters   *Women in Early Modern Britain, 1450–1660*
Barry Reay   *Rural Workers, 1830–1930*
Richard Rex   *Heresy and Dissent in England, 1360–1560*
John Rule   *Labour and the State, 1700–1875*
Pamela Sharpe   *Population and Society in Britain, 1750–1900*
Benjamin Thompson   *Feudalism or Lordship and Politics in Medieval England*
R. E. Tyson   *Population in Pre-Industrial Britain, 1500–1750*
Garthine Walker   *Crime, Law and Society in Early Modern England*
Andy Wood   *The Crowd and Popular Politics in Early Modern England*

Please note that a sister series, *British History in Perspective*, is available which covers all the key topics in British political history.

Social History in Perspective
Series Standing Order
ISBN 0–333–71694–9 hardcover
ISBN 0–333–69336–1 paperback

(*outside North America only*)

You can receive future titles in this series as they are published by placing a standing order. Please contact your bookseller or, in case of difficulty, write to us at the address below with your name and address, the title of the series and the ISBN quoted above.

Customer Services Department, Macmillan Distribution Ltd
Houndmills, Basingstoke, Hampshire RG21 6XS, England

WOMEN IN BRITAIN SINCE 1900

Sue Bruley

First published in Great Britain 1999 by
MACMILLAN PRESS LTD
Houndmills, Basingstoke, Hampshire RG21 6XS and London
Companies and representatives throughout the world

A catalogue record for this book is available from the British Library.

ISBN 0–333–61838–6 hardcover
ISBN 0–333–61839–4 paperback

 First published in the United States of America 1999 by
ST. MARTIN'S PRESS, INC.,
Scholarly and Reference Division,
175 Fifth Avenue, New York, N.Y. 10010

ISBN 0–312–22375–7

Library of Congress Cataloging-in-Publication Data
Bruley, Sue.
Women in Britain since 1900 / Sue Bruley.
p. cm. — (Social history in perspective)
Includes bibliographical references and index.
ISBN 0–312–22375–7 (cloth)
1. Women—Great Britain—History—20th century. I. Title.
II. Series.
HQ1593.B78 1999
305.4'0941'0904—dc21   99–18545
                                                   CIP

© Sue Bruley 1999

This book is printed on paper suitable for recycling and made from fully managed and
sustained forest sources.

10   9   8   7   6   5   4   3   2   1
08 07 06 05 04 03 02 01 00 99

Printed in Hong Kong

CONTENTS

ACKNOWLEDGEMENTS

The completion of this book has been a long haul over several years during which many people and organizations have helped me along the way. As I cannot mention them all by name my first duty is to say thank you to everyone who has helped with this project. Second, I would like to thank my oral contributors, including the use I made of the Oral History Archive, Southampton City Council. Third, I owe thanks to the staff of the Department of Documents, Imperial War Museum, London, and the research division of Brixton Library for their co-operation. My grateful thanks also to all those who gave permission for me to quote from unpublished papers. Every possible effort has been made to trace copyright holders. Where this has not been successful, I would be very happy to include them in future editions of the book. I have made extensive use of the inter-library loan service at the Frewen Library, University of Portsmouth, and I would like to thank them for their very efficient service. Also thanks to the Equal Opportunities Commission for their prompt response to all my enquiries. Elizabeth Crawford and Jane Bell, specialist secondhand booksellers, have also sent me regular supplies from their excellent catalogues. Other people have helped in different ways. Jeannie Sharpe suggested the title for Chapter 2. Helena Cole guided me to the political statistics in Chapter 6. Students of my courses on 'Feminism' and 'Women, War and Social Change' at Portsmouth also provided me with stimulating insights. I owe particular thanks to Ligia Kasanin, Den Barry, Jacqueline Smith, Tracey Legge James and Jonathan Hamill. All my colleagues in the School of Social and Historical Studies have been very supportive during this period. I have also profited from a sabbatical semester from Portsmouth for which I am extremely grateful. I have been working in the area of 'feminist history' since the late 1970s. During this time I have benefited, along with hundreds of others, from the help and support of Anna Davin, whose unstinting encouragement of feminist history has been a great inspiration. Thanks Anna, from all of us. I would also like to take this opportunity to say a public thank you to Jane Lewis and Jeffrey Weeks for their path-breaking work. I must also acknowledge some more personal debts. The love, support and encouragement of my parents, Vi Bruley and the late Joe Bruley, have been one of the great features of my life. I could have achieved nothing without them and to them I dedicate this book. I am also grateful to all my friends who have listened patiently to my moans and groans about the book over the years and who have given me valuable advice and support, especially Brenda Kirsch, Siri Lowe, Martin Durham, Jane Garratt, Mari Reynolds, Jane Elliot, Sue Laurence, Marie MacNay and John Shiers. Jane Gardner has provided childcare and other domestic back-up for the last seven years. Words cannot fully express what I owe to her. My final thank you is to Barry Edwards for sorting out so many of my technical problems. Without him this book would not have seen the light of day. The very last word of all is for my children who have too often been told, 'Don't ask me to do it – I'm trying to write a book!' Now that the book is written and it's time to let go, it's actually quite hard to do it, but when I think about Eric, Charlotte and Rowan I know that everything has its place.

Sue Bruley

INTRODUCTION

An integral part of 'New Wave' feminism of the 1970s was a realization that the dominant historical discourses were male centred and defined and that women were either marginalized or invisible. Since then a great deal of work has been done to recast what we know as 'history' to include recognition of gender difference and to record the changing lives of women. This project has explicitly rejected any essentialist view of femininity. Joan Scott, Denise Riley and others have shown the need to historicize gender.[1] This enables us to view feminine identity as an historical construction which has been malleable and shifting over time, constantly being reworked and renegotiated, adapting to changing pressures and challenges. As we approach the end of the twentieth century it is apparent that there has been a transformation in femininity. It seems, therefore, an appropriate point to take stock of where we are at, to sum up 'women's century of change'. What did it mean to be a woman in 1900, how does it differ today and how did these changes come about? The aim of this book is to answer these questions by drawing on (selected) primary sources and specialist secondary texts to create a synthesis which will give us an overview of twentieth-century femininity in Britain.

I have to confess to a personal element in writing this book. My maternal grandmother, Daisy Oakham, was born in 1883; her youngest daughter Violet, my mother, was born in 1923; I was born in 1951 and my older daughter Charlotte was born in 1984. We four women traverse the century. Coming into maturity at either ends of the century, Daisy and Charlotte tell us a great deal about the changing lives of women in Britain. Daisy was born into a labouring family in rented rooms in Fulham, west London. She worked 'in service' after an elementary education and had moved to factory work by the time of her marriage to a carriage-hand

1

in 1906. Once married, her life revolved around the needs of her growing family. She had nine children, seven of whom survived into adulthood. The family only had two bedrooms between them: consequently beds were always shared. Money was an ever present problem. Daisy went out cleaning and did other casual work typical of women in her situation. Her life, both at work and in the home, was circumscribed by the boundaries of gender division of her time. Once married, her husband was held in awe and respect by both Daisy and the children. But beneath the outward appearance of submission she often resorted to devious means to exert her will. Daisy's great-granddaughter, Charlotte, was born almost exactly a century later only a few miles from Fulham and has benefited from the unprecedented rise in living standards over the century. Material want does not dominate her life as it did that of Daisy. Charlotte has her own bedroom, has enjoyed several foreign holidays and keeps up with her peer group by wearing the latest in teenage fashion. Unlike Daisy, she does not see a life of domesticity stretching out ahead of her. She will almost certainly stay at school until she is 18, attend university and establish financial independence and a professional career, perhaps having one or two children on the way. Charlotte does not hesitate to stand up to any other member of the family when she feels she needs to defend her interests. All three children receive equal treatment so her older brother does not enjoy any privileges which will not be bestowed on her, and she is not asked to undertake any domestic work which is not required of her brother.

So far we have referred only to a collective identity of 'woman' and without this unity this project would founder. But clearly within the category of 'woman', difference must be acknowledged. It is obvious from the above that the life of Daisy Oakham was as much marked by class division as it was gender. My particular family has been upwardly mobile, as I was able to take advantage of the post-war increased access to higher education and enter university and subsequently gain secure professional employment. Therefore my children undoubtedly live out a middle-class lifestyle. Class must play a major role in any attempt to reconstruct women's lives over time. Here it must be acknowledged that, without entering into all its complexities, class has also changed over the century. It is my view, however, that there has been throughout the century a recognizable working class, albeit in changing form, and I make no apologies for centring this book around the experiences of these ordinary working women. In addition, I am conscious of the danger of generalizing from the experiences of white women when, from the late 1940s, we have had substantial immigration of women from other ethnic groups. The last two chapters have attempted to chart some of the experiences of West Indian and Asian women in Britain. The emergence of a lesbian identity and its changes over the century has also been sketched out. Recognition has been given to age differences by the charting of generational patterns. Finally, where particular examples are cited, attempts have been made to use evidence from as many different geographic regions as possible.

The organization of this text could have been either thematic or chronological. Both strategies have disadvantages. I have chosen to give primacy to context, to divide the book into chronological chapters and to further divide each chapter thematically. Each period has a recognized unity and coherence which will, I hope, be helpful to students. The reader should bear in mind, however, that the divisions between these chronological periods are not as fixed as they appear. In reality there are no rigid divisions between periods, only the seamless web of history. The war years have been given particular emphasis as these were times when accepted notions of femininity were most challenged, and detailed treatment is necessary. The war chapters should not be read in isolation, however, as the impact of both wars reaches well into the post-war years.

Ultimately, the overriding rationale for the chronological approach is that it is my intention to locate women firmly within the overall history of the period. It is, therefore, a 'woman-centred' history of Britain in the twentieth century. Critics may oppose this approach, arguing that we have to focus on gender as a whole, masculinity as well as femininity. I fully acknowledge that 'women's history' in isolation is not a meaningful concept. In writing this history, therefore, I have inevitably written about changes in masculinity. The dynamic between masculinity and femininity is such that one cannot explain changes in one without reference to the other. But, beyond this, the central focus of the book is clearly set on female agency and female experience. In doing this I am recognizing that this text may have a political, as well as academic, currency. Every movement is empowered by a sense of its own history and to this extent my purpose is to give women a collective sense of their recent past. This text is intended primarily as a survey for those new to the subject. Given the need to keep the book to a manageable size (and therefore cost) the emphasis has been on a broad-brush treatment of major themes. I am aware that many areas and themes have had to be omitted and others could have been more extensively developed. I have concentrated on major developments in the social, political, economic, and to a lesser extent cultural, history of women in these years. Readers who have grasped an awareness of these broad themes will then be ready to tackle more in-depth specialist work which is beyond the scope of this text. In concentrating my attention in the way described I have been guided by several principles. The first has already been stated: my major focus has been on the experiences of working-class women. Middle- and upper-class women have been given less attention. Likewise, there is some coverage of 'stars' and celebrity women but they are not central. On the other hand, women in collective action constitutes a dominant theme throughout, particularly feminist movements where women have explicitly organized as women for feminist or socialist-feminist objectives. In addition I have tried, whenever possible, to weave personal testimony into the narrative, to bring a generalized account to life by relating it to individual experience. I am also aware of the danger of losing reader interest by overburdening the text with statistics and 'official' information. Consequently, I have tried to keep such material to a minimum.

My final guiding principle is that I have stuck rigidly to the brief of a country study. This was necessary for reasons of space and to maintain coherence, but I am cognisant of the limitations of such an approach. By looking at one country in isolation it is not possible to follow through the international connections: British women in India; GI brides in the USA; women emigrants to Australia in the 1950s and 1960s; the lives of Asian women before they came to Britain in the 1960s and 1970s, and so on. Neither have I been able to compare the British women's movement with women's movements abroad. Nor have I examined in depth the international influences acting on British women. Fortunately, we already have one major study of British and American women.[2] I hope very much that readers will not study British women in isolation but will seek out similar texts covering other countries and international themes. I am very much aware that this book is a mere part of a much broader picture.

1

THE BITTER CRY OF OUTCAST WOMEN, 1900–1914

The years between the turn of the century and the First World War were ones of rapid social change and upheaval. Internationally, the once dominant British economy was increasingly under threat from new industrial powers, such as the USA, the newly unified Germany and Japan. With the British Empire at its height, notions of colonial domination and racial superiority form an inescapable aspect of the age. Imperial pomp and splendour, and rising living standards for many, masked the enduring misery of the underclass. The rise of social science and investigation uncovered wretched living conditions for as many as a third of the population. Many of these researches, such as Maud Pember Reeves' study of Lambeth, *Round About a Pound a Week* and Lady Bell's study of Middlesborough, *At the Works* contain much valuable material concerning working-class women.[1] An increasingly interventionist state introduced a major period of social reform. Although the origins of this movement are complex, it certainly had more to do with nationalism than any desire to ameliorate the lives of the poor.

This time of 'inherited traditions' also witnessed major cleavages in the social fabric. The rise of labour and collective action led to a vigorous and assertive trade union movement. Irish nationalism, with its incessant demand for Home Rule, was also continually on the boil. Finally, the women's suffrage movement formed one of the largest popular movements ever known in Britain. Also of historical significance was the declining birthrate.

The trend towards smaller families, discernible in the middle classes from the 1860s, continued throughout these years. The concept of voluntary motherhood among the working classes, however, did not have a decisive impact until the inter-war years. The title of this chapter, taken from a late nineteenth-century book about outcast London, seems no less apt to describe women in this period.[2] The remarkable publications of the Co-operative Women's Guild, *Life as We Have Known It* and, *Maternity, Letters from Working Women*, reveal lives of struggle, hardship and pain.[3] Although many retained a fierce spirit, the deep bitterness of labouring women is unmistakable. The title is also apt in another sense. Although the women's movement had made important gains from the 1870s in many areas, women's status in society was still fundamentally unequal. As several writers have acknowledged, the women's movement was at heart a struggle for a new definition of femininity which would transform 'male' public space and thereby burst open the public/private divide that regulated and defined women's lives.[4] The demands of feminists for the vote as a symbol of this new vision of womanhood still resonate down the century to us today.

Family, Motherhood and Sexuality

Home for the majority of people was very rarely a self-contained unit. Whilst a significant number of families in urban areas only had one room, most had between two and four small rented rooms. Running water was usually available only at ground-floor level, so all water required by upstairs tenants had to be carried. Conditions were almost always cramped, with often only two beds for the whole family, no wardrobe space or storage space for food. Those who could afford it had cooking ranges or the newer type of gas oven, but it was still common to cook on an open grate. For many women, doorstep conversations were their only form of interaction with the community, apart from daily visits to local shops and stalls. Perambulators (prams) were prohibitively expensive so babies usually had to be carried.

Middle- and upper-class married women did not concern themselves greatly with the running of the household. An army of housemaids, parlour maids, cooks and nannies relieved these women of all routine housework, releasing them for an endless round of socializing and 'good works'. Even the most down-at-heel, barely middle-class family had a maid-of-all work who was usually a young woman brought in from the countryside to be a live-in drudge. The wives of skilled craftsmen and other good earners could also command the assistance of a weekly char or help on washday. But for poorer married women there was no escape from the constant round of cooking, washing up, scrubbing, sweeping, and polishing. Ranges and grates had to be black-leaded regularly, which was a very messy job. The weekly wash was a huge undertaking as everything had to be vigorously pounded in a dolly tub then pushed through a mangle and hung up to dry. As the children grew older it became a little easier. In large families the oldest girl was expected to take on some duties, particularly baby-minding, from an early age. Cooking from cheap ingredients was a very time-consuming process, although in urban areas ready-cooked food, such as fish and chips, was now available for those who could afford it.

Although the running of the home was the mother's responsibility, fathers did have some clearly defined duties, such as boot-repairing and tending vegetable plots and chicken coops. They would usually only take on other tasks in extreme circumstances like maternity or serious illness of the mother. In general, however, the father's main role was to bring in the weekly wage. Both *At the Works* and *Round about a Pound a Week* provide detailed breakdowns of family budgets. Where men earned less than a skilled wage budgeting was a serious problem, particularly if there were several dependent children. The wives of these men would often only have about a pound a week to manage on, of which about 8s would have to be allocated for rent. The father would take 1s 6d–2s for his own purposes such as fares to work, 'smokes' and perhaps a glass of beer. Overtime earnings and other perks would be regarded as his own.

It was regarded as axiomatic that the breadwinner should have special food, usually some sort of meat or fish known as 'titbit' or 'relish'. As Ellen Ross has observed, the eating of meat performed a symbolic function separating women and children from the superior world of men.[5] As 3s 6d was regarded as the absolute minimum for the father's food, the rest of the family had to rely on a mainly bread-based diet, with very little meat or milk. Mothers would often go without in order to provide for their children. As one of the women who wrote in *Maternity* put it, 'My husband has never earned more than from 23s to 25s a week, and many a time I have had to go without many a thing that would have done me good.'[6] If the husband gambled or drank, the household would be in a perpetual state of want. Arthur Jasper was born in Hoxton, East London, in 1908. Although his father was a good earner his mother never received more than about 6s or 7s a week, due to his father's drinking habits. In his autobiography Arthur wrote that when his older sister managed to steal a few coins from their father's purse, 'we always had a good feed the next day'.[7] Finding funds for unexpected expenditure was a problem for most families. If a very sick child needed special food, or medical expenses were incurred, it was up to the mother to somehow 'make do', which usually meant increased deprivation until the debt could be paid off. If the family became deprived of its main income for any reason, then the whole family could be plunged into destitution within weeks. Everyone lived close to the margin of disaster. In cases such as unemployment or sickness, neighbours would usually rally round, at least for a few weeks, and provide food in an effort to stave off the terrifying prospect of the workhouse for the family concerned.

As one would expect, the experience of motherhood was largely a matter of social class. For the better off, nannies and nursery maids would undertake all routine duties. In her autobiography Mary Stocks refers to her children's nurse, 'beloved Sarah who put me to bed, got me up, brushed my hair, mended my stockings and saw to it that I washed my neck thoroughly.'[8] In such households motherhood often involved rather distant interaction with children. In working-class families, as Florence Bell wrote, 'the pivot of the whole situation is the woman'.[9] She was essentially a worker, a provider of meals and a home, and had very limited opportunity for playful interaction, and especially not for excursions of any kind. That does not mean that she was not fond of her children, but that circumstances dictated that her love for them had to be expressed through work rather than any other means. Infantile and childhood diseases took their toll. In Liverpool, Agnes Little, grandmother of Bessie Braddock MP, lost two children of her six children in one night to scarlet fever.[10] Most families could expect to lose at least one child. Class is also very evident in the circumstances surrounding maternity. As Florence Bell put it:

> The woman who is well-to-do makes her health the first consideration ... She rests as much as she chooses, ... The moment of child birth among the prosperous is surrounded in these days in every direction by extremes of antiseptic precaution to ensure healthy conditions ... Gallons of water boiled for several days previously stand ready for use, the room is spotlessly clean and airy, a well qualified doctor is ready to be summoned, a trained and experienced nurse is in attendance as well.[11]

Such women would be kept in bed for nearly three weeks following the birth. However, the poor woman would be at her usual routine right up to the birth and would be expected to make all the necessary preparations, including a thorough spring-clean, herself. She would have to give birth in the cramped conditions of the family bedroom. She would be attended for the actual birth and would usually have help for up to a week following. During this lying-in period she would be surrounded by all the usual noisy comings and goings of the household. At night she would have to share her bed with her husband, the baby and probably the ex-baby, as there would be nowhere else for them to go. After a few days or perhaps a week she had to be on her feet. No wonder that so many women wrote such tales of misery in *Maternity*. One mother of six wrote, 'what a terrible time it is, to be sure'.[12] Many letters spoke of poor treatment by doctors, although they were aware that there was very little that could be done to change the situation. As one put it, 'When we are poor, though, we cannot say what must be done; we have to suffer and keep quiet.'[13] The stress of continual pregnancies, overwork and poor nourishment left many women with permanently damaged health. As one woman wrote, 'I had seven children and one miscarriage in ten years and three months. This left me at the age of thirty a complete wreck.'[14]

Some women were beginning to realize that they could do something about it. Several of the *Maternity* letters make references to birth control, such as this woman with four children:

we do not feel justified in having any more children if it can possibly be avoided. I love children dearly, another reason why I do not wish to create them to be badly fed, clothed badly, uneducated etc. on a mere pittance.[15]

The most usual methods pursued were withdrawal and abstention. Of course, these methods involved the active consent of the husband. If this was not forthcoming, the wife would have to resort to avoidance of various kinds such as keeping a child in the bed. Once an unwanted pregnancy had occurred, abortion was the only way out. Although illegal it was a common practice. Referred to coyly as 'drugs' in the *Maternity* letters, there are several references to abortion. One example is of a woman whose baby and toddler were both sickly. She was faced with the prospect of a third child in under three years, 'I confess without shame that when well meaning friends said, "You cannot afford another baby; take this drug," I took their strong concoctions.'[16] Many abortifacient remedies failed, as they did in the case of the woman above. Moreover, newer methods such as quinine, lead compounds and rupturing of the amniotic sac, were highly dangerous and sometimes resulted in death.[17]

The conditions of maternity was one of the great issues of the Co-operative Women's Guild. Founded and established as part of the co-operative movement in 1883, it became the largest organization of working-class women before 1914 with nearly 32 000 members. Its membership, consisting largely of full-time housewives of skilled workers, had overall control of the organization through its annual congress, although its central committee did have great influence. The Guild became an important pressure group. It supported adult suffrage, industrial reform and mounted a campaign for improved health care for mothers and infants. It successfully campaigned for the inclusion of maternity benefit in the National Insurance Act of 1911 and within two years had amended the act to allow the benefit (39s for wives of insured workers) to be paid directly to the woman.[18] On several issues it came into conflict with the Board of the Co-operative Union. Its defiant stand for easier access to divorce led eventually to recognition of its right to an independent voice.[19]

The Women's Co-operative Guild was campaigning on issues which had recently become the focus of government attention.

Concern about Britain's inability to maintain its position of world leadership led to fears of 'racial decline'. The parameters of the debate were largely set by the eugenics movement, which held that national prestige and power was derived from the quality of the 'racial stock'. The results of social investigations such as those of Booth and Rowntree, combined with the revelation that about a third of the Boer War recruits were unfit, led to a growing impetus for government intervention. Following the Interdepartmental Government Committee on Physical Deterioration Report of 1904, the government focused on infant mortality as a major cause of national decline. More than one child in five was dying in infancy. This culminated in a series of measures which essentially redefined the role of mothers. Motherhood was now seen as a national duty. The quality and quantity of the population was its greatest asset and it was the responsibility of women to bear and successfully raise children for the state. If national decline was to be reversed, the mothers of the labouring classes had to be taught mothercraft. The infant welfare campaign resulted in the growth of 'Schools for Mothers'. The status of midwifery was raised and from 1904 health-visiting schemes were introduced. Taking advice from traditional sources, grandmothers or neighbours for example, was now viewed as irresponsible as women were encouraged to follow 'expert opinion'.

Infant death was seen largely as a matter of maternal irresponsibility. 'Feckless mothers' were blamed for sickly children, whilst virtually no recognition was given to the fact that mothers had to rear their infants in circumstances over which they had no control. Women's groups, such as the Co-operative Women's Guild railed against the 'guilty mother' syndrome and pointed to poverty as the major cause of infant mortality, arguing that mothers were being expected to 'make bricks without straw'.[20] The government, in refusing to tackle poverty head on, preferred to emphasize the value of self-help and cookery lessons to make the best of meagre incomes.[21] Maternal health, which is essential to the raising of healthy children, was simply ignored. Infant mortality did fall in the years before the First World War, although it is by no means certain that this was a result of the government's infant welfare campaign. Ellen Ross points out that at the Bell Street Clinic in Marylebone, 'all the clinic's quite plausible rules for infant feeding were broken routinely by most working-class mothers'.[22] The increased regulation and professionalization of midwifery was probably beneficial. Reforms affecting older children, notably increased provision for school feeding (1906), were distinctly advantageous to poor mothers of large families. Home visits, no doubt beneficial in some cases, were resented by many women for their intrusive nature and impractical advice. All the discussions about infant welfare assumed that mothers had the support of a male breadwinner. This was by no means the case, and as the potential earnings of women with dependent children were appalling their situation was often acute.

Little has been written so far of the relations between men and women. Davidoff and Hall have written of the development of an ideology of 'separate spheres' developing from the late eighteenth century.[23] Although increasingly challenged, particularly from the 1870s, the notion of profound sexual difference was still dominant in the Edwardian period. The stress on women's role as wife and mother was reinforced by the new idea of women as 'mothers of the race'. As irrational and emotional beings, women were excluded from culture, political power and public space. They were, in fact, seen as 'little more than walking wombs'.[24] The only alternative view of women was that of the 'despised prostitute' which was not an enviable role as it lacked the moral force of the 'revered mother'.[25] Feminists, whilst often mobilizing arguments for the moral superiority of women, based on their maternalism, were increasingly challenging the biological reductionist view that femininity rested on a physical notion of woman. Elizabeth Blackwell, for example, 'was appalled by the widespread medical opinion that women were ruled by their reproductive systems'.[26] Intellectual women were also resisting the idea that marriage and motherhood were the only goals for women. Cecily Hamilton's vitriolic *Marriage as a Trade* outlined the 'essential servility of woman's position in the eyes of man'.[27] Hamilton pitted herself forcefully against the view that woman was 'a breeding machine and a necessary adjunct to a frying pan'.[28]

In matters of sexuality a double standard was applied. As Lucy Bland writes, 'unchastity for men was understandable and even necessary for health, but for women it was unforgivable'.[29]

Women could only belong to 'respectable society' if they retained a state of modesty. To step outside the accepted boundaries would mean being cast into a state of 'vice'. Modesty included chaperones for unmarried women, excessive dress and censored reading matter. Masturbation was thought to be a shocking example of self-abuse, almost certainly indicating insanity. Women were not expected to exhibit any form of independent sexual desire. The wife's role was to endure rather than enjoy sex. Although not yet expressed in the working classes, the idea of an independent women's sexuality was slowly emerging and found expression in contemporary fiction around the theme of the 'new woman', the most well-known example being that of H.G. Wells' *Ann Veronica* (1909). F.W. Stella Browne is a rare example of a feminist asserting the sexual rights of women. Linking feminism, socialism and sex reform, she wrote a remark-able series of letters to the intellectual journal *The Freewoman* in 1912. Initially writing anonymously but eventually declaring her identity, she defended 'auto-eroticism' and argued that sexual experience was 'the right of every human being'.[30] Although influenced by eugenics she was keenly aware of issues of class as well as gender, particularly the plight of poor mothers with many mouths to feed. She staunchly defended the right of women to control their fertility, 'our right to refuse maternity is also an inalienable right. Our wills are ours, our persons are ours; nor shall all the priests and scientists in the world deprive us of this right to say "No".'[31]

Although the *Freewoman* discussion circle aroused great inter-est, leading feminists involved in the suffrage movement were anxious to disassociate themselves from it. Called a 'nauseous publication' by Maude Royden, it did not strike a chord with mainstream feminism.[32] An alternative view of sexual relations, most notably promoted by Christabel Pankhurst, was that of sexual danger. Linking with earlier traditions of moral purity, *The Great Scourge and How To End It* urged women to renounce complicity in the double standard of morality and refrain from committing 'race suicide' with male partners infected with venereal disease.[33] This argument must have added weight to the rising credibility of the single woman. Viewed largely as an object of pity during the nineteenth century, the spinster was now developing a more satisfying public role. As more work opportunities opened up for educated women it became economically viable for them to live outside of family structures and create independent lives. The late nineteenth century also witnessed the emergence of a homosexual sub-culture in Britain. Jeffrey Weeks has documented this movement and has also pointed to a smaller, less vibrant female version. This lesbian sub-culture was 'overwhelmingly upper-class' and dominated by the figure of Radclyffe Hall who was living openly as a lesbian from the early 1900s.[34] The lesbian identity, in so far as it was recognized at all, was seen as a rather pathetic victim of a congenital perversion. Sexologists referred to it as 'inversion' and claimed that lesbians adopted masculine characteristics and tried to rival men for female sexual attention. The 'feminine' lesbian who did not display these characteristics was not a real lesbian at all, but had merely been 'led astray'. Historians are divided on the role of the sex reform movement in relation to lesbians. Sheila Jeffreys argues that intimate, romantic friendships between women had been regarded as acceptable from the eighteenth century and that sexologists, fearful of rising female independence, labelled and stigmatized lesbianism in order to create a ghetto which would separate lesbians from other women.[35] This analysis is too simplistic. As Bland has pointed out, sexual theorists were not homogenous and many were actually pro-feminist.[36] Sexologists could not impose the formation of a lesbian sub-culture. The new lesbian identity, however flawed and stigmatized by medical stereotyping, did have some positive attributes; they were no longer invisible; they could find each other, create their own culture and enjoy sexual fulfilment.

Education

By 1900 considerable progress had been made in establishing girls' education. Although it was still common for upper-class girls to be educated by governesses, increasingly, middle-class girls were sent to school, some of which were boarding. Schools such as Cheltenham Ladies College (1854) were already very firmly established. The proliferation of day schools for girls from the 1870s led to the formation of the Girls Public Day School Trust in 1906. Whether girls could be educated exactly the same as boys or have a different curriculum, acknowledging girls' future role as wives and mothers, had been hotly debated in the late nineteenth century. By the early twentieth century the academic quality of girls' private education was recognized, although it was common in day schools for the girls to finish at lunch-time in order to be able to spend the afternoons with their mothers learning 'domestic arts'. Dora Russell attended Sutton High in Surrey where academic standards were high and competition intense. She spent her school career struggling to hold her top position in the form against her friend who was placed second.[37] Dora went on to study modern languages at Girton College. Certainly for the academically minded, it was possible to progress to higher education. But these were the minority and for the majority a life of domesticity loomed. Mary Stocks recalls that even after an excellent education at St Pauls, 'it was counted as no disgrace for a girl to pursue no profession, do no systematic work, and "come out" as a young adult female available for invitations to dances or proposals of marriage'.[38]

Gender socialization and expectations also profoundly influenced state education for girls. From 1870 primary education became compulsory and both boys and girls attended elementary board schools, which by 1914 meant they were educated up to the age of 14 (or earlier if the half-time system was still in operation). Unauthorized absence was a major problem, particularly for girls, and it is not difficult to understand why. Hard-pressed mothers of large families depended on older daughters. A girl of 12 or 13, sometimes even younger, could be entrusted with the babies and toddlers whilst mother got on with her work. Girls often missed two or three half-days of school a week.[39] Washdays were particularly bad. Although educated together as infants, boys and girls were separated from the age of seven. For girls a practical element was introduced as it was thought necessary to instil into them the elements of house-wifery. Needlework, cookery and laundry were regarded as essential. Needlework was thought to be especially useful as it was regarded as a sedative, dulling high-spirited girls into docile acquiescence. Concern about the 'racial deterioration', particu-larly infant mortality, led to a new emphasis and by 1910 girls were also being instructed in infant care.

Domestic instruction for girls, which was given at expense of maths, science and other academic subjects, came under ferocious attack from feminist teachers and parents. Although some were prepared to recognize a differentiated curriculum, the huge amount of time given over to domestic work led to complaints that the more able girls were being held back. Parents took the view that they did not send their children to school to learn to be household drudges. As socialist-feminist Ada Nield Chew put it:

> Slaves should break their chains and those who want to be free should help in the chain breaking and not try to rivet the links closer by advocating domestic training for all schools for all girls, fostering in the minds of girls that simply because of their sex they must inevitably some day be ready to cook a man's dinner and tidy up his hearth.[40]

It was certainly the case that by 1914 academic opportunities for bright elementary school girls were increasing. Girls' grammar schools were established and from 1902 the number of girls in secondary education rose, but there were far fewer than boys. Here domestic subjects failed to become an integrated part of the curriculum and were associated with the less able.[41] Some girls managed to progress by becoming pupil-teachers in elementary schools. Ellen Wilkinson attended elementary school in Manchester. In 1906, at the age of fifteen, Ellen won a pupil-teacher bursary which meant she attended Manchester Day Training College for half the week and in return she taught the other half. As she was only slightly older than her pupils and only four feet ten inches tall, this must have been quite a task! She qualified as a teacher after two years and went on to do matriculation and entered Manchester University in 1910 under a scholarship scheme.[42] This was the first generation of working-class girls who could aspire to enter higher education, but the opportunity was only offered to a tiny number. In 1910 70 girls from elementary schools entered English and Welsh universities with scholarships.[43]

Across the country, the university extension movement meant that women, mainly middle-class, were attending part-time courses in a great variety of subjects. According to Carole

Dyhouse, women constituted about 15 per cent of the student population by 1900.[44] Women students were less of a rarity, but they were not usually allowed to study for the same qualifications as men in the same environment. London University was very much a pioneer in awarding women degrees from 1878, but when Marie Stopes went to University College in the early 1900s 'she was amazed by the extent of prejudice against women'.[45] Many women, like the young Vera Brittain in Buxton, had to fight parental resistance to enter university at all. And once there they were hidebound by elaborate restrictions and rules for chaperonage, although these were easing off a little by 1914.

Paid Work and the Labour Movement

The weight of ideology hung heavy on the shoulders of women workers. As Isabella Ford put it, 'everything is against working women'.[46] The prevalent notion of the adult man as breadwinner led to the assumption that adult women were dependent wives and mothers. Although it was not thought to be respectable for married women to work, this outlook could not be sustained in practice for large sections of the working class. In addition, there were many single women (spinsters, widows, deserted wives etc.) who were in the labour market. As it was widely held that skilled work, that is, highly paid work of protected status, was the preserve of men, women's employment opportunities were severely restricted. As the sectors which employed women were over-supplied, market forces brought down the price of women's labour. On average women's earnings were only about 40 per cent of men's earnings. A 14-year-old girl would usually start industrial work at about 3s a week. This would rise with age and experience, but few women earned 15s which was regarded as the minimum subsistence wage for an adult. Hours of work were long, usually at least 60 a week and, in manufacturing, heavy fines for bad work (often unspecified) or misdemeanours were common. Women were employed in a variety of industrial trades: Lancashire cotton, Yorkshire wool, small metals in Birmingham, fish-curing at the ports, rope-making in London's East End, hosiery in Nottingham and so on. London and most cities employed many women in tailoring, millinery and sweated trades such as sack-making, box-making, tennis-ball-covering and artificial flowers, where women worked at home and were often forced to compel their children to work with them. Conditions in these trades were often deplorable. Laundry work was also common in urban centres.

Cotton textiles were an exception, where a rate for the job regardless of gender was established in the late nineteenth century. In practice, the labour process in cotton was divided along gender lines, except for weaving where both men and women worked on the same piece-rate system. Some male weavers took home more pay as they worked heavier or more complicated cloth but, on the whole, cotton-weaving represented the nearest thing to equal pay in British industry.[47] Consequently, women weavers in Lancashire (there were 150 000 of them) could earn about 25s a week, making them the highest-paid women in industry. In the weaving towns such as Blackburn and Burnley, the practice of married women working was widely accepted, not least because the other side of near equal pay was that men were not breadwinners and it was necessary for married women to work, at least until the oldest child became a wage earner.

Official statistics of women's employment are almost certainly underestimates. Married women, for reasons already explained, were extremely reticent to identify themselves as workers. The 1900 census identifies only 13 per cent of married women working, but much of the work they did was casual and not recognized as work: charring, taking in washing or sewing, keeping lodgers, child-minding, etc. This work could be performed under the illusion that the woman was still a full-time housewife. The largest single employer of women was domestic service. Here women were not fully proletarianized as they lived in and were kept by their employers. Wages were minimal and paid infrequently. Time off would be restricted to an afternoon a week and employers would attempt to exert moral surveillance of their domestic staff. As many young women found these conditions undesirable, particularly in urban areas where other employment opportunities were opening up, girls were often brought in from the countryside or obtained from workhouses and orphanages. Not surprisingly, such vulnerable girls were prey to sexual exploitation.

From the 1870s, white-collar work had expanded fast due to the growth of Britain's tertiary industries, especially in London. The 'white blouse' revolution, as it became known, was created from a number of growth sectors: retail stores, particularly the new large department stores; the civil service and local government; state and private education. Meta Zimmeck has estimated that the number of women clerks rose from 2000 in 1851 to 166 000 in 1911.[48] As a proportion of the total this represents a rise of from 2 per cent to 20 per cent. Technological change was altering the gender divisions in clerking – the nineteenth-century male scribe was giving way to the female typist. Clerical jobs were much in demand as this work was seen as an ideal occupation for middle-class girls. They were kept segregated from male clerks, had very limited opportunities for promotion and led sheltered lives at home with their parents. In local government and the civil service a few women graduates were able to move beyond clerical positions. There were women sanitary inspectors and factory inspectors. Nursing had become professionalized in the late nineteenth century, but conditions were still extremely poor. Nurses had to live in and were expected to be completely devoted to the job with little regard for such matters as pay or hours of work.

Large numbers of women went into teaching. Elementary school teachers, who usually taught classes of 50 to 60, were not usually graduates, although some took an external degree whilst working. Women teachers were paid less than male teachers. They could rise to the level of headmistress, but could not become inspectors, except for domestic subjects. Women graduates who were inclined to teach tended to think elementary schools were beneath them and would opt for a private day or boarding school. A few women graduates were managing to break into teaching in higher education, mainly as mistress in charge of training women teachers, but the status of these women academics was often ambiguous. According to Dyhouse, Mrs Mackenzie of University College, Cardiff, may have been the first full woman professor in Britain when she became Professor of Education in 1910.[49] For all these professional and white-collar women, no matter how elevated their status, a marriage bar was almost universally applied. This could be a formal rule or merely a matter of informal pressure. For 'respectable women' marriage was regarded as a full-time occupation. Although its justification was ideological, its implications were economic: enforcing women's dependence on men and ensuring a continuous supply of young, cheap female labour for employers. Women's subordinate position in the labour market had a direct impact on their position in the labour movement. In 1900 only a small number of women were in unions, but the trend was upward and by 1914 there were over a third of a million women workers in trade unions. Over two-thirds of these were in textiles, the remainder being mostly in clothing, distribution and clerical unions. But as Deborah Thom has written, 'the question should thus be, not why did so few organise but why did so many, against such considerable odds?'[50] Working long hours and burdened down by domestic commitments, few women had time or inclination to attend meetings. Besides doing a double shift, married women often faced disapproval if they attempted to go out alone in the evening unaccompanied. In addition, male trade unionists were not always supportive and were sometimes downright hostile, expressing the view that if men earned a 'decent wage' wives would not have to work at all. Even in cotton-weaving, where women were numerically dominant and collectively constituted the most organized and self-conscious group of women workers in Britain, they made virtually no inroads into the union apparatus.

Socialists and feminists among the new breed of social reformers were concerned by women's vulnerable position in the labour market. The Women's Trade Union League actively promoted women's trade unionism and succeeded in securing a platform within the TUC to raise women's interests. The Women's Industrial Council, like the League, consisted of middle-class women but, unlike the League, it did not promote women's trade unionism but concentrated more on education, legislation and investigative work. From its formation in 1894 to 1913 it conducted investigations into 117 trades and also made separate studies on the conditions of home workers and married women.[51] Such was the picture of poverty and degradation depicted in these and similar studies that a powerful momentum gathered for government intervention in the sweated trades. In 1906 the Anti-Sweating League was formed with Mary Macarthur, the dynamic shop assistants' organizer from Glasgow as one of its leading members. In the same year Macarthur formed the National Federation of Women Workers (NFWW), a national women's union, which women could belong to in addition to a specialist union. In the period before the war the NFWW concentrated on minimum wages legislation to alleviate the plight of sweated women workers. The Liberal government eventually accepted the view that sweating was an offence against morality and in 1909 passed the Trades Boards Act. The act established regulatory boards and minimum rates in four trades (chain-making, box-making, lace-making and finishing, and readymade clothing) and was later extended. The effect was dramatic; in lace-making average weekly earnings rose from 7–8s to nearly 12s, in paperbox-making they rose from 8s 5d to 13s and tailoring from 8s to just over 14s.[52] The adverse side of it was, as Thom has pointed out, that the necessity for state intervention for women was emphasized (with the implication that women were weak and needed protection), that minimum rates rapidly became maxima and the notion that motherhood was women's primary role was never challenged.[53]

Women were becoming more assertive and demonstrating their ability to take independent action, especially in the wave of general labour unrest which occurred 1910–11. The strike of chain-makers in the Cradley Heath area of Birmingham is an example of this. In chain-making the board decided on an increase which would give women chain-makers a rise from 4–6s a week to 10–11s for a 55-hour week. The act allowed employers six months to implement the new rates. Macarthur argued for immediate implementation. By September of 1910, 700 women chain-makers were refusing to work at the old rate. They were isolated home workers and spread over a large area, but they received tremendous support from the Anti-Sweating League and many labour movement bodies. Strike pay enabled them to hold out for ten weeks until the employers gave in and agreed to pay the new rates.[54] Several very successful local women organizers emerged during this period, both working for separate women's unions or in general unions. Mary Bamber was an official for the Warehouse Workers Union in Liverpool and was well known in the local labour and socialist movement. In 1912 Julia Varley, a Birmingham activist, became the first women's organizer for the Workers' Union. Altogether, by

1914 women's industrial trade unionism had greatly improved from 1900. The NFWW had 20 000 members under the leadership of Macarthur, and there were many more women in general unions. Outside of TUC-affiliated unions, women white-collar workers were also getting organized. The rising number of women clerks was a great concern to male clerks as this letter to the *Liverpool Echo* in 1911 reveals:

Your co-respondent ... seems to think that the female clerk should receive the same wages as the male clerk for similar work. Surely ... this is a gross piece of audacity on the part of that small, but bombastic, section of clerical labour. Seeing that they are so fond of comparing the product of their labour as equal to that of the male clerk I would suggest that these intrepid 'typewriter pounders' ... should fill in their spare time washing out the office and dusting same, which you will no doubt agree is more suited to their sex and maybe would give them a little practice and insight into the work they will be called upon to do should they so far demean themselves as to marry one of the poor male clerks whose living they are doing their utmost to take out of his hands at the present time.[55]

Unlike the respondent above, the National Union of Clerks decided that, in view of the numbers of women coming into clerking, the only realistic response was not only to admit women, but to also adopt a policy of equal pay. This demand, for a minimum wage of 35s (27s 6d in rural areas), for all clerks, was unparalleled for many years by any other union.[56] In practice, only a small proportion of women clerks were unionized and women clerks rarely did get comparable pay to men. A greater proportion were unionized in teaching, where rivalry was not a major problem because of gender-segregated education. The National Federation of Women Teachers was founded as a pressure group inside the National Union of Teachers (NUT) in 1903, with its principal aim the fight for equal pay. By 1914 it had 58 branches but remained within the NUT until after the war.[57]

Suffrage and Citizenship

Feminist ideology and feminism as a social movement were both well established by 1900. A note of caution is necessary here as, clearly, feminist ideology took different forms and there was not one but many feminisms. Feminist influence was felt in many areas, some of which have already been mentioned. In general terms one can identify a broad movement of women (and men) who sought, with varying degrees of emphasis, to raise the political, legal, social and economic status of women. The central tenets of liberal feminism were laid out by John Stuart Mill in his *The Subjection of Women* (1869) and from this time the overwhelming demand of rank and file activists was for women's suffrage. Late nineteenth-century liberal feminists based their arguments for equality largely on grounds of social justice. Increasingly, this was also combined with the belief that women in political life would imply the abolition of patriarchal cultural hegemony. So votes for women would abolish the public/private divide and allow women to bring their nurturing (and other 'womanly') qualities to the benefit of the public domain and inaugurate social reform. Socialist-feminists, of various orders, were keener to focus on the unequal economic position of women. They sought to combine a class and gender analysis and believed that ultimately women could only be emancipated in a socialist society.

In the area of local government, women had already made gains. During the nineteenth century the growth of local government and the increasing range of provision meant that a very large number of elected officials were involved in running local services such as schools and sanitation. Women succeeded in becoming members of school boards, vestries and many other local bodies, although they tended to be well off and in practice much of their work blended in with philanthropy, which had long been a pastime of ladies. In 1894 the property qualification for Poor Law Guardians was removed, enabling many married women to stand for office. A few working-class women became guardians, such as Selina Cooper in Burnley.[58] Women guardians were known for their attention to detail and desire to humanize the harsher aspects of the workhouse regime. They struggled to raise the standards of diet and medical care and to place workhouse children into ordinary elementary schools. In other areas of local government the 'ladies elect', as Patricia Hollis refers to them, promoted parks, baths and other amenities.[59] Women guardians and councillors either stood as independents or were supported by the Liberals or Labour, in some form. From 1907 women ratepayers could stand in borough and county council elections. Few were successful and only about 50 women were borough or county councillors by 1914. The big metropolitan areas were particularly difficult for women. Hollis attributes this partly to a 'cordon sanitaire' which was erected between local and national politics.[60] Local government service had come to be seen as an appropriate activity for women, but national politics was still seen as a man's world. City and county councils were regarded as too close to the national scene for women to be welcome. So, although by 1914 over a million women could vote in local elections and 1800 held elected local office, the hopes of feminists that this example of public power could be used as a springboard to national politics were in vain.[61]

Women were not entirely absent from the national political scene, however. Following the growth of a mass electorate in the late nineteenth century, local and national party structures had emerged for the purpose of mobilizing the electorate. Women became members of the Primrose League, which sought to promote popular Toryism, but they were not expected to play a political role. Liberal women had their own separate organization, the Women's Liberal Federation, which by the turn of the century had 470 branches and 80 000 members.[62] Many of these women were involved in local government and at times Liberal feminists found that their Liberalism conflicted with their commitment to women's suffrage. The links between socialism and feminism were rather more complex.

From the 1880s the British socialist movement had grown in strength and influence. The movement around the Independent Labour Party (ILP) paper *Clarion* embraced the idea that socialism involved a transformation of all aspects of life, not just economic structures. The probing into personal life which was an essential part of this necessarily involved an analysis of the position of women. Edward Carpenter wrote that women under capitalism could be divided into three types: 'the "lady", the household drudge and the prostitute ... it is hard to know which is the most wretched, which is the most wronged ...'[63] Both Carpenter and his contemporary Olive Schreiner were influenced by Engels and both tried to develop his ideas. Schreiner's *Woman and Labour* argued passionately that not only should women enter public industry, as Engels had written, but that they should not be restricted by gender:

> There is no post or form of toil for which it is not our intention to attempt to fit ourselves; and there is no closed door we do not intend to force open; and there is no fruit in the garden of knowledge it is not our determination to eat ... And, for today, we take all labour for our province.[64]

Socialist-feminist intellectuals also made a visible presence in the Fabian Society, who had their own women's group from 1908. The work of Reeves has already been referred to above. Fabian women were particularly interested in women's economic position. The Fabians were the first socialist group to take seriously the idea of state endowment of motherhood.[65] There were also many women activists who worked within the labour and socialist movement raising feminist issues. Isabella Ford, who was based in Leeds, was a leading member of the ILP and author of the influential pamphlet, *Woman and Socialism* (1907). As June Hannam has written, Ford emphasized that 'women's suffrage and the emancipation of all working people had to go hand in hand'.[66] Ada Nield Chew had no formal education beyond the age of 11, but she became a formidable speaker, writer and organizer. Chew was a forceful exponent of the right of married women to work. She was bitterly opposed to endowment of motherhood, arguing that it would further imprison women in their domestic drudgery. Instead she proposed state nurseries and co-operative housekeeping.[67]

British Marxism, as manifested in the Social Democratic Federation (SDF) did not support the 'socialism of the new life' which many of the *Clarion* socialists of the ILP followed. As the SDF regarded the unequal position of women as something which could only be resolved in a future socialist society, it became an irrelevance to the party leadership. There were, however, individual SDF women, Dora Montifiore for example, who sought to work on women's issues within this limited theoretical framework.[68] The acceptance of limited property-based women's suffrage by the main suffrage organizations as a first step led to accusations that working-class women were to be duped by 'bourgeois feminists'. Marxists argued that women's suffrage as the key to emancipation was in any case an illusion, as only   socialism could bring about a real transformation of women's position. No doubt many socialist men used this anti-feminist Marxist fundamentalism as a means of defending patriarchal privileges. Belfort Bax, a leading member of the SDF, was open about his belief in the profound inferiority of women and would not accept that this compromised the socialist principle of equality.[69]

Socialist-feminists were, therefore, in a real dilemma – to stay in the socialist movement or to work outside it. By 1914 the Women's Labour League had a sizeable membership of women inside the Labour Party.[70] Labour women did sterling work on many women's issues, but the League's position in the party was always marginal and it had to struggle (not always successfully) to avoid the danger of sliding into the political ghetto of tea-making, sewing banners and other duties which the male comrades regarded as 'women's work'. This led many, including Dora Montifiore, Ada Nield Chew and Isabella Ford, to decide eventually to concentrate their efforts in the autonomous women's movement. Here, other dangers were evident, such as the lack of a class perspective and the unrealistic expectations of what women's suffrage could actually achieve. Effectively, socialist-feminists were forced to make a choice, to become woman-centred and join a women's suffrage organization or to give the class question a higher priority and stay within the socialist movement.

Suffrage narratives have mostly been organized on the basis of a clear distinction between the constitutionalists of the National Union of Women's Suffrage Societies (NUWSS) and the militants of the Women's Social and Political Union (WSPU). This distinction emanates from the administrative separation of the two bodies and the divergent strategies and tactics employed. In fact, this distinction has been somewhat overplayed. In the early years particularly, dual membership was common and there was no irreconcilable break between the two groups until 1912. The

Women's Coronation Procession of 1911, the most spectacular of all the suffrage demonstrations, united all the women's suffrage organizations. Although the suffrage movement was divided over how the vote could be achieved, it was ideologically homogenous.[71] Neither constitutionalists or militants sought to deny sexual difference, but the right to redefine it. Both utilized conventional Edwardian female dress, with its flouncy dresses and wide-brimmed impractical hats, in an effort to assert that feminism was not incompatible with the 'womanly woman' and was indeed an essential part of it. Both groups were served by artists who created a range of women's suffrage images which saw no basic distinction.[72]

These observations noted, it seems appropriate at this point to set out some of the major developments in the two suffrage organizations, beginning with the NUWSS and its radical suffrage offshoot. It was formed in 1897 from an affiliation of the sprawling network of suffrage groups which had sprung up from the time of the 1866 Reform Bill. It grew steadily and established it own paper *The Common Cause*, its own premises and paid staff. It was organized on democratic principles and its President, Millicent Fawcett, was elected. It was the largest of all the suffrage groups, with 53 000 members in 1914 organized in 480 different groups.[73] The constitutionalists adopted the conventional methods of pressure groups politics: they lobbied MPs, pressed for a private members' bill, organized petitions and peaceful public meetings and demonstrations. It was an uphill struggle, particularly as the more dramatic activities of the WSPU captured most of the press attention (and also, in due course, interest from historians). Although many leading figures in the NUWSS were prosperous Liberals, as was Millicent Fawcett, the membership was extremely diverse and included many working-class women. The content of *The Common Cause* reflected this diversity and included articles across a broad spectrum of women's issues.

From the start, the women's suffrage movement had a strong following in Lancashire and Cheshire where working-class women activists linked suffrage, socialist and labour movement involvement. The centre of suffrage agitation in the north-west was the North of England Suffrage Society, which linked a network of local groups and in turn affiliated them to the wider movement through membership of the NUWSS. From the early

1890s the textile women activists and their friends began to develop a separate working-class women's movement, which was only brought to light in 1978 by the publication of *One Hand Tied Behind Us: The Rise of the Women's Suffrage Movement* by Jill Liddington and Jill Norris. Women such as Selina Cooper, Helen Silcock and Sarah Dickenson became committed to 'womanhood suffrage', that is, one woman one vote. They wanted suffrage in order to instigate a programme of radical social reform. The radicalism of the textile women distanced them from the more conservative elements in the North of England Suffrage Society. At the same time the radical suffragists (as Liddington and Norris refer to them) were becoming equally disillusioned with the formal labour movement. Women weavers had contributed substantially to the election of David Shackleton of the Darwen Weavers' Association, as MP for Clitheroe in 1902, and to his subsequent salary.[74] The textile women were thus in the anomalous position of paying (6d a week) for an MP whom they were denied an opportunity to vote for. Shackleton was only the third Labour member to be returned and the textile women had high hopes for him in Parliament. Despite numerous petitions and delegations, Shackleton's promises to promote women's suffrage came to little. This appears to have been the final straw which provoked the radical suffragists to launch their own group. The long-winded title of Lancashire and Cheshire Woman Textile and Other Workers Representation Committee was adopted at the formation of the group in the summer of 1903. Unfortunately, the new organization did not thrive.[75] Although the movement built up a real momentum in Lancashire and Cheshire, it did not travel well beyond this area. The committee developed many contacts outside the textile region, but it remained an essentially localized phenomenon arising from the particular circumstances and conditions prevailing in textiles. Equally important to the movement's failure was that the radical suffragists never received the wholehearted support of labour which they so badly needed. Hostility to women's suffrage, from powerful male interests in both the early Labour apparatus and local weavers' and miners' organizations, destined it to political isolation and impotence.

The whole question of the Labour Party's approach to women's suffrage was complex. Thanks to the work of Sandra Holton, we have a detailed account of the relationship between the NUWSS and the early Labour Party. In those years, over a third of adult men were still without a vote. This led the Labour Party in 1904 to adopt a policy of adult suffrage rather than a specific commitment to women. The Labour leadership were suspicious of any limited women's suffrage bill on the grounds that it would advantage only 'fine ladies' at the expense of their poorer sisters. The National Union, which was prepared to support a limited bill on the 'half a loaf is better than none' principle, was equally suspicious of Labour's concept of adult suffrage, fearing that it would eventually turn out to be manhood suffrage only. As the NUWSS well understood, hiding behind the adult suffrage tag were Labour men who were completely hostile to any women's suffrage measure. This stalemate and the NUWSS's official commitment to be non-party went on for several years, although in practice many rank and file activists continued to hold joint membership of Labour organizations, particularly the ILP and the National Union. At the same time there was increasing frustration at the inability of the NUWSS to successfully steer a bill through Parliament, despite increasing evidence of majority support.

Eventually a Conciliation Committee was formed of suffrage MPs of all sides which sought to achieve a compromise. The resulting Conciliation Bills of 1910 and 1911 and their defeat made the NUWSS realize that its best hope lay with Labour. The Labour Party Conference of January 1912 voted not to support any electoral reform measure which did not include women, which removed any remaining doubts among the NUWSS leadership that an alliance was desirable. Following the defeat of the third Conciliation Bill in March 1912, formal negotiations were opened and Arthur Henderson, for the Labour Party, and Kathleen Courtney, for the NUWSS, hammered out the details of a new policy of mutual support.[76] Between April 1912 and the outbreak of war the National Union supported Labour candidates in by-elections and undertook joint campaigning. This activity also included a successful trade union campaign. The new policy provoked disquiet amongst Liberals in the NUWSS, particularly in view of the forthcoming General Election. It seems certain that some Liberal NUWSS support fell away, but as Holton points out, the new policy created many more recruits than those who defected.[77]

The Women's Social and Political Union (WSPU) originated in Manchester in 1903. Emmeline Pankhurst and her daughters Christabel and Sylvia had deep roots within the ILP and the North of England Suffrage Society. The Pankhurst women tried to motivate ILP men towards the suffrage issue, but found little interest. Emmeline and Christabel were also impatient with the constitutional policies of the National Union and became increasingly convinced of the need to put direct pressure on the Government, rather than relying on private members' bills. Militant tactics began in 1905 with the heckling of Ministers at public meetings, symbolizing women's right to access to male public discourse. Between 1906 and 1907 the WSPU broke its remaining ties with Labour and moved offices to London. A spiral of militancy followed, culminating in mass window-smashing, destruction of property, including art treasures, and arson. No life was put at risk except their own. Thousands of women across the country were swept up into the campaign. Viscountess Rhondda led a privileged life in London and at the family estate near Newport. The suffrage movement came 'like a draught of fresh air into our padded, stifled lives'.[78] After various small acts of militancy her local WSPU branch decided that they ought to attempt something more dramatic, 'I decided that we had better try burning letters' on the grounds that 'setting fire to letters in pillar boxes was amongst the easiest of the things we could find to do'.[79] Jane Wyatt, a young teacher in Leicester, became an ardent follower. 'One early morning ... a friend and I burnt with vitriol VOTES FOR WOMEN all over a local golf course, the secretary of which was unfortunately a sympathiser and his wife a member, but the only other course was miles away'.[80]

Working-class women were also involved in the campaign. Hannah Mitchell, a young mother from Ashton-under-Lyne, was a member of the ILP and a Poor Law Guardian. She met the Pankhursts and became a WSPU organizer in Oldham. In 1906 she went to London and spoke at several rallies. She recalls in her autobiography that on the way home she was keen 'to get a few hours' rest on the journey, as I knew that arrears of work, including the weekly wash, awaited my return'.[81] It was not easy to combine the heavy demands of suffrage (let alone militant) activity and running a household and very soon ill-health forced her to give up the WSPU. For working-class women who were imprisoned for the cause, the conflict was even more severe. Mrs Towler went to a conference in London in 1908. She spent the week before baking to ensure that her husband and four sons would be well supplied. In London she participated in a raid on the House of Commons and was arrested and imprisoned.

After a fortnight had gone by Mrs Towler became extremely agitated thinking of her family who, by now, would have eaten every crumb of her baking. So great was her distress that Mrs Pethick-Lawrence was asked to bail her out. This done, she fled home to Preston and put her oven on.[82]

Over a thousand women were imprisoned for suffrage activities. Medical doctor Elizabeth Chalmers Smith and artist Ethel Moorhead were caught red-handed trying to burn down an empty house in the west end of Glasgow. They both received eight-month sentences, in spite of the fact that Chalmers Smith had six children.[83] As Millicent Fawcett wrote, 'all through 1908 and 1909 every possible blunder was committed with regard to the suffrage prisoners'.[84] The refusal of the government to grant them political status led to hunger strikes from 1909 and a horrific regime of force-feeding, which those enduring it likened to rape.[85] The young Lady Constance Lytton was imprisoned in Newcastle Gaol and received preferential treatment on account of her social status. When she was arrested again in Liverpool in disguise as a working woman, she was force-fed eight times with great brutality.

Then he put down my throat a tube which seemed to me much too wide and was something like four feet in length. The irritation of the tube was excessive. I choked the moment it touched my throat until it had got down. Then the food was poured in quickly; it made me sick a few seconds later ... The horror of it was more than I can describe ... I was sick over the doctor and the wardresses, and it seemed a long time before they took the tube out. As the doctor left he gave me a slap on the cheek.[86]

This torture was performed without the necessary prior medical examination. Had this been done it would have revealed that

Constance Lytton was suffering from heart disease. Her health broke down soon after and she was an invalid until her death in 1923.

Force-feeding was not the only aggressive act shown toward the suffragettes. Attempts at public meetings were often met with showers of rotten eggs and tomatoes or by the speaker being dragged bodily from the platform. There were men who supported women's suffrage, and some of these were prepared to act as bodyguards for suffrage speakers. Clearly there was also a great deal of male anger and hostility towards feminists of any type, particularly suffragettes. This came to a head on 18 November 1910, subsequently known as 'Bloody Friday'. When it became known that Prime Minister Asquith was not going to allow any time for the Conciliation Bill, Mrs Pankhurst called for a march on Parliament. The charge of the suffragettes, symbolically demanding access to forbidden places, and the police retaliation, created a battle lasting for six hours. There were 119 arrests and many injuries caused by the aggressive tactics of the police, which included dragging women into side streets for a beating.[87]

Faced with such opposition it is perhaps not surprising that the movement developed a quasi-military ethos, combined with a religious fervour and making extensive use of ritual and symbolism. Although all women were welcome inside the WSPU, it soon became clear that women of 'means and influence' were the preferred membership of this army.[88] Democratic procedures such as annual conferences for policy-making were dropped and unquestioning obedience to instructions from the leadership was demanded. Christabel, the acknowledged leader from 1907, would not tolerate any compromise solutions. When Janie Allan, the chief WSPU Scottish organizer, made an agreement with the Glasgow Lord Provost that during the forthcoming royal visit no militancy would occur providing the suffrage prisoners in Perth were not forcibly fed, she was sacked.[89] For Christabel such a deal meant bargaining with the enemy, which could not be tolerated as only the granting of votes for women could end militancy.

Increasingly, Christabel saw the struggle as a sex-war and focused on the destructive aspects of women's relationships with men, particularly the male regulation of sexuality and the dangers of male-inflicted venereal disease. She stressed female

power, female solidarity and the factors which united women and
not those that divided them, such as class. From 1912 the
movement was at fever pitch. Driven by an unyielding opposition,
and its renunciation of constitutionalism, to more and more
desperate acts, the movement reached the limits of militancy.
Christabel, Emmeline and other WSPU leaders had become
virtual outlaws. By early 1914 most of the rank and file were burnt
out and exhausted.

Not all of the WSPU membership lasted this far. There was
early disquiet at adoption of an autocratic structure. Formidable
women such as Charlotte Despard and Teresa Billington Grieg
could not tolerate the loss of internal democracy and split off to
form the Women's Freedom League (WFL) in 1907. The WFL
developed a policy of tax resistance and also organized a boycott
of the 1911 Census. The League retained strong links with
Labour and in 1912 fell in with the NUWSS-Labour alliance.
The second Pankhurst daughter, Sylvia, also developed misgiv-
ings. A talented artist, she designed many WSPU banners and
emblems and also participated fully in the campaign. During a
tour of the provinces in 1912 she had a message from Christabel,
'Would I burn down Nottingham Castle?'[90] Sylvia thought that
such a deed would be morally wrong and would not help the
cause. Unlike her mother and sister, Sylvia retained her links
with the labour movement and favoured building up a working-
class women's movement, which they considered futile. The
turning point came soon after when George Lansbury resigned
his seat in Poplar, East London, and fought the by-election on
the suffrage issue. Sylvia and a squad of WSPU women were sent
to help Lansbury, although they were under strict instructions to
work independently and not take orders from men. After
Lansbury had been defeated, the WSPU leadership favoured
pulling out of the area, but Sylvia was captivated by the East End
and stayed for twelve years.

Sylvia Pankhurst succeeded in building around her a base
of working-class women such as Mrs Savoy, a brushmaker and
Mrs Payne, a shoemaker, with whom she lodged, into the East
London Federation of Suffragettes (ELFS). Like the radical
suffragists, they were not interested in the vote for its own sake
but to alleviate sweated labour, maternal and infant mortality and
other evils, and to build a more equal society. She built close links

with the local labour movement, particularly the Lansbury's. Sylvia's socialist-feminism increasingly alarmed the WSPU leadership and, in January 1914, it was finally decided that a split was necessary.[91] Within two months, and with some help from wealthy friends, the first issue of *The Women's Dreadnought* appeared. The ELFS developed a distinct following across the many districts of the East End, but it remained a localized phenomenon.

In later years Sylvia Pankhurst's account of the suffragette movement became the standard text. During the socialist-feminist revival of the late 1970s it was especially favoured and Sylvia became something of a socialist-feminist icon. Both Liddington and Norris' book and Garner's *Stepping Stones to Women's Liberty* follow Sylvia's interpretation of events, particularly the degeneration of Emmeline and Christabel into deranged man-hating traitors. This demonization of the two WSPU leaders as traitors for breaking their links with Labour (and focusing exclusively on gender), has been challenged by more recent work from a more radical feminist perspective. Jane Marcus' introduction to the Pankhurst anthology argues that Sylvia has led us to ask the wrong questions: not why did the militants abandon Labour but 'why did Labour reject and repudiate the suffrage movement?'[92] Marcus sees Sylvia's text in the context of the family split, with Sylvia skilfully weaving the narrative to denigrate her mother and sister and to present herself as the heroine of the suffrage struggle.[93] Vicinus has sought to emphasize the revolutionary nature of the militants, seeing Emmeline and Christabel as feminist revolutionaries, leading a crusade of martyrs who were prepared to sacrifice themselves to create a new vision of womanhood.[94] The difference in the two perspectives comes out very clearly in the issue of sexuality. Sylvia argues that Christabel cynically used sexuality as an issue which would not offend wealthy Conservative women.[95] Subsequent writers saw this issue as fairly marginal to the movement overall. Susan Kingsley Kent regards this as a mistake, arguing that the struggle for sexual autonomy and a new sexual culture was central to the creation of a new female-centred value system.[96]

Putting aside these historiographical issues, there is one aspect of the whole suffrage campaign which is unequivocal. From the recorded memoirs of all kinds of women who were involved in the movement, both suffragists and suffragettes, it is clear that the shared vision, solidarity and sisterhood generated by the struggle was a richly rewarding and positive experience which they cherished for the rest of their lives. As Jane Wyatt put it:

The companionship and friendship of many wonderful women, charming, gracious, highly intelligent, and anxious to serve humanity and make a better life for everyone, I shall always venerate and honour, and for that alone everything was worthwhile.[97]

2

NO TIME TO WEEP: THE FIRST WORLD WAR, 1914–1918

In many ways the First World War was a watershed for British society. Those four years of national crisis and extreme nationalist fervour left an indelible imprint. For the majority, brought up on the popular culture of the imperial myth, it started as the ultimate 'Boy's Own' adventure, but as the full horror gradually unfolded and the casualty lists escalated many developed a more critical attitude. After the terrible losses of the battles of 1915 and 1916 practically everyone was grieving for a lost relative, neighbour or friend. The long duration of the war, brought about by the changing technology of warfare, led to a situation of 'total war' which required extensive new areas of state intervention for the necessary mobilization of resources. This had far-reaching repercussions for almost every area of life.

Conventional histories of the war focused almost exclusively on the military aspects of the conflict. With the exception of a flawed account by David Mitchell in 1966, it was not until the 1970s that women in the war began to elicit the interest of historians.[1] Fuelled by popular interest, especially from 'second-wave feminism', which sought out positive images of women breaking traditional gender boundaries, Arthur Marwick's *Women at War*, was a pioneering attempt at bringing the role of women in the war to the foreground.[2] Marwick's optimistic work was followed by a detailed analysis by Gail Braybon of the changes which the war brought about in women's employment.[3] During the 1980s, the focus shifted from women workers to the feminist movement as it became clear that many pre-war feminists did not join with Emmeline and Christabel Pankhurst in supporting the war. The split in the movement and the subsequent participation by British women in the attempts to procure a negotiated settlement are reflected in works such as that of Jill Liddington, Jo Vellacott and Joanna Alberti.[4] Martin Pugh has focused more on the workings of the political elite in relation to feminism.[5] He also goes to some length to minimalize the demographic impact of the war and to explode the myth of the 'lost generation' of women who were forced to remain spinsters. In a new approach, Susan Kingsley Kent has done much to illuminate our understanding of how the war itself was conceived in gendered terms and how that in turn influenced understandings of gender.[6] Clare Tylee's *The Great War and Women's Consciousness* provides a comprehensive survey of women's writings on the war.[7]

Work – Paid and Voluntary

Although the First World War is often associated with widening opportunities for women workers, initially the opposite was the case. The declaration of war in early August created an immediate sharp downturn in employment for both men and women. The wave of patriotism created by the war and the uncertainty about the future induced people to dispense with domestic servants and defer purchase of luxury items such as evening dresses and confectionery. The Lancashire cotton trade, the biggest employer of industrial women, was also immediately hit by a plunge in cotton exports upon which it was heavily dependent. To make matters worse, well-off women, fired by a patriotic desire to support the war effort, volunteered to do sewing and other war work which deprived working-class women of an income.

After protests from women trade union leaders, particularly Mary Macarthur, some effort was made to steer volunteers in other directions and to focus on providing relief work for women who would otherwise be in distress. Queen Mary's Work for Women Fund and other similar schemes initiated a number of workrooms for women, mainly employing them to do sewing. Wages, which did not exceed 11s 6d a week, were similar to the 'sweated' trades. No attempt was made to train women for industrial work. It's not surprising that Sylvia Pankhurst was forthright in her condemnation of 'Queen Mary's Sweatshops'![8]

As the economy adjusted to arms production new opportunities for women's employment began to be created. By the end of the year unemployment among women began to decline and by early 1915 industry was looking hungrily at women workers to help fulfil the enormous demands now placed upon it by war production and the loss of male workers to the front. The question of substitution raised complex issues which involved the state, employers and unions, as well as the women themselves. Of course, there were examples, particularly in the service sector, of direct substitution arranged informally within families – women doing milk rounds, chimney-sweeping etc. for absent husbands, brothers or fathers. But for arms production, where large-scale substitution was required, more formal arrangements were necessary. Since on average women earned less than half the wages of men, and the whole edifice of patriarchal power rested on the idea of the male breadwinner, this was a particularly urgent issue for the male-dominated labour movement.

In March 1915 the Board of Trade made a public request for women to volunteer for war service. It announced the creation of a Register of Women for War Service. Lloyd George was now united with Mrs Pankhurst in backing her 'right to serve' campaign, which reached its peak in the summer of 1915. The only problem was that in virtually all branches of industry, organized labour (that is, male labour) was opposed to the introduction of women workers.[9] The government were at this time in the process of introducing widespread powers over the control of labour, including the outlawing of strikes and prohibition of the free movement of labour. The engineering union, the Amalgamated Society of Engineers (ASE), was an elite craft union which fiercely defended the pay rates and privileged status of its all-male membership. Although it resisted the introduction of women into munitions work ASE realized that, if it did not compromise, a solution would be imposed upon it. To this end it formed a seemingly unlikely alliance with the National Federation of Women Workers (NFWW) in the summer of 1915.[10] The general principles of a policy towards women workers were hammered out between employers, unions and the government during 1915 and continued to evolve in the next two years. The women workers themselves were not represented. The unions agreed to relax their restrictions on the employment of women, but only for the duration of the war. This principle was also a key point in the alliance between ASE and the NFWW. Macarthur, leader of the NFWW, supported this principle, but she was also realistic enough to know that it was politically unavoidable. It was established that where women replaced men on piece work, existing rates would be maintained. Women would not get equal-time rates, but a specially introduced 'women's rate' for the job.

In practice, women were largely assigned to time-rate work, so the question of equal pay was avoided. Within arms production it appears that only women welders, who numbered only a few hundred, managed to achieve equal pay. The skilled male workers were relatively successful in preserving the higher paid, high-status work for themselves.[11] This position was eroded, however, by the gradual introduction of new work processes which broke down skilled work into a large number of small, repetitive tasks. The work was then regarded as unskilled and therefore suitable for women 'dilutees'. Peggy Hamilton, a middle-class volunteer, describes in her memoirs how tedious the work was in the New Fuse Factory at Woolwich: 'I'll do twenty more and then look at the clock, I'd tell myself.'[12]

In these circumstances women workers were often paid as little as 13–15s a week. Macarthur, on behalf of the NFWW, campaigned vigorously for a £1 a week minimum for women war workers on a standard 60-hour week. (This demand, supported by ASE, was the price it had to pay for the alliance with the NFWW.) Macarthur argued, with some justification, that since government controls now prevented women workers from switching to higher paid work and thus taking advantage of increased demand for their labour, the government was morally

bound to pay them a decent wage. By early 1916 the argument
for the £1 a week minimum was largely won at ministry level, but
there were many problems in enforcement. In any case, by then
wartime inflation had eroded the value of money considerably.
By 1916 very large numbers of women were involved in war
production of one sort or another. The idea of an influx of
middle-class women, such as Peggy Hamilton, into munitions
work is largely a myth as the women concerned were overwhelmingly working class. Popular opinion is that these were
new workers; indeed, official figures for women's employment
increased by about one and a half million. Braybon argues that it
was, in fact, a question of transference as most of the women
concerned were already working in some capacity or other, often
in casual or sweated trades which were not officially recognized.
These hidden workers shifted into war production to increase
their incomes.[13] In engineering, the increase was particularly
staggering, from a relatively insignificant number in 1914 to over
half a million in 1918.[14] In 1914 there were 125 women at the
Woolwich Arsenal in south-east London; by 1917 it had grown
to 25 000.[15]

Conditions at work improved enormously during the course
of the war. The government took over responsibility for this and
became acutely aware that workers would not optimize their
output unless their conditions of work were at least tolerable.
With women often working a 70–80 hour week on rush jobs, it
became vital to introduce canteens and other welfare facilities.
In 1917 the Treasury approved grants for nurseries and in 1918
£21 000 was allotted to 41 nurseries.[16] Unmarried mothers were
no longer shunned but allowed to return to work, although at
Woolwich the children of these women were cared for in a separate nursery from the children of married women.[17] Medical
checks and other health benefits became common, especially
where women were working with dangerous substances such
as TNT and cordite. Even with inflation women workers in
munitions, particularly by 1916–17, were better off than almost
all categories of women workers before 1914.

Women's experiences in the rest of industry were extremely
varied. As Sylvia Walby notes, much depended on the strength of
patriarchal organization within each industry.[18] Some groups
of male workers, such as the Liverpool dockers, successfully

resisted all attempts to introduce women workers. The most notorious example is that of the cotton-mule spinners, who relentlessly campaigned against any suggestion of employing women. In transport the introduction of women was also resisted, but with far less success. As a result the numbers of women in transport grew from 18 000 in 1914 to 117 000 in 1918.[19] On the railways women were employed as carriage cleaners, porters, booking clerks and ticket collectors. The National Union of Railwaymen accepted women members and argued for equality in basic rates. Women became tramdrivers and conductors. Women bus conductors, along with the welders, were the only women workers who achieved equal pay. After a short period of training they were put straight onto the full rate of £2 5s a week.[20] Many trade unions, among them those for silkworkers, bookbinders and electrical trades, took in women members for the first time during the war.

Not surprisingly, the war period can be seen as a golden age of women's trade unionism in many ways. The number of women in unions increased threefold from 433 679 in 1914 to 1 209 278 in 1918.[21] This was, however, still very much a minority of women workers. Although women in textiles remained the largest single group of organized women, huge advances were made in other areas, particularly the general unions. The NFWW was the most outstanding of these, with approximately 80 000 members in 1918.[22] This figure represents a fourfold increase during the war period.

By 1917 women were becoming much more confident as workers and there are some indications of militant activity. At the Woolwich Arsenal women began to claim equality in wage rises instead of what the government decided was fair treatment. But, as Deborah Thom points out, their lack of representation on the shop stewards' committee put them at a great disadvantage.[23] In August 1918 women tramworkers in London struck against the introduction of a new 5s bonus, which was paid only to male workers. The industrial action spread rapidly and threatened to draw in women munition workers. By the end of the month the full 5s bonus (backdated) had been awarded, to all muni-tion workers as well as tramworkers.[24] By the time of the armistice, organized women were really beginning to get into their stride which made the events after November 1918, when the inevitable backlash appeared, particularly depressing for the labour movement.

On the whole it is clear that working-class women who joined the labour force in industry during the war were likely to benefit from wartime circumstances. Almost all industrial work on offer was an improvement on the pre-war options which were primarily domestic service or the sweated trades. It is also the case that increased opportunities did not radically transform the sexual division of labour at work. With very few exceptions, women failed to gain access to higher paid work which was recognized as skilled. The work which they did gain access to was offered only grudgingly, with the all-important proviso of 'for the duration only'. Organized male labour was understandably suspicious about the threat of women workers, as women's pay rates would undermine their own pay. This could only have been overcome by the labour movement arguing for equal pay and that would have drastically undermined the patriarchal ideology which was so central to masculine identity. Consequently, the labour movement's overtures towards equal pay were framed entirely in terms of the necessity of protecting male standards rather than improving the lot of the woman worker.

For the great majority of working-class women, the wages which they earned were the central feature of their working experience. The motivations of middle- and upper-class women were more complex. Many such women had a strong desire to make some visible contribution to the war effort. For very well-off women there was a great deal of continuity between pre-war philanthropic work and war work. Katherine, Duchess of Atholl, whose husband was a foremost Scottish aristocrat, threw herself into all kinds of war work. When news came that soldiers in the highland regiments were suffering from cold knees because of their kilts, she designed a knitted garment to be worn underneath. Within three weeks, 15 000 of them had been knitted and dispatched to France.[25] Later she turned part of her castle home into a convalescent hospital.

For the professionally qualified woman the war opened up new horizons. Mary Stocks was an academic living in London. She continued to lecture in economics throughout the war, despite giving birth to two children in 1915 and 1918. Her autobiography makes it sound like simply a matter of hiring a nanny, but one wonders whether it would have been that easy before the outbreak of war.[26] In medicine, women made a major impact during the war, particularly Scottish women doctors. The work of Dr Elsie Inglis is legendary in this regard. At the outbreak of war she went to the war office personnel in Edinburgh and offered mobile hospital units, staffed by women, for service overseas. She was told that all that was required of women in the war was to 'go home and keep quiet' as the commanding officers did not want to be bothered with 'hysterical women'.[27] Instead, she and her colleagues, largely funded by the National Union of Women's Suffrage Societies (NUWSS), sent hospital units to France, Serbia, Corsica, Salonika, Rumania and Russia. The unit which left for South Russia in September 1916, for instance, had 76 personnel (all women) in 18 vehicles.[28] Not surprisingly, the War Office soon changed its tune about women doctors and by 1915 complaints were heard that it couldn't get enough of them.

In practice, most war work associated with medicine was far more mundane, as women were much more likely to be nurses than doctors. At the beginning of the war there were only a few thousand trained military nurses. Their numbers were hastily augmented by a variety of voluntary organizations, the most significant being the Voluntary Aid Detachments (VADs). Founded in 1910 under the auspices of the Red Cross, they developed an important wartime role. Although rigorously selected from 'good backgrounds', they were expected to perform hard, menial labour, which often included cooking and cleaning as well as nursing. Discipline was harsh and petty regulations ruled their lives. Nurse Bowcatt lost her half day's leave at her hospital in Dorset as the Sister did not think that she had dusted the castors on the beds in her ward adequately.[29]

The most well known of all the VADs is Vera Brittain, whose *Testament of Youth* (1933) really brings home the horrors of the Great War. Vera gave up her studies at Oxford University to become a VAD in south London in 1915. From London she moved to Malta and eventually concluded her war service near the front in France. In her *Testament* she recalls what was expected of these young, totally untrained women. Whilst in France, she arrived for duty one morning to find that her 'light medical' hut had become a surgical ward overnight with 40 desperately wounded men. She found herself

> gazing, half hypnotised, at the dishevelled beds, the stretchers on the floor, the scattered boots and piles of muddy khaki, the brown blankets turned back from smashed limbs bound to splints by filthy blood-stained bandages. Beneath each stinking wad of sodden wool and gauze an obscene horror waited for me.[30]

The war sprouted a plethora of women's paramilitary organizations, some of which had overlapping functions, the Women's Police Volunteers and the Women's Police Service being one example. As Susan Grayzel points out, many women were keen to be in uniform as a visible sign of patriotism at a time of national crisis.[31] The idea of women in khaki aroused fears of the blurring of gender boundaries, and army commanders were extremely resistant to the introduction of women for any purpose. The severe shortage of manpower during 1916, however, led to the formation of the Women's Army Auxiliary Corps (WAAC) in January, 1917. It operated under the principle that 'no woman was to be employed unless a soldier was released for other purposes'.[32] Consequently, the role of the WAAC was to perform duties such as cooking and clerking in order to release men for combat duties. They were very strictly regulated so as to have as little contact as possible with the men. Before the end of the war both the naval and the air force branches of the services also developed women's units: the Women's Royal Naval Service (WRNS) and the Women's Royal Air Force.

The Women's Land Army (Women's National Land Service Corps) was not formally connected with the armed services at all, but it did work closely with related government departments. About 33 000 women went on the land during the war in the three areas of agriculture, timber-cutting and forage.[33] They were poorly paid (18–22s week) and subject to a very strict regime, although women often found a way round the rules. Despite the fact that some educated women gave up professional jobs to join the Land Army they were not welcomed by farmers, who preferred child labour, which was even cheaper, and doubted women's ability to perform heavy manual labour.

In addition, farmers did not want the discipline problems involved with employing young women.

Finally, mention should be made of the involvement of women in the 'white blouse' revolution and the service industries generally. The whole area of work was already increasing rapidly before 1914. The burgeoning role of government created much new employment for women. In 1914 65 000 women worked in the Civil Service, including the Post Office. By 1919 it was 170 000 and the highly segregated work atmosphere of the pre-war years had been somewhat relaxed.[34] Some women seized the opportunity which the war provided to launch themselves into business. The war letters of the affluent Berryman family from Surrey reveal that Jane ('Jinny') Berryman and a friend opened a café-cum-cigarette shop in central London. Reservations were voiced by the enlisted Berryman menfolk about whether this was appropriate work for them to do and whether the two women were capable of managing their own business. In the event, it was a roaring success and the objections of Jinny's brothers were soon forgotten.[35]

Feminism and Votes for Women

Emmeline Pankhurst seemed relieved to be able to call a suspension of militant tactics upon the declaration of war. The militant campaign had exhausted itself and all the leading activists were battle weary. *The Suffragette* ceased publication. Suffragette prisoners were released. Grass-root activists awaited new directives. Within a week the Pankhursts had swung the Women's Social and Political Union (WSPU) behind the government and began an ultra-nationalist campaign to support the war effort. Christabel returned from exile in France, talking not of feminism, but 'the German peril'.[36]

Mrs Pankhurst held recruiting meetings and called upon men to 'go into battle like knights of old'.[37] Her supporters dispensed white feathers to men of military age who were in civilian dress. In the spring of 1915 *The Suffragette* reappeared as a pro-Government paper. Later renamed *Britannia* it was suppressed by the government for its wild accusations about 'traitors'. The Pankhursts encouraged the persecution of naturalized Germans and called for their internment. With extreme racism and xenophobia they called for 'purification of the blood'. They were strong supporters of military conscription for men and industrial conscription for women. Mrs Pankhurst was horrified by the attitude of the organized labour movement towards the introduction of women. With the encouragement of Lloyd George (from May 1915 the Minister of Munitions) she launched the 'right to serve' campaign, which culminated in a 'national procession' in July 1915 when the Pankhursts pulled out their supporters for one last great rally. The difference this time was that it was supported and funded by the government. Both Emmeline and Christabel travelled abroad promoting the British cause. Jaqueline De Vries argues that, contrary to received opinion, there is much continuity between the pre- and post-1914 Pankhurst positions.[38] According to De Vries, the Pankhursts always saw the vote as part of a wider struggle towards national regeneration. This gendered patriotism did not cast aside feminism during the war but rendered up its own elitist, xenophobic version of it. Thus, role models of women patriots such as Joan of Arc were relentlessly promoted.

There is no evidence that more than a tiny handful of WSPU activists actually followed the Pankhursts down this road. The once mass membership rapidly melted away. The decline in numbers forced the WSPU leadership to move to smaller, less prestigious offices. In 1917, when the constitutional suffragists were pressing for a women's enfranchisement clause in the forthcoming Reform Bill, the Pankhursts took little interest, indicating that enlisted men had a greater cause. Only when some form of women's suffrage seemed certain to come about did they take any interest. In November 1917 the WSPU was relaunched as The Women's Party, under the slogan 'Victory, National Security and Progress'. Although it did have demands which related to women it was clear that the old days were over and it soon fizzled out, thus providing the final epitaph to the militant movement.

After the outbreak of war the gulf between Sylvia Pankhurst and her mother and sister became a chasm which remained for the rest of their lives. Whilst Emmeline and Christabel became jingoistic supporters of the war, Sylvia condemned it. The East London Federation of Suffragettes (ELFS), now formally separate from the WSPU, continued to build a socialist-feminist movement in the East End of London, based on the independent self-activity of working-class women. Always much more broadly based than the narrow campaign for the vote, the Federation was now launched into whole new areas of work by the energetic Sylvia. Many East End men joined up, leaving near-destitute families behind. Bureaucratic procedures meant that separation allowances took some time to come through.

Appalled by the increasing distress, the Federation began a milk distribution scheme for destitute babies, with money begged from wealthy sympathisers. This work soon escalated and at its height in 1915–16 the Federation was responsible for two cost-price restaurants, five mother and infant welfare clinics, a toy factory for unemployed women, a nursery, a Montessori school and a women's employment bureau.[39] The nursery, a disused public house transformed from 'The Gunners' Arms' to 'The Mothers' Arms', made use of volunteer labour supplied by some of Sylvia's old WSPU chums. Funding for these enterprises was always a problem. All services were offered at cost price or whatever people could afford. As a result, most of them were permanently in deficit. Although Sylvia fervently believed in an autonomous working-class women's movement, in practice she was heavily reliant on a small group of wealthy supporters, particularly Nora Smythe.[40] As Sylvia's anti-war views became more well known, her middle-class friends deserted her, particularly as she shifted further to the left. She also met with hostility within the East End for her anti-war views. In 1916 the ELFS became the Workers Suffrage Federation and ceased to make a particular appeal to women. The Russian Revolution had a major impact on Sylvia, which is reflected in another name change in 1918 to the Workers Socialist Federation.[41] Sylvia, now an integral part of the British revolutionary left, spoke incessantly of class warfare and hardly bothered to mention women. Not surprisingly, almost all of her original ELFS supporters melted away.

The other major split from the WSPU, the Women's Freedom League, also opposed the war. Determined to keep the suffrage issue alive, it formed the Women's Suffrage National Aid Corps with the indomitable Charlotte Despard as its president. Numerous relief projects followed, many of which were located in the London area, particularly in Battersea where Despard was already well known. The Corps opened milk clinics, soup kitchens and a guest house for exhausted mothers.[42] Although inclined to take a rather pious approach to her philanthropic work, Despard remained politically solid and campaigned against conscription and invasions of civil liberty as well as more directly women's issues.

The largest women's suffrage society, the NUWSS, the umbrella grouping for all the non-militant, constitutional suffrage groups, had a more complex approach to the war. Unlike the WSPU, being a democratic organization there was bound to be a variety of opinions about such a controversial subject. For women such as Millicent Fawcett and Ray Strachey, the pressure to rally round the men in the cause of patriotism was overwhelming. For them, once war had been declared, any talk of a negotiated peace amounted to treachery. Such opinions alarmed other more pacifist inclined NUWSS leaders such as Kathleen Courtney and Maude Royden, editor of the Union's paper, *The Common Cause*.[43] Eventually, the NUWSS resolved to support a negotiated peace, but not peace at any price.[44] The inability of the pacifists to push the Union any further led to a split in 1915. Half the executive resigned, including Courtney, Royden, Alice Clark and Isabella Ford. Some of the activities of the 'pro-peace' feminists are described below.

NUWSS activists recognized the urgent necessity of immediate relief work, particularly for the quarter of a million Belgian refugees who had fled from the invading German army. Inevitably this humanitarian aid broadened out into more general support for the war effort. Local groups became involved in a large variety of different projects, most of which managed to tie in the cause of women with the war effort. Many women abandoned the NUWSS altogether as, for them, the only reality became the war and they threw themselves into war work as nurses, drivers, stretcher-bearers and doctors. As Alberti observes, 'the terrible seduction of danger' made them want to share the experiences of the men by becoming directly involved.[45] For other women workers it was the same. Women who become breadwinners and work 70–80 hours a week do not have much time for meetings. Not surprisingly, as women became increasingly bound up with the war, the Union lost its mass base, particularly its working-class membership. Although the NUWSS remained loyal to the cause of women, women did not remain loyal to it. The links with Labour, which had taken so long to establish, were now pushed to one side. By 1918 the NUWSS was behaving much more like a middle-class pressure group and the mass movement of women for democratic reform became nothing more than a memory. The traditional explanation for women's enfranchisement in 1918 was their contribution to the war effort. This view has been challenged by Pugh who argues that the long fought for suffrage came about almost by accident, as a bi-product of wider electoral reform.[46] Whilst there is an element of truth in this argument, it is certainly not the case that the women's movement played no role in the granting of the suffrage, as Pugh implies. More recently, Kingsley Kent has argued that fear of renewed militancy, hence 'sex war', played a part but it is difficult to see that this threat was real as there were no forces within the movement ready to resume militancy.[47]

Within a year of the war starting, electoral registers became practically worthless as the male population was so transient. Even when functioning efficiently the franchise did not allow large sections of the male population to vote (hence the adult suffrage argument). With such men at the front dying for their country it was a matter of some political urgency to extend the franchise. In May 1916, when Sir Edward Carson and a group of MPs began to agitate for a reform bill, the NUWSS pressed their case for inclusion. By late summer the proposal for an all-party conference on electoral reform, under the chair of the Speaker, had been accepted and most people expected some sort of 'votes for women' clause to be included. Despite the vigorous efforts of Sylvia Pankhurst and other adult suffragists for full, universal adult suffrage, the mood was very much one of compromise. The change of government at the end of the year benefited women as Labour, which supported women's suffrage, now had a place in a Coalition government.

Public opinion had changed. The suffragette campaign had been suspended and most people were preoccupied with the war. Such opinions that were expressed about women's suffrage were now generally in favour. Asquith and other public figures made it public that they had changed sides and were now supporting votes for women. It seems difficult to assert, as Pugh does, that women's contribution to the war was insignificant in bringing about the franchise.[48] If this was so, why did the anti-suffrage movement collapse so suddenly during the war? Most local branches ceased to function and only a few die-hard public figures, such as Mrs Humphrey Ward and Lord Curzon, were left aboard the rapidly capsizing anti-suffrage boat. Nevertheless, the 'anti's' still had some cards to play. They argued that women's enfranchisement would endanger the country, as full women's suffrage would give women voters a majority. In addition, the anti's argued that the links between feminism and organized labour, which was increasingly radicalized by the war, would destabilize the country and steer it towards revolution.[49] These arguments did have some influence and the bill which made its way through Parliament in the summer of 1917 included an age qualification for women voters of 30 (as against 21 for men). On 6 February 1918, the Representation of the People Act finally became law. The new law gave the vote to eight and a half million women, which meant that women formed just under 40 per cent of the new electorate.[50]

Ultimately, the explanation for the enfranchisement of women is inextricably bound up with the experience of war, particularly women's experience of war, and not a simple bi-product of it as Pugh implies. The war broke down the seemingly impenetrable deadlock between the suffragists and anti's. As Balfour later admitted, the war provided the excuse for a number of people who realized that they had been wrong to change sides.[51] Pugh points out that, given that a large number of MPs were in favour of women's suffrage before 1914, it was only necessary for a fairly small number to change sides to bring about the required majority.[52] This shift was possible not just because of women's war effort but because the whole of society had changed.

Feminism and Pacifism

As the threat of war hung over the country, women's peace rallies were called for 4 August 1914. Events overtook them and the meetings were held on the day that war broke out. The London women's peace meeting, sponsored by the NUWSS and reluctantly chaired by Millicent Fawcett, was packed to capacity with representatives from suffrage, Co-op and trade union organizations.[53] The meeting did not offer outright opposition but urged mediation to end the conflict. The overwhelming feeling was shock and bewilderment. The peace rallies came to an abrupt end when Germany invaded neutral Belgium. Refugees and stories about German atrocities, many of which were overtly sexualized, flooded in. Mary Stocks, who had attended one of the Manchester peace meetings, describes in her autobiography the 'revulsion of feeling' which the German aggression created. This 'monstrous, wicked, unprovoked act of aggression' meant that for her, and her circle of friends, there had to be a 'farewell to peace activities'.[54]

The country was gripped by a wave of anti-Germanism and war hysteria but there were some courageous women who spoke out against the war. NUWSS leaders Helena Swanwick, Maude Royden and Kate Courtney were sickened by all the talk of 'killing the Hun'. Their views were shared by a surprisingly diverse group of women, bringing together the Leeds socialist-feminist Isabella Ford, Emmeline Pethwick-Lawrence (previously of the WSPU), Sylvia Pankhurst, Charlotte Despard, Mrs Barton of the Co-operative Women's Guild and many others.[55] The Union for Democratic Control of Foreign Policy (UDC) was formed soon after the outbreak of war. Although dominated by male intellectuals it had a feminist presence, including Kate Courtney, Helena Swanwick and Isabella Ford.

Feminist intellectuals wrestled with the connections between feminism and pacifism. The NUWSS had always argued that they did not want the vote for its own sake but to transform society. As Jo Vellacott recognizes, the abolition of militarism and the creation of non-violent methods of decision-making was an important part of this.[56] Maude Royden got to the crux of the problem when she identified masculinity as being inextricably bound up with militarism.[57] She understood that women could be militaristic, but argued that feminism as an organized movement could not be militaristic as militarism could never be integrated with feminism.

There was an international aspect to this movement right from the start and a framework for action was created through the International Women's Suffrage Alliance (IWSA). A proposal was made to hold an international women's peace congress in the spring of 1915 at the Hague in Holland. The IWSA leadership did not sponsor the Hague Congress, which was the work of a group of individual IWSA women, including British women Chrystal MacMillan and Kate Courtney. The British co-ordinating committee organized a 180-strong delegation, which included such names as Margaret Bondfield the labour leader, Charlotte Despard, Olive Schreiner the writer, Alice Clark the historian, and many other well-known women.[58]

Due to the blocking tactics of the government, only three British women (Emmeline Pethwick-Lawrence, Chrystal Mac-Millan and Kate Courtney) actually made it to the Congress. Due to similar difficulties, no French or Russian women attended. A dozen countries were represented, including Germany. The Congress urged the warring governments to seek peaceful means to settle their differences and sent diplomatic envoys to all the major European governments and to President Wilson of the USA. Wilson's 14 points, issued in January 1918, which were very influential in the eventual peace settlement, bear a striking similarity to the resolutions of the Hague Congress. The Hague delegates also laid the basis for an international women's peace movement with the formation of the International Committee of Women for Permanent Peace (ICWPP), which established a base in Amsterdam.[59] The British branch of the ICWPP was officially launched in October, 1915 as the Women's International League (WIL). By the end of 1916 34 local groups had been estab-lished.[60] Activists such as Maude Royden and Kate Courtney often met with physical abuse at public meetings and pacifist women were sometimes disowned by their families.

Early in 1916 the government introduced conscription and by the middle of the year this was fully in force. At the same time, news was pouring in from France of staggering casualty figures, sometimes amounting to 20 000 men in a single day. Men posted to France had a more than even chance of being killed, wounded or missing. In these circumstances it is not surprising that the peace movement gathered enormous momentum during the year. The No Conscription Fellowship (NCF) was formed and feminist-pacifists such as Katherine Marshall became involved in it. The movement, no longer dominated by pacifist intellectuals, drew in much larger numbers of ex-suffragists, socialists, organized labour and religious groups. In April 1917, when

Sylvia Pankhurst and Charlotte Despard organized a peace rally in Victoria Park, Hackney, staff and wounded soldiers stood outside Poplar Hospital and cheered the procession, which marched under the heading 'Spring and Peace Must Come Together'.[61]

There is evidence, especially in the north, that working-class women, albeit a minority, identified with the peace movement. Hannah Mitchell, in her autobiography, describes the 'agony of mind' which she went through when her son was making up his mind whether or not to become a Conscientious Objector: 'I couldn't bear to live if I knew he had killed another woman's son'.[62] Like Mitchell, Selina Cooper, NUWSS organizer in Nelson, Lancashire, opposed the war from the beginning. Cooper was inspired by the women at the Hague and keenly followed developments in the international women's peace movement.[63] Alice Wheeldon and her daughter Hettie, both ex-WSPU members from Derby, became involved with the undercover work of the NCF and helped to put up men on the run. After being tricked by an agent provocateur, they were charged with plotting to assassinate Lloyd George. Alice was released two years into a sentence of ten-year penal servitude due to her broken health and died soon afterwards.[64]

The growing number of women, particularly working-class women, opposed to the war culminated in the formation of the Women's Peace Crusade. Initiated by the Scot Helen Crawfurd, an ex-suffragette, it rapidly took off in 'Red Clydeside', which had already experienced a working-class women's movement against rent rises (see below). A national network was quickly established and a whole series of demonstrations were held during the summer of 1917, including Manchester, Bradford, Leeds and Birmingham.[65] Cardiff also developed a strong women's peace movement. The Crusade produced a pamphlet, *An Appeal to Women* by Charlotte Despard, which sold more than 100 000 copies.

Life and Death

The increasingly interventionist role of the state has already been noted. Measures which would have been virtually unthinkable in peacetime were accepted with little fuss. Some of this legislation was of direct benefit to women, such as the restrictions on the opening times of public houses. More significantly, the separation allowances for dependants of servicemen marked a major advance in state responsibility. Although not generous, the allowances paid were graduated for each dependant, so that a wife with four dependent children would get almost twice as much as one with only one dependent child. These allowances would provide for about half the weekly needs of the families involved.[66] This acknowledged for the first time the varying needs of families and thus helped to pave the way for the family allowances advocated by Beveridge after the Second World War. As was to be expected, the war heightened interest in 'national efficiency', particularly the care of mothers and infants. Training for midwives was extended and the number of health visitors increased. Grants to local authorities were increased so that by the end of the war the government were covering half the costs of ante-natal and childcare clinics.

The impetus for new legislation did not emanate entirely from above, rent control being a major example of this. Wartime inflation and pressure for housing in areas around munitions factories led to an upward drift in rents during 1915. A wave of rent strikes followed in many cities. Glasgow, which had some of the worst housing in Britain, eventually had 25 000 tenants withholding rent.[67] Women such as Mrs Barbour of Govan and Mrs Ferguson of Partick led an army of women who beat off with flour bombs, rotten fish and other missiles all attempts to collect rent. Eventually, when the munition workers on the Clyde came out in support of the rent strike, the government gave in and rushed through a rent control act. Although not completely effective, the new act did mark the first real attempt by the state to intervene in the housing market.

One of the ironies of the war is that women on the whole emerged in 1918 healthier and enjoying a higher standard of living than in 1914. Unemployment had been virtually wiped out and with it much of the grim destitution of the pre-war era. Women workers were benefiting from subsidized canteens and other welfare measures. More importantly, they were earning more than ever before, as a 'levelling up' of wages eroded differentials with craft workers. Although large numbers of men were away from home and (consequently) fewer babies were born, more milk, potatoes, bread, flour and oatmeal was consumed per family than in 1914.[68] Better diet was no doubt a major factor in the falling rates of virtually all categories of female mortality from 1915.[69] Winter writes that evidence of reduced social inequality was accompanied by a decline in deference and an unwillingness to put up with poverty and powerlessness.[70] This must surely apply to working-class women who were one of the most disadvantaged groups in society in 1914. Proof of this can be seen in the unwillingness of women to return to domestic service in the post-war years.

The habits and conventions of personal life underwent important changes for women during the war. Young women, in particular, became much more independent and assertive. Old ideas about morality could hardly be kept in force when women were earning a wage and living in a hostel far from parental influence. Everyone was far too busy to be bothered with chaperones any more. Women were now seen together, without men, in public houses and restaurants. Skirts were shorter and in some cases had been abandoned altogether for trousers. Many factories organized women's football teams as they could no longer sustain the usual men's teams. Such changes were not universally welcomed. Complaints were made about women munition workers who were sometimes apt to be rather boisterous in public when they were out enjoying themselves after their long hours of toil. As Braybon notes, no one complained about soldiers on leave letting off steam.[71] Olive, a landworker, recalled for Southampton Oral History Project the reaction of villagers in Fairoak when she appeared with a friend in breeches, 'the Fairoak people stoned us because we were in breeches. Threw stones at us; in those days they were so shocked to see women in breeches they stoned us.'[72]

The war raised awareness of sexuality in a number of ways. In the early months, teenage girls swooned around barracks in a phenomenon dubbed as 'khaki fever'. As Angela Woollacott observes, this blatant display of sexual desire was a challenge to the prevailing notion of respectable femininity.[73] As the casualty figures rose and as women themselves became more directly involved in the war, khaki fever subsided. Casual sexual encounters became more common as young people felt that they should 'live for today'. Increased availability of sex and the enhanced employment opportunities for women actually reduced the level of prostitution during the war. Although sales of condoms boomed, a steep rise in the number of births outside marriage was recorded. Attitudes towards unmarried mothers were slightly relaxed, but on the whole the future for such women was still bleak.

Although the war has been popularly associated with an element of personal liberation for women, this has to be set alongside the tragedy of war. When an American woman, Mabel Daggett, made a tour of Britain and other war-torn countries of Europe in 1918 she wrote, 'Everywhere I turn I am looking on men with broken bodies and women with broken hearts.'[74] Over one and a half million men were permanently disabled as a result of the war.[75] Some were so badly maimed that they spent the rest of their lives in institutions. Others, with missing limbs, blinded, chests ruined by poison gas or forever traumatized by shell-shock, were cared for by mothers, wives and sisters. Another three-quarters of a million men did not return at all. About an eighth of all enlisted men were killed. Women like Vera Brittain had to come to terms with the sudden, violent death of their loved ones. After the death of her fiancé, Roland Leighton, Vera 'wondered however I was going to get through the weary remainder of life.[76] With formal mourning and the wearing of crepe no longer observed, many women fell into a kind of perpetual mourning.[77] Some attended seances in the hope that they could overcome the final barrier of death.

For many grieving women, particularly those from the working class, the problems brought about by the loss (or maiming) of a husband or father were of a practical as well as emotional nature. The death of a breadwinner was likely to bring financial ruin to a young family. Gilbert and Annie Nash were a close couple with two young daughters and a baby son, living in High Wycombe. After leaving for army training soon after the start of the war Gilbert wrote tender letters to Annie full of affection and concern for her and the children. He missed them all terribly and longed for letters from home. Within a few weeks of arriving in France in the spring of 1915, he was dead and Annie was left to bring up the family alone and unsupported, except for a tiny widow's pension.[78] Whilst it may be true that there was no 'lost generation' it is also undoubtedly the case that the losses amounted to millions of personal tragedies. The Nash family is but one example of a family torn apart by the war and these stories of misery must surely form a crucial element of the legacy of the First World War.

3

A NEW FEMININITY, 1919–1939

This 'long weekend' of British history witnessed many important shifts towards contemporary society. But there was a sense in which the First World War could not be left behind. The individual and collective mourning, visible everywhere in human grief and stone memorials, were the outward signs of a society which could never quite come to terms with the trauma of the so-called Great War. Historians are still assessing the impact of the war on British society. Recently, Susan Kingsley Kent has put new emphasis on the paramount need to reassert traditional gender differences after their apparent blurring during the duration of the conflict.[1] This has led to a vigorous debate about the nature of 'new' feminism in these years. It is apparent, however, that 'first wave' feminism as a mass movement was dead, but feminist issues were still doggedly pursued by a dedicated group of predominantly middle-class women.

The war also produced a shock to imperial confidence from which it was never to recover and so began a long slow retreat from empire. The Peace Congress at Versailles did not create a permanent peace and the German 'problem' was soon to reassert itself on the European stage. By the mid-1930s the threat of fascism dominated both the national and international agendas. At home, the Labour Party became the second party of state and for two brief periods a governing power, although its minority status and conservative economic philosophy prevented far-reaching social reform. Both politically and socially these years were dominated by conservatism. Restructuring of the economy

59

meant that the areas of traditional industries, mainly in the north, declined steeply leaving behind mass unemployment and distress. But alongside the gloomy picture of the 'hungry thirties' there was new hope in the booming consumer industries of the midlands and the south. Improved living standards for many people were reflected in the growing leisure industries, especially cinema, dancing and holiday resorts. Such activities were made possible by a fall in working hours as well as a growth in disposable income for those in work.

The falling birthrate created the small nuclear family of modern times and with it came a new ideal of womanhood, based more decisively than ever on an ideology of domesticity. Four million new homes meant that many couples achieved the dream of a home of their own, in marked contrast to the rented rooms which was the unfortunate lot of their parents. The new suburban housing estates, complete with such luxuries as modern kitchens, bathrooms and front and back gardens, encapsulated the popular ideal of privatized family life. The rapid growth of radio broadcasts to individual homes from 1922 emphasized this new family-centred world, where the new woman could contentedly care for her family and the new man could acquaint himself with his children, potter about in the garden and engage in home maintenance and improvement. Paradoxically, despite the pressures to bury themselves in domestic life, women's employment expanded in these years, particularly in the new consumer industries.

In studying this period, we are fortunate in that it has generated many more autobiographies than had earlier years, giving us many accounts of girls growing up in working-class families.[2] We also have women's testimony from many other sources, including the Women's Health Enquiry of 1939 which revealed a great deal of information about the poor state of health of the nation's women, and letters to Marie Stopes about birth control in the 1920s.[3] In addition, women's testimony has been collected in numerous oral history studies which cover this period.[4]

Paid Employment and the Labour Movement

The move to dismiss women workers from munitions began after the collapse of the eastern front at the end of 1917. This steady trickle became a flood as soon as the armistice was signed in November 1918. Overall, 775 000 women had either left voluntarily or been dismissed within a year.[5] The Aintree Aircraft factory in Liverpool shed 8000 women.[6] The Woolwich Arsenal in East London employed over 25 000 women workers at its peak in 1917. By March 1919 only 5000 were left and these were soon to go.[7] Government departments, local authorities and businesses also dismissed women, particularly if they were married. The War Office alone dismissed 700 women at the end of 1919.[8] A formal marriage bar came into force in many areas for women teachers, clerks, nurses and civil servants. This vicious backlash against women workers was officially sanctioned by the 1919 Restoration of Pre-war Practices Act, which enforced the 1915 agreement between engineering employers, unions and the state allowing women workers to be introduced into industry for the duration of the war only. Its application went far beyond the original agreement and was even used to dismiss women in firms which had not existed before 1914. As Martin Pugh points out, with the demobilization of four million men it was seen as essential for the reestablishment of male self-respect for men to be restored as the breadwinners for their families.[9] The Labour Party and the labour movement pursued this patriarchal ideology vigorously. Even the National Federation of Women Workers did not resist. In 1921, its leader Mary Macarthur died and the Federation lost its independence with the merger into the General and Municipal Workers Union. Thereafter a distinct women's presence was completely obliterated.

The expulsion of the female workforce was accompanied (and assisted) by a transformation in public and media perceptions of women workers. As Irene Clephane, who witnessed this at first hand, wrote:

> women, whose able fulfilment of their duties had won them ecstatic praise, found themselves no longer wanted in a changed world where all the doors that had so miraculously opened to them were relentlessly closing again. From being the saviours of the nation, women in employment were degraded in the public press to a position of ruthless self seekers depriving men and their dependants of a livelihood.[10]

The frenzied and emotional atmosphere amongst ex-servicemen in the post-war period produced many acts of violence. Women workers were a favourite target. Women tram and bus conductors were particularly prone to attacks from ex-servicemen.[11] Unemployment created by the depression following the war was widely attributed to women workers and reinforced the pressure to eradicate them from the work force. Although married women workers were not tolerated, it was single women who were especially vilified in the media as being useless members of society. Many women conformed quietly to these pressures, but there is evidence that at least a minority resisted. In London in December 1918 there was a demonstration of 30 000 munition workers protesting about lost jobs.[12] Very often domestic service was all that was offered to discharged women. Many went unwillingly, the alternative being starvation as they were denied unemployment benefit if they refused. Not the woman in Portsmouth, however, who was deregistered for turning down a domestic service post at 8s for a working week of over 70 hours.[13] In 1919 Labour Exchanges placed 195 000 women in domestic service positions.[14] Government training schemes for 'Homecraft', which started in 1921, were also intensely unpopular, but again compliance was enforced through the threat of withdrawal of benefit.

Despite its unpopularity, domestic service remained a major employer of women, employing about a third of all working women, extending even a little beyond this in the depression years of the early thirties. 'Service' could range from a single 'maid of all work' in a lower-middle-class home to being a member of a large, hierarchically organized servant community in a very wealthy household. The latter usually fared rather better than the former who were treated as household drudges. The middle classes were particularly keen to hang on to their servants, not least for the fact that even one general maid was an instant bearer of social status. In areas where alternative work was available, recruitment was often difficult. Many young girls took the view of Mary Hewins' older sister in Stratford-upon-Avon in preferring factory work on the grounds that 'you knows when you's a-goin' to start an' when you's a-goin' to finish. And you gets your money on Friday night.'[15] This being so, employers had to resort to orphanages and depressed areas to recruit female labour. Mary Wade's autobiography, set in a mining community in Northumberland, recalls that local employment for girls was almost non-existent.[16] Dire poverty forced many families to send much-loved daughters long distances to take up work in service. Winifred Foley was desperately unhappy at leaving her family in the Forest of Dean. She knew though that her younger siblings were seriously undernourished and by going away there would be one less mouth to feed.[17]

As the lowest job in the servant hierarchy was the kitchen maid, this is where many young women started. Margaret Powell started domestic work in the 1920s as a kitchen maid in Hove. For £2 a month she was expected to work from 5.30 a.m. right through into the evening. She finished early at 4 p.m. one day a week and on alternate Sundays. After these conditions had been explained to her she 'felt like I was in jail at the finish'.[18] Employers were known to take advantage when they felt they could get away with it. Foley met a servant from the neighbouring house who explained that she had little time to talk as it was her afternoon off and 'these buggers always want you to do them a favour if you hang about'.[19]

Both servants and masters understood that they were a race apart and great lengths were taken to preserve distinctions of status. Powell was appalled to find out that she could not hand anything over by hand to the mistress of the house unless it was placed on a silver salver.[20] After being given her first supper in the kitchen while the family ate in the living-room, Foley thought it 'strange to be considered not fit to eat in the same room as other human beings'.[21] Young women increasingly resisted the more draconian aspects of servant life. Powell went out without permission one evening as she got fed up with sitting in an uncomfortable kitchen with dreary company. This was a great shock to the mistress of the house who said that she 'had never heard of such a thing as a servant going out above the stipulated time for her outings'.[22] With a high labour turnover and rising forms of alternative work, employers were forced to negotiate compromises. Gradually, the whole idea of 'living-in' became harder to sustain and many mistresses turned to 'dailies', often making use of local ex-residential staff who had left for marriage.

In the industrial sector, female labour suffered under the impact of the catastrophic decline in the world market for British textiles. The women of this declining sector fiercely resisted wage cuts, which were the employers' main method of reducing costs in a vain attempt to win back lost markets. In the Yorkshire woollen industry, where 60 per cent of the workforce were women, most of whom were poorly paid and unorganized, these troubles came to a head in the spring of 1930 when the whole industry erupted into crisis over the threat of wage cuts. With over 20 per cent of woollen workers already unemployed, the woollen unions were prepared to accept an across-the-board wage cut. The Communist Party, which had a small base in Bradford and Shipley and was at this time in the middle of its ultra-left 'Third Period', led the rank and file into industrial action.[23] The Party's strategy was to concentrate on the wool-combers, the most male dominated and highly organized section of the industry, without whom the other sectors could not work. It worked and over a hundred thousand workers came out on strike, many of them desperately poor women with no strike pay to fall back on. Although the party organized some communal feeding, the strikers could not hold out and within a few weeks the strike collapsed. Three months later, when another wage cut was imposed, there was a further strike involving 20 000 woollen workers, but they were again forced to return defeated.

In contrast, women in the Lancashire cotton industry were more organized and as a result enjoyed higher wages than the women woollen workers. The slump, starting in the early 1920s, deepened in the late twenties, so that in some cotton towns unemployment approached 50 per cent of the labour force. Here, too, employers went on the offensive. From 1928 cotton workers were resisting wage cuts. Reference has been made earlier to the fact that women in the weaving side of the industry worked in conditions more approaching equality than anywhere else in British industry. Traditionally, women stayed at work after marriage until the oldest child entered employment. This was soon to be challenged by a group of mill owners in Burnley, who introduced a rationalization scheme in 1929 whereby fewer weavers would work more looms (for more pay) with the clear intention of sacking married women.[24] The mill owners initially won the co-operation of the weavers' union which, despite its predominantly female membership, was dominated by a patri-archal male bureaucracy. This position could not be sustained, however, as it soon became clear that rank and file opposition to the new scheme was intense. Mass pickets, often erupting into violence, were organized around mills operating the new scheme. When leading mill owner Tertious Spencer attempted to explain the 'more looms' system at a public meeting, he was heckled by women weavers asking, 'What about those thrown out of work?'[25]

The 'more loom' experiment was never generally adopted and the industry descended into chaos as 'rebel' employers sought to go it alone and undercut recognized wage lists. In a desperate attempt to retain a recognized wage agreement, employers decided to suspend all previous agreements on wages and conditions, thereby laying open the way for another round of cuts. The result was a county-wide lock-out in the summer of 1932 involving nearly half a million cotton workers, over half of whom were women.[26] The dispute, arguably the most important of the inter-war period after the General Strike of 1926, ended in defeat after five weeks. Altogether there were five separate sets of wage reductions before conditions at last began to improve again in the mid-thirties, by which time the industry had shrunk considerably. The women weavers who fought to protect their wages and living standards and right to work have been largely ignored by labour historians.[27] Outstanding militants like Bessie Dickinson and Amy Hargreaves appear to have no place in labour history's 'hall of fame'.

As was to be expected, the unemployed movement of these years was based in the depressed regions, principally South Wales, the north and industrial Scotland. The National Unemployed Workers Movement (NUWM) like the industries of these areas was heavily male dominated, although wives of unemployed miners, engineers, etc. did participate in the movement. The exception was the textile districts. Here women did form a presence, arguing for equal unemployment benefit, a national minimum for all and the right to work. Although the unemployed movement's leader, Wal Hannington, opposed women's participation in hunger marches, he eventually gave way and women's contingents formed part of the national marches from 1930. The women marched separately from the men and sometimes had to resort to the workhouse if no hospitality was offered by the local labour movement. This they did with dignity, refusing to submit to strip searches, forced work and petty regulations. As they had been living on 13s 6d a week, the women usually ate better on the march than at home. Maggie Nelson, a Burnley weaver and mother of three, remembers chanting, 'Work, work, work, We want work, An end to the means test, Slave camps and the rest.'[28] Class unity was always a strong element, as seen in another of their chants, 'March along, working women, march along, In the ranks of the workers you belong.'[29]

In 1931 the Labour government passed the Unemployment Insurance (Anomalies) Act, which was mainly targeted at the removal of married women from the register. Within 18 months, approximately 200 000 women had been denied benefit on the basis that they were 'not genuinely seeking work'.[30] The NUWM, largely orchestrated by the Communist Party, resisted the Anomalies Act and did much valuable casework for individual women in its local branches. However, it must be said that by the mid-thirties the increasing pressure on married women to see themselves primarily as housewives was felt within the organization, as indeed it was everywhere. This was reflected in the NUWM's propaganda such as Maud Brown's pamphlet 'Stop this Starvation of Mother and Child'.[31] From 1934 the most vocal women in the movement were the wives of unemployed men rather than women who defined themselves as unemployed.[32]

Alongside the decline in traditional women's trades, notably textiles and clothing, came the rise of a new breed of woman worker in the growth industries of the midlands and the south east. Electrical appliances, synthetic fibres, chemicals, car and bicycle manufacture, food processing and many other new industries took in over a million and a half women workers in this period. A typical example is Peak Freen, biscuit makers of south London, which mechanized production and expanded to about 3000 workers in the 1920s, over half of whom were women.[33] The women tended to leave work on marriage (or be sacked), although gradually the practice of staying on until the first pregnancy was taking hold.

Learning from the 'dilution' experiences of the First World War, the employers in the new industries organized mass production techniques avoiding the costly use of skilled male labour, and defined basic assembly as 'women's work' (although a new breed of male technician also emerged). These young women, who earned a fraction of what skilled men would earn, had the additional advantage of lacking a tradition of labour organization, let alone militancy. Despite the rising numbers of women in light industry, the formal labour movement expressed little interest in recruiting them. The Amalgamated Engineering Union opened new sections in the late twenties to take in unskilled workers, but this did not include women even though the industry was experiencing a huge growth in the numbers of women in electrical engineering.[34] Assembly-line production was potentially a very intensive form of labour. Certainly, oral evidence from early production lines indicates workers' resentment at the loss of autonomy and the increased pressure to maximize output. Violet Ryan worked at Mullards in south London making radio valves in the 1930s. She worked on the end of a belt which had women threading wires which then had to be clamped into red-hot glass bulbs, the air pumped out (that was her job) and then sealed. It was very hot and strenuous work,

> and they are coming at you at 400 an hour! And of course you couldn't go out to the toilet unless you had someone to relieve you ... you are at it all the time. You can't stop to blow your nose or nothing.[35]

Not surprisingly, workers felt very stressed and there are examples of women running out screaming or resorting to sabotage. Miriam Glucksmann argues that this new production process created a new set of relations between capital and labour, notably the 'collective worker' as an individual could not be separated from the team on the line.[36] Certainly the women had to learn to work together, but we should be guarded, however, in assuming that assembly-line work was automatically more exploitative than ordinary assembly. My own research in several south London factories revealed very mixed feelings about assembly-line work, with some respondents insisting that they did not feel that it was more stressful.[37] Probably workers on the earliest conveyor belts were subjected to a nightmarish regime. But by the late thirties many employers had realized that production would be enhanced if the belt was kept at a reasonable pace and proper rest breaks and cover for toilet breaks was allowed.

In any case, individual assembly could also be stressful as workers were usually on piece rate and the pace had to be maintained in order to earn a decent wage. In collective assembly, the women learned to act in unison and developed techniques of helping each other out to overcome bottlenecks. For many this resulted in a bonding which they found very rewarding.

Britain's changing industrial structure was reflected in regional female employment patterns. For example, between 1921 and 1931 women's employment in the north west shrank by 1.5 per cent whereas it grew by 2.6 per cent in the south east.[38] Not all of this can be accounted for by the rise of the new industries. The 'white blouse' revolution, started before 1914, led to the continued expansion of clerical, retail and leisure industry employment for women. Many of these jobs and, of course, those in the professions, required qualifications and that meant a grammar school education. Here, many a bright working-class girl had her hopes dashed. Margaret Powell passed a scholarship exam at 13 and hoped to be a teacher:

> My parents saw my headmistress but when they found out that I couldn't possibly earn any money till I was eighteen and up to that time they would have to keep me, and not only keep me, but buy me books and clothes, they just couldn't do it.[39]

As we saw above, Powell became a domestic servant. The great majority of girls stayed at elementary school and left at 14. Of those who made it to grammar school, or were privately educated, only a tiny minority went into higher education. Even if qualified, the social climate, particularly in the early twenties and the slump years 1929–33, made it difficult for women to enter the professions. In theory, the Sex Discrimination (Removal) Act of 1919 opened the door but in practice few got through it. There were, for example, still less than 200 women lawyers in 1935. Women doctors made more headway with 2810 by 1931.[40] Understandably, little progress was made towards equal pay, although women civil servants did achieve some limited gains. The Burnham pay scales for elementary school teachers, introduced in 1919, fixed a maximum wage for women teachers of four-fifths of the male rate, prompting equal pay activists to declare 'No pay for Friday!'.

The most pressing issue for women white-collar and professional workers was not equal pay, but the marriage bar. The practice of sacking women on marriage, not exactly unknown before 1914, became much more extensive in the years following the war. The civil service and local government enforced it vigorously. Nurses, doctors and many secretarial workers in private businesses also suffered from it. As the majority of women married by the age of 30, their working lives were rarely more than 12 years. They had no pension rights, although it was usual to award a small gratuity 'to help set up home' on leaving. As always, some women found ways of resisting these pressures. A woman interviewed by Teresa Davy for an oral history project on shorthand typists reported that

> Most girls would leave an office on marriage but conditions in my home were such that I felt my mother should not be left without some continuing help. I had a very hard time from some of the other girls who were resentful that I 'was taking a single girl's place', and I tried hard to find other employment which took until 1929. To do this I took off my wedding ring and called myself 'Miss Adams'.[41]

The most persistent and organized pressure against the marriage bar came from the teachers. It was a major issue for the National Union of Women Teachers (NUWT). Nan MacMillan entered teaching in London in 1926 and became a leading activist for the NUWT, becoming president of the London region in 1934. In an interview she revealed how strongly she felt about the issue: 'I came into the profession when you couldn't marry. Now this was another thing that incensed me, and I felt was wicked.' Her commitment to the issue was deeply influenced by her own circumstances as she was living with another teacher in secret: 'If it had got about, we both would have been sacked for immoral conduct. So life was very difficult. I was very keen to get the marriage bar removed.'[42] Nan and other NUWT activists worked closely with Agnes Dawson, ex-teacher and London County Council councillor, who persuaded Herbert Morrison to set up a working party. The result was the removal of the marriage bar for women teachers, doctors and nurses in the LCC at the end of 1935. It was an important but isolated victory,

as most other local authorities continued to operate a marriage
bar until the war.

Finally, a reminder that not all women married. The 1931
census revealed that there were over one and a half million
women over 35 who were unmarried. War losses and injuries
made it inevitable that some women would remain spinsters.
Almost all of these women were dependent on their earnings and
some were supporting aged parents. At a time when single
women were widely despised, they often banded together for
support and solidarity. Hilda Keane has shown, for example, how
women teachers formed their own communities in these years.[43]

Reconstructing Femininity; Marriage, Family, Health and Sexuality

British society in the autumn of 1918 was in a state of profound
trauma. Old values and constraints had been torn apart, pre-
scribed codes of behaviour abandoned. Deeply fearful of the
unfolding possibilities for radical change, dominant forces in
society asserted the need to return to what was held to be
'normal life'. Integral to this resurgence of conservative values
was the necessity of reasserting gender divisions, separate
spheres ideology and, after the war losses, an insistence on the
need for women to procreate. As we saw in Chapter 2, the war
did not bring about any fundamental change in women's
position in society. It did, however, bring women into the
public domain more than ever before. Middle-class women, in
particular, gained in confidence and working-class women
showed that they could be breadwinners and mothers. Styles of
dress and hair were indicative of a new mood, with an emphasis
on simplicity and freedom of movement. All this was acutely
disturbing to patriarchal forces in society. Kingsley Kent asserts
that the most fundamental step in the post-war search for peace
and security was 'an insistence upon gender peace; a relationship
of male–female complementarity in which women did not
compete with men in the public sphere'.[44]

As the section above reveals, these forces were powerful and
effective in promoting a 'gender backlash' immediately after
the war. However, in considering the fabric which constituted

inter-war British society, we should be mindful of the fact that it is a complex picture, involving a whole constellation of inter-related factors, the aftermath of the war being just one of them. The falling birthrate, for example, began long before the war and reached its nadir in the inter-war years, creating a norm of one to two children by the 1930s. As we know, middle-class women had long been limiting their fertility, but now working-class women were also choosing to have fewer births, and war losses only temporarily halted this trend. Until recently, it had been accepted that poorer women had simply copied their better-off sisters, that middle-class values and aspirations had somehow 'filtered down' to the working class. Diana Gittins has successfully challenged this notion and shown that the changing working-class family size did not come about because working-class women were copying the middle classes, 'but rather the result of their changing relations to the socio-economic system'.[45] Working-class women were operating according to their own changing dynamics and these need to be examined according to a number of criteria such as occupational experience before marriage, after marriage and after childbirth, husband's occupational experience and so on.[46] Although statistically the small family became the most common type, in practice there were very wide variations and there is ample evidence of the continued existence of larger families, particularly in the poorest communities.

Methods of controlling fertility had always been known to the working class, with abstinence, withdrawal and the safe period being the most commonly employed. Now that large numbers of women were motivated to actually practise birth control, they quickly saw the shortcomings in all these methods. The search for reliable and safe contraception is apparent in the flood of letters, from both women and men, sent to Marie Stopes after she started her birth control campaign towards the end of the war. Here is one woman's plea, reproduced as she wrote it.

> I wonder if you can help me. I am married and the mother of five children and live in dread of having any more children. My husband who is a Catholic does not believe in stopping life by any means when I say I do not want any more he gets very nasty with me he wont try and keep me right and I feel now

that if only I can manage to keep myself right life mite be
worth living as it is one horrable dread.... Can you let me
know what I can do if possable unknwon to my husband.[47]

The small family was an essential part of the new vision of privatized family life in which women were encouraged to think that
they could find complete fulfilment in looking after home and
family. New women's magazines such as *Woman's Own* (1932)
and *Woman* (1937) gave women recipes, handy tips for sewing and housework and ways to keep their man content.
Circulation soared as women strived to live up to the media
image of the ideal woman. With the introduction of electricity
and new consumer goods, such as electric washing machines,
irons and vacuum cleaners, women were made to feel that far
from being household drudges they were technicians in charge
of an advanced scientific workshop, which could be manipulated
at their command. These trends were all exemplified in the
building of the new suburban estates. The London region was a
key location for many of the new 'garden cities'. Almost three-
quarters of a million new flats and houses were built between
1919 and 1938 in the London area.[48] The London County
Council (LCC) itself built nearly eighty thousand of these.

It is clearly very important for historians to understand why
domesticity became such a central part of women's identity in
this period. The new anti-heroic, less romantic and more inward-
looking Britain of the 1920s offered new roles for both men and
women. Rising standards of living became inextricably bound up
with notions of privacy. Women who had been living in over-
crowded rooms, collecting water from an outside tap and waiting
their turn for use of the cooker on the landing longed for their
own sense of personal space. In a very material sense, a 'home of
their own' gave them a better life and this necessarily involved a
decisive break with mutuality and therefore weakened community bonds. Judy Giles argues that within this context working-
class women 'found a cultural ideal and a social space in the
figure and practices of the housewife and adopted the discourse
of housewifery in order to develop their own forms of identity
and self-definition'.[49] To gain respectability and recognition as
useful members of society, women developed a feminine identity
acceptable to themselves and the outside world. There was,

however, a price to be paid for this 'cultural space'. Giles argues that to resist the ever present surveillance of health visitors and other welfare agencies women developed the mechanism of 'keeping themselves to themselves'. This retreat from emotional intensity and intimacy distanced them from their children, husbands and other women.[50]

It is important though not to over-generalize on the basis of rising living standards achieved mainly through improved accommodation as not everybody benefited from this. Ena Chamberlain called her autobiography, *29 Inman Road*, a street in south-west London where she grew up in the 1920s. Although not a slum, she describes it as not 'entirely respectable'. Her mother's dream was to buy one of the new houses in Morden and once she even dragged Ena off to see a show house. But slowly the dream faded and Mum had to reconcile herself to the situation, brushing it off with 'chin up, make the best of it'.[51] Local authority housing was only allocated to those who were deemed to be 'good tenants'. In any case, it was beyond the reach of the poorest as the new rents were far in excess of what was paid for the old squalid rooms. Rose Gamble spent seven years of her *Chelsea Childhood*, as her autobiography is termed, living in one room with parents and four siblings. (Her descriptions of the eating and sleeping arrangements are memorable.) The move to a nearby local authority flat was only made possible by the earnings of the two older girls as the rent was more than double what they had been paying.[52]

Poverty was still a major social problem, especially so in the depressed regions. Nowhere was this more apparent than in the findings of the Women's Health Enquiry, set up in 1933 with representation from a wide cross-section of women's organizations. The report, published in 1939, analysed the evidence provided by 1250 married working-class women and referred to the enquiry by health visitors and other welfare agencies.[53] Although not necessarily entirely representative of working-class women as a whole at this time (for example, most of the women have large families) its findings are important. Many of the women were living in inferior accommodation, particularly those in Scotland and the north. Mrs S. of Glasgow, aged 32 and mother of four is described as living in 'the usual one room and kitchen'.[54] Mrs T. of Arbroath was living on the first floor of a tenement with husband and five children. With no indoor sanitation, all water had to be carried in and a single toilet shared with 24 others.[55] The evidence provided by the Women's Health Enquiry is alarming. Less than a third of the women were in good health. At the opposite end, about the same number were described as being in a 'grave' state with serious chronic conditions. Those in-between were suffering from various forms of ill-health, particularly maternal morbidity brought about by poor diet and repeated pregnancies. The Enquiry team were insistent that women had not exaggerated their health problems, in fact the reverse, as most had sought to underplay them. The Enquiry felt that a major cause of ill-health was undernourishment and this is amply documented in the descriptions of women's diets. Mrs N. of Rotherham, who had six children under 14, is perhaps a typical example. The report describes her diet thus; 'she drinks a great deal of tea, has an imported egg twice a week, a bit of fish once a month, no supper and for the rest a slice of bread and marg'.[56] Tuberculosis was a very serious problem. Mary Wade describes it as being 'rife' in her Northumberland mining community.[57] Angela Hewins' account of the decline and death of her sister Jess from the disease in Stratford is heart-wrenching – abandoned by her boyfriend of three years and her life ebbing away over an agonizing length of time.[58]

Women's mental health suddenly came into the public view in the 1930s when social workers began to report the new phenomena of 'suburban neurosis'.[59] Many women found life on the new suburban estates boring and lonely after the hustle and bustle of the inner city, with kin usually at hand and workplaces not far away. Housewives with small children became isolated and 'nervy'. Those with children at school and few social contacts often had little to do and were also prone to this new form of mental illness. This link between domesticity and illness, identifying suburban neurosis as a form of deviant femininity, opened the way for later feminists to develop a critique of women's role within the modern family.[60] The women who were most likely to succumb to suburban neurosis were in the lower middle class and upper working class. Those more affluent than this often kept up hobbies and interests outside the home, such as music, church, welfare or local council work. Poorer women had little time on their hands and tended to be totally preoccupied with the day-to-day struggle to 'make ends meet' and retain at least an outside façade of respectability. An essential component of the ideology of domesticity was the requirement that women appear to be better off than they actually were. Jan Lambertz and Pat Ayers' discussion of marriage in Liverpool underlines the necessity for a woman to be seen to be 'a good manager'.[61] This often involved quite unrealistic expectations on the part of husbands who had, at all costs, to be seen to be the breadwinners of the family. As a result, women often had to keep quiet about some of their money-making sidelines, creating a largely female 'shadow economy'. Activities such as casual street-hawking, home assembly and cleaning could often be performed without the husband's knowledge.

All this stands somewhat uneasily with the notion that the inter-war period witnessed the rise of the 'companionate marriage', with greater companionship and equality between husband and wife. We do, however, have autobiographical evidence for a greater involvement of men with children. Winifred Foley's father, a miner, 'never minded being woken up at any odd hour to help with a fretful baby' and when seeing her off to her first job in service told her tenderly ' 'ow much your mam and I wish we could kip thee at 'ome.'[62] Phyllis Willmott's family of five lived in a cramped flat in south-east London. Saturday nights were bath night when 'my father had the job of drying us one by one as we were handed out to him by Mum'.[63] The family Sunday morning treat was provided by Dad who brought everyone tea and biscuits in bed. On the other hand, Phyllis Wilmott makes it clear that her painter and decorator father did not expect to help with the household chores. He did not see this as an appropriate activity for a man even when he was 'on slack' and his wife was out charring.

A new recognition of female sexuality and the importance of sexual compatibility was an intrinsic component of the concept of 'companionate marriage'. This change can be illustrated in the attitude of the Church of England. As Olive Banks notes, as late as 1913 the Church was maintaining that sex, even within marriage, indulged in for its own sake was a sin but, by the 1930s, the Church recognized that sex was an important part of married life.[64] The new approach to sex can be partly attributed to the writings of Sigmund Freud, which had their first comprehensive English translation in 1922. It was also facilitated by the growth of expert 'sexologists' such as Havelock Ellis and Magnus Hirschfield. All these writers underlined the importance of sexual desire, in both men and women, as a vital part of the human psyche.

In terms of popular writings, it was Marie Stopes who gave voice to women who wanted their sexual desires to be both recognized and fulfilled. *Married Love*, published in 1918 and instantly a bestseller, argued that mutual sexual satisfaction was an essential part of married life. Stopes encouraged couples to experiment with different positions to enhance their sexual performance. She told men what they must do to stimulate their wives sexually and specifically mentions the clitoris as the site of female orgasm, although she does not seem to encounter the possibility that it might come about by anything other than penetrative sex.[65] For women who had been brought up with the idea that sexual desire outside of procreation was depraved, these were liberating ideas.

It does need to be reiterated that Stopes was writing exclusively for married couples and campaigned fiercely against sex outside marriage. There were a few sexual radicals, such as Dora Russell and Stella Browne, who did not feel that sexual desire should be contained within marriage, but their views were seen as quite scandalous at the time. Stopes went to enormous lengths to argue that women's sexual satisfaction, and indeed general psychological well-being, was entirely dependent on sex with men. As Sheila Jeffreys notes, her view that women benefited from the absorption of men's secretions through the vaginal walls has never been scientifically proved.[66] For Kingsley Kent, changing views on sexuality are all part of her argument that women's oppression was 'psychologised' in these years.[67] So rather than being constrained primarily by legal and institutional barriers, as they had been before 1918, women were bound by the internalization of patriarchal values: enjoying sex with your husband was now necessary in order to be a good wife.

Marie Stopes' writings on sex were explicitly for the 'educated middle-classes'. As we know, working-class women certainly sought to prevent unwanted pregnancies, but there is little direct evidence to link this with a more positive sexuality. Giles writes that, in the historical imagination, these women have been largely constructed as one-dimensional figures: long suffering, stoical, once married overwhelmingly maternal.[68] Sex was something to be endured, husbands who largely left them alone were said to be 'good' or 'considerate'. Alternative images, particularly regarding the intimate subject of sexual relations, are difficult to locate, although we can find the occasional glimpse of overt sexual desire in younger women, as in Mary Hewins' longing for the banished boyfriend who had made her pregnant:

> I couldn't help thinking about him – and Sis. What does she think of me? I wondered. I dreaded her mouth. I dreaded what she'd say. She was married, she'd had a fella alright, seen a man in all his glory. It seemed a long time since I had. Yes, I'll confess it, I was aching in my heart for him. I would a-done anything to see him, hear his voice, feel him, anything. I knowed it was wrong, wicked, but you can't help feelings.[69]

Although still publicly condemned, sex outside marriage was in fact increasing. One indication of this is the decline in 'professional' prostitution in these years. According to Stephen Humphries, there were about 25–35 000 pregnancies a year outside marriage.[70] Recognition of this can be seen in the foundation of the National Council for Unmarried Mothers in 1918. Maximum pressure was placed on the father, if known, to marry the young woman concerned, and in the majority of cases this succeeded. When this did not happen, the fate of the woman was not an enviable one. She was often disowned by her family, but this could be as much out of poverty as of shame. Many had no alternative but the workhouse (termed Public Assistance Institution after 1929), as in the case of Ada Haskins, reported by Humphries in *The Secret World of Sex*.[71] Ada was 'wheedled' into sex by her boyfriend in County Durham when she was 19 in 1930. After the boyfriend fled to sea, Ada's mother forced her into the workhouse to have the baby and then brought up the child as her own, sending Ada off to work in service. It was a typical story. It was also common to force the pregnant woman into agreeing to adoption. More rarely, abandoned pregnant women were certified under the Mental Deficiency Act of 1913 and detained indefinitely in asylums. Many of these sad cases remained in mental institutions for the rest of their lives for no other reason than the 'crime' of becoming pregnant outside marriage. Lesbians were another group of 'deviant' women who received the full force of public disapproval in these years. In 1921, no doubt as another consequence of the post-war backlash, an attempt was made to make lesbianism a criminal offence as was male homosexuality. After passing through the Commons, the move met problems in the House of Lords, where members were caught between the desire to condemn it and the fear that if they acknowledged its existence it might convert women to it. As a result, it failed to become law. A series of novels with lesbian themes aroused little attention but the publication of Radclyffe Hall's *The Well of Loneliness* in 1928, with a clear moral and didactic stance on the life of 'inverts', caused a public outcry verging on the hysterical. Amid almost universal condemnation, the publishers were prosecuted for obscenity. Even the defence lawyer for the publishers attempted to argue that the book was not about lesbianism, until Hall intervened as her purpose in writing the book was to gain public tolerance and understanding (and that was, of course, why the book was prosecuted).[72] The book was banned but it was already a bestseller. As the title indicates, the book depicts a depressing picture of the life of the 'invert'. Paradoxically, Hall's own life appears to have been happy and fulfilled, living openly as a lesbian for over 30 years with Una Troubridge, indulging in many other affairs and supported by a wide circle of friends.[73] Hall was, of course, an upper-class figure, and the stereotype of the rich 'butch' lesbian appears to have been the only way in which lesbianism impinged on public consciousness. As this was a figure of denigration, there was really no way that more ordinary women could be openly identified as lesbians at this time. Radclyffe Hall wrote that 'thousands have turned to me for help' which appears to indicate that there were many women who felt emotionally and sexually drawn towards other women.[74]

Feminism and the Public Domain

There was no mass base for militant feminism to resume at the end of the war and Christabel Pankhurst's Women's Party quickly fizzled out. Christabel herself no longer had any serious interest in feminism and, after a difficult period of adjustment, devoted herself to an evangelical form of Christianity. Mrs Pankhurst, whose politics had steadily drifted to the right, spent six years lecturing in the USA and Canada. After her return she became a prospective parliamentary candidate for the Conservatives in the safe Labour seat of Whitechapel in east London, but her health deteriorated and she died in 1928. Sylvia Pankhurst had lost most of her socialist-feminist support by the end of the war and became increasingly preoccupied with ultra-left wing communist politics. Of all the militant groups and splits, only the Women's Freedom League appears to have survived. Although much reduced in size and mainly active in the London area, it continued to campaign on feminist issues throughout this period and, indeed, right up until 1961 when it finally expired.[75]

The largest suffrage organization, the non-militant National Union of Women's Suffrage Societies, also survived in a somewhat reduced form. Once (limited) suffrage had at last been conceded in 1918 the National Union felt that a change of name was required to symbolize the need to broaden the basis of its work, and the following year it became the National Union of Societies for Equal Citizenship (NUSEC). Soon after, Millicent Fawcett, who had led the constitutional movement for over half a century, felt that it was time for her to make way for a younger woman as president. Eleanor Rathbone, the new leader, was almost certainly the most significant inter-war feminist and her book *The Disinherited Family* (1924) arguably the most important feminist tract of the time. As Banks has pointed out, Rathbone's 'new feminism' was distinct from the equal rights feminism of the suffrage period, which had its origins in the Enlightenment.[76]

Rathbone owed much more to the evangelical tradition of moral reform, which gave women a special superiority and commitment to social reform, and gave her strong links with 'new Liberalism'. Rathbone's most distinctive contribution to feminism lies in her campaign for family endowment. In *The Disinherited Family* and earlier works she argued forcefully against the concept of a 'family wage'. She pointed out that the wage structure was built upon the idea of an adult man having to support a family, yet less than half of adult men were in fact supporting dependants.

This patriarchal policy was used to justify unequal pay between men and women as women were assumed not to have any dependants. Rathbone argued that as a result of this practice men without dependants were able to squander unnecessary income, whilst large families were left in extreme poverty: 'the greatest cause of primary poverty is the failure of the wage system to adapt itself to the needs of variously sized households'.[77] Rathbone noted that during the war medical officers in most major cities had reported that children's physiques had improved. This realization that, prior to 1914, income that had been paid to 'family wage'-earning fathers was not necessarily being used to support children, helped to convince her that income must be paid directly to the mother for the maintenance of children. Rathbone wanted all workers to be paid on the basis of a single adult wage and children to be catered for separately through payments to the mother. In her view, this would lead to true equal pay as there was no longer any excuse to pay men more. She would not support equal pay in isolation as she felt that it should only be implemented as part of a new wage structure, with family endowment as an integral part.

This almost exclusive concentration on motherhood was deeply disturbing to the feminists of the equal rights tradition. Rathbone's desire to make feminism relevant to the broad mass of women, at a time when it appeared to be stagnating, led to accusations of betrayal from those who felt that Rathbone was attempting to institutionalize the domestication of women. This is also the view of historians such as Kingsley Kent, who argue that Rathbone's feminism was a return to separate spheres ideology.[78] Defenders of Rathbone have argued that she did not turn her back on equal rights feminism and that she believed that women must be given viable choices – neither to be forced into domesticity nor to be forced into the labour market.[79] And, as Jane Lewis writes, Rathbone showed 'the necessity to get away from defining equality on men's terms'.[80] Giving women economic power meant undermining the material basis for patriarchy, which was ultimately much more important than any formal rights. Rather more difficult to defend are Rathbone's eugenicist views, which were fairly common at the time, and her refusal to include unmarried mothers in her family endowment schemes.

Rathbone's determination to steer 'the new course' in NUSEC was set on a collision course with the 'equalitarians'. The split occurred in 1927 over the issue of protective legislation specifically for women, opposition to which had always been an integral part of equal rights feminism. According to this view, protective legislation equalled restrictive legislation. Rathbone's narrow victory in shifting the NUSEC from absolute hostility to a position closer to conditional support, led to the resignation of 11 members of the executive of 23.[81] Maude Royden, Mary Stocks, Kate Courtney and Margery Corbett Ashby stayed loyal to Rathbone whereas Lady Balfour, Elizabeth Abbott, Chrystal MacMillan and Monica Whatley were among those who opposed 'the new course' and continued to press for equal rights, equal pay and equal opportunities. The equal rights tradition continued in several smaller groups, principally the Open Door Council, the Six Point Group, and, of course, the Women's Freedom League. Lady Rhondda was a particularly vociferous opponent of protective legislation, arguing that any distinction between men and women at work ultimately worked against women: 'it will never be possible to persuade public opinion that women are independent, fully responsible human beings and complete citizens, so long as the law protects them specially in ways it does not protect men'.[82] Winifred Holtby's *Women* (1934) contained a vitriolic attack on the enforced domestication of women; 'the tradition of woman as home-maker encumbers her intellectual and economic progress at every turn'.[83] She favoured the rather drastic measure of complete abolition of private homes for a generation, arguing that, 'we pay too high a price for our good housekeeping'.[84]

Another strand of NUSEC began to detach itself in the late 1920s with the formation of the Townswomen's Guilds. The guilds grew in response to the huge success of the Women's Institutes (WIs) which had started during the war for rural women. The Guilds, in the towns, and the WIs, mainly in the countryside, focused on traditional crafts and 'home making' activities.[85] This division was made complete in 1932 when the National Union of Townswomen's Guilds became a separate organization. Whilst the WIs and their urban equivalent went from strength to strength, the activists of the NUSEC appear to have become increasingly isolated, amounting to a middle-class urban pressure group. It did, however, maintain an influence. Rathbone's assault on patriarchy became considerably diluted from the late 1920s as she concentrated increasingly on the alleviation of family poverty. Here her critics have a point, as her feminism appears to have been overwhelmed by the need to prevent children suffering in primary poverty and the dominating weight of revitalized domestic ideology. She also became very engrossed in international issues, particularly the growth of fascism, as we see below.

Women's involvement in the political process and the impact of feminism at this time has been extensively surveyed by Martin Pugh. Between the Representation of the People Act 1918 (allowing women over 30 the right to vote) and the Equal Franchise Act of 1928, there was a welter of legislation affecting women. These measures, which were mostly passed with little contention, were largely concerned with the role of women as wives and mothers, but it could also be argued that politicians were now more willing to listen to women's demands.[86] The tendency for women to vote Conservative in larger numbers than men must have also helped to prompt Baldwin in his decision to support an equal suffrage measure. The Parliamentary Qualification of Women Act 1918 allowed women to stand for Parliament as well as vote, but attempts to gain entry for women to the House of Lords failed. Only 36 women actually became MPs in this period and their marginality is underlined by the fact that most of them were in office for less than three years.[87]

Constituency associations tended to be reluctant to select them for anything except a hopeless seat. Prejudice against women with children worked against them, although this did not stop Nancy Astor, who had six, or Edith Summerskill, who had two. Once in Parliament, the overwhelmingly male ethos struck them. Summerskill, who was elected for Labour in West Fulham in 1938 after a long search for a seat, felt that it was 'a little like a boys' school which had decided to take a few girls'.[88] Although elected members in their own right, they still faced restrictions on use of the Commons dining room and other humiliations. Not surprisingly, they tended to stick together, especially in the early years. Their insights into the workings of the House of Commons were sometimes illuminating as well as humorous. Ellen Wilkinson, Labour MP, once remarked that 'Every woman member, with apologies, I include myself, always speaks to the House as one who simply cannot get accustomed to the collective stupidity of so many men.'[89] The only independent feminist to get elected was Rathbone who sat for the Combined English Universities (plural voting for graduates existed until 1948) from 1929. Ironically, she represented middle- and upper-class interests but took it upon herself to be the leading spokesperson for working-class women.

Apart from the work of Pugh referred to above, there has been little detailed work on the impact of feminism on the major political parties between the wars. The only detailed account of a major political party is Pamela Graves' *Labour Women, Women in British Working Class Politics 1918–1939* (1994). About 150 000 women surged into the Labour Party from 1918 to 1924.[90] Expectations of genuinely infusing labour ideology and policy with gender politics were not fulfilled. The tone was set in 1918 when male Labour activists made it clear that they looked to the party to put women back into the home. The Labour Party was one of the major forces behind the Restoration of Pre-War Practices Act of 1919, which feminists regarded as a betrayal of women's interests. This, and the decision of NUSEC to support all women parliamentary candidates after the war, meant that the alliance with Labour of 1912 was firmly broken. The split deepened in the twenties as Labour women put their class interests first, and feminists felt that Labour women were defending patriarchal forces. Most of the women who joined the party were housewives, often wives of trade unionists who felt that 'women's place was in the home'. The majority of the new women members joined the newly formed Women's Sections and seem to have been happy to opt for the 'separate but equal status' which the new constitution accorded them. The few women who were not housewives tended to take part in more mainstream party work. It soon became clear, however, that the party expected women members to be primarily interested in questions of welfare concerning women and children. Publications of the period address women as 'housewives'.

Only nine women were elected as Labour MPs in the entire inter-war years, including the first woman minister, Margaret Bondfield, in 1924. These women, and National Women's Officers Marion Phillips and later Mary Sutherland, rarely stood up against the male leadership. As Graves describes, the women who did struggle to establish equality of gender interests in the party were defeated at every turn.[91] Labour feminists such as Dora Russell and Frieda Laski, who promoted access for working-class women to birth control literature, had considerable grass-roots support. Between 1924 and 1927, the Labour Women's Conference consistently pressed for birth-control measures (much to the annoyance of the women's leadership who defended the leadership and opposed birth-control resolutions) but with no impact on national policy. The same story applies to family endowment. Apart from payments in kind, school meals, etc., the party were not prepared to go down this road. The TUC, many of whose members were Labour Party activists, was implacably opposed to any monetary payments to mothers as it would undermine family wage ideology. The fact that the annual Labour Party Conference was prepared to continually vote down resolutions on these and other issues that had been almost unanimously passed by the Women's Conference reveals the weakness of the women's position. As Graves remarks, the 'separate but equal' status did not pay off: 'treated as a distinct group for some purposes but as equal to male members for others, they had no access to power in either capacity'.[92] Labour feminists were accused of trying to generate 'sex antagonism' and 'separatism' whenever they attempted to exert views different from the leadership. At a time of heightened class antagonism, especially in the twenties, most Labour women felt that the necessity for class loyalty had to outweigh feminist considerations. Sadly, this meant that many Women's Sections were relegated to a servicing role and focused most of their attention on fund-raising and social events.

The other major parties also integrated women into the party apparatus during the twenties. Both the Conservatives and the Liberals came to depend on a large army of women supporters, who often sustained the local party organization. Responding to women as voters, more interest was shown in welfare policies and 'the interests of the homemakers'. Neither party showed any great interest in promoting women candidates in winnable seats, though this was obviously a problem for the Liberals as they were declining at this time and so had fewer safe seats. As a result, many able Liberal women were prevented from becoming MPs.

Some of these had been suffrage campaigners. For example, Margery Corbett Ashby stood unsuccessfully for Parliament on eight different occasions. Turning to the minor parties, the research of Martin Durham shows that the thinking of the British Union of Fascists (BUF) on gender was more complicated than one would expect. Surprisingly, although women's inferiority in the movement was obvious, it did not universally promote patriarchal interests.[93] Even so, one of the most enduring images of the inter-war years must be that of the BUF's leader Oswald Mosley pronouncing that 'we want men who are men and women who are women'. As we see below, fascist Germany's attempts to exaggerate sexual difference met with vigorous responses from feminists. In contrast to the far right, the small, but influential, Communist Party openly proclaimed sexual equality. In practice, as the work of the author shows, it was dominated by the weight of organized labour, particularly 'labour aristocrats' such as the engineers who were the very embodiment of patriarchal ideology.[94] This tension, as in the Labour Party, was never resolved. The party also promoted women's sections, but their denial of feminist interests ('class war not sex war') meant that the women's groups occupied a very inferior position. This picture changed somewhat with the adoption of Popular Front policies from 1934 as the party made an effort to accommodate itself to feminist interests.[95]

At the local level, women were able to make more of an impact, although according to Patricia Hollis they were still less than 15 per cent of elected members in the 1930s.[96] Many ex-suffragists found a natural home as councillors, JPs or Poor Law Guardians (until 1929 when the latter were merged with local authorities). Here they were able to argue, not always successfully, for such measures as baby clinics, school meals, secondary school places and public wash houses. Many aspiring women politicians gained their political spurs in local government. Thelma Cazalet-Keir, for example, was a Conservative member of the LCC from 1925 to 1932, prior to her becoming an MP. Hannah Mitchell was a very active Independent Labour Party councillor in Manchester from 1924 to 1935 and a JP from 1926 to 1946, consistently promoting working-class women's interests. Unlike Cazalet-Keir, who was immensely wealthy and therefore not expected to undertake domestic work, Mitchell found the conflict between home and her public duties troublesome. In her autobiography she writes vividly of how imprisoned she felt by the inescapable round of meal times:

> I feel my greatest enemy has been the cooking stove – a sort of tyrant who has kept me in subjection ... the cooking, preparing and clearing away of four meals a day – which I do not want – are the things I hate with an undying hatred, and I would sell both my loaves any day to buy roses.[97]

Fortunately, Mitchell was able to ameliorate the problem by paying a neighbour to help so that she could stay out of the house for longer than the time between dinner and tea. She well understood though that the circumstances of most women made this impossible.

This chapter would not be complete without more sustained reference to the social movements which gained popular momentum in these years. Sexual radicals had always supported birth control, but in the early twenties there was greatly increased popular interest. Stella Browne, for example, Communist and member of the Malthusian League, spoke to large audiences at meetings around the country.[98] Marie Stopes was a more central figure in the birth-control movement. Her advice on increasing sexual gratification for women depended on the use of birth-control techniques, which she tirelessly promoted. Her commitment to birth control sprang from a number of motives, not least of which was eugenicist. In *Radiant Motherhood* (1920), the sequel to *Married Love*, she states that 'our race is weakened by an appallingly high percentage of unfit weaklings and diseased individuals. The work of the Empire is hindered'.[99] Although her writing on sexuality was chiefly for the 'educated classes', Stopes felt that her mission to the working classes was to bring them safe and reliable birth control. This led her to open Britain's first birth-control clinic in Holloway in 1921.

As we saw above, Labour Party members (and Co-operative Women's Guild members) were also taking up birth control openly for the first time. Annual conference resolutions show that both groups consistently argued that birth-control information and services be adopted as part of local authority maternity services. Opposition mainly came from the Roman Catholic

Church. Fear of alienating Catholic voters certainly played an important part in steering the Labour Party leadership away from any involvement with birth control. Failure to get the 1924 Labour Party Conference to pass a pro-birth control resolution and the need to make a socialist-feminist (as opposed to eugenicist or Neo-Malthusian) case for birth control precipitated the formation of the Workers Birth Control Group.[100] Despite persistent efforts between 1924 and 1927, and eventually even with the support of the miners, the group never succeeded in getting the Labour Party to take up the issue as national policy. The group's efforts were not in vain, however, as in 1930 the Ministry of Health issued a circular allowing local authorities to disseminate birth control information at clinics. Within a year, 36 local authorities were giving out birth control advice.[101] As 'family planning' gradually became respectable, the feminist movement also shifted its position. Traditionally, feminists had staunchly kept to the view that any involvement with sexual matters was not respectable. By the mid-1920s, in view of the popular support for birth control, this view was no longer sustainable and the NUSEC responded accordingly. Altogether, the birth control movement in the 1920s was impressive but, as Gittins reminds us, this did not in itself create the reduction in family size: 'it did, however, make the means by which the desired family size could be achieved safer, more reliable and, for some, also more accessible'.[102]

In contrast to birth control, the campaign for access to abortion remained very much a minority interest, promoted by sexual radicals such as Janet Chance, Dora Russell and Stella Browne. The latter had been writing on this issue from before the First World War, arguing for women's unrestricted access to abortion.[103] Despite its illegality, the practice of abortion was widespread and the back-street abortions, carried out every day in unhygienic conditions by untrained personnel, formed a major element in the large incidence of maternal mortality at this time. In 1936 the issue came out of the shadows with the launch of the Abortion Law Reform Association, which promoted the decriminalization of abortion. The group remained isolated, however, as the issue was never seriously taken up by feminists or the labour movement. On the other hand, maternal mortality did become an issue. About three thousand women a year were

dying in childbirth and, unlike infant mortality, the maternal
death rate showed no sign of abating. Following the birth of
her son Richard in 1927, Sylvia Pankhurst investigated maternity
services and published the results in *Save the Mothers* (1930).
The labour movement tried to establish a link between malnu-
trition and maternal deaths, but this was really a contributory
rather than a direct cause.[104] During the Popular Front years,
particularly 1936–9, maternal mortality was taken up as a
popular cause in many cities. In Sheffield, for example, there
was a Mothers Action Group which included representatives
from various labour movement and women's organizations.[105]
The group campaigned for a hospital bed for every first-
time mother.

The link between feminism and pacifism continued. The
Women's International League for Peace and Freedom, established at the Hague Congress of 1915, never had a mass base but
a small group of feminists, most notably Helena Swanwick and
Kathleen Courtney, worked under its auspices. The most
important working-class women's organization in this field was
the Co-operative Women's Guild, which consistently campaigned against militarism and for disarmament and peace
education. Some feminists found themselves drawn into the
newly formed League of Nations, on which rested many hopes
for peace. It was soon obvious, however, that women would not
be integrated into the League structure for anything other than
giving advice on 'The Traffic in Women and Children'.[106]
During the late twenties and early thirties, pacifist opinion was
gaining strength. Vera Brittain, who lectured for the League of
Nations Union in the 1920s, gradually formulated her pacifist
convictions at this time. Her book *Testament of Youth*, chronicling
the devastating impact of the First World War on her family and
friends, immediately struck a chord with a still grieving nation
when it was published in 1933. The book was acclaimed as
a 'woman's view of war' and became something of a national
monument, though Mary Joannou has recently undermined
this view by making explicit Brittain's limitations, particularly
her adherence to traditional concepts of masculinity and the
class system.[107] By the mid-1930s, confidence in the League
had declined sharply and in 1937 Brittain transferred her
support to the Peace Pledge Union. She tirelessly promoted the

peaceful reconciliation of international disputes, opposing armed resistance under any circumstances.

Virginia Woolf's *Three Guineas* (1938) is a much more discursive work than *Testament of Youth*, and has received a great deal less attention. The text is written in the form of an answer to an anonymous male respondent who asks her how war can be avoided. Openly referring to 'the patriarchy', she links masculinity with militarism and the growth of totalitarianism on the one hand, and feminism with pacifism on the other. Her references to 'The Society of Outsiders' reveal a deep sense of women's detachment from the patriarchal institutions of the nation state, 'as a woman, I have no country. As a woman I want no country. As a woman my country is the whole world.'[108] For Woolf, feminist emancipation and pacifism go hand in hand. She recognizes that women cannot completely detach themselves from men: 'a common interest unites us; it is one world, one life', but she declines to join with her respondent to fight war.[109] Instead she hopes that by infusing 'the patriarchy' with female values, society will gradually move against militarism.

On a European-wide level, the post-war backlash, reimposing rigid concepts of gender difference unsettled by the demands of war, received its most extreme expression in the fascist view of women. Feminists voiced concerns about the totalitarian governments of Italy and Germany from an early stage. Holtby wrote in 1934, 'The pendulum is swinging backwards, not only against feminism, but against democracy, liberty, and reason, against international co-operation and political toler-ance.'[110] Graves indicates that, although Labour Party women's membership grew in the 1930s, the Women's Sections declined: 'the crises of the thirties discouraged gender segregation in the political labour movement.'[111] Whilst it does seem true that there was a stronger comradeship between socialist men and women in the thirties than the twenties, there is also evidence for the view that the need to oppose the extreme sexist ideology and policies of the fascist states created a new bond between women. The inauguration of Popular Front policies in 1934, allowing Communists to undertake joint work with 'all progressive forces' opposed to fascism, facilitated joint work between Communists and feminists for the first time in the party's history. This policy was increasingly successful and leading feminists, including

Monica Whatley, Maude Royden and Vera Brittain, were drawn
into Popular Front work in the form of the Women's Committee
Against War and Fascism. This group also managed to attract
affiliations from the NUWT, the Association of Women Clerks
and Secretaries, the Six Point Group and other women's
organizations. The Committee launched a Women's Charter
which included demands which went far beyond the defence of
women from fascism, including the right of women to work, free
maternity hospitals, access to birth control information and the
decriminalisation of abortion.[112] The Committee and other
feminist organizations attempted to defend individual women
under threat in Germany, for example, Selina Cooper and
Monica Wheatley travelled to Munich for this purpose in late
1934, but with little success.[113] In another case, Eleanor
Rathbone, Ellen Wilkinson, Lady Rhondda and others struggled
in vain to prevent the execution of Liselotte Hermann for
attempting to publicize abroad Germany's preparations for war.
     The issue which really took off for the Popular Front
movement was Spain, where a military uprising had overthrown
the elected reformist government in July 1936, and in so doing
initiated a bloody civil war which was to last for three years. Over
50 women volunteered to go to Spain, almost all of them
connected with the International Medical Service. The great
majority were nurses who worked in appalling conditions. The
interest and response shown by the public at home in Spain was
remarkable. Fired by films such as Ivor Montague's *Defence of
Madrid*, Aid Spain Groups sprang up all over the country,
numbering about 850 at the movement's height.[114] Support
for Spanish relief came from a very broad base, including
progressive Conservatives, Liberals and clergy in addition to
labour and feminist groups. Labour Party women's sections and
Co-operative Women's Guild Groups contributed to the supply
of humanitarian relief. The Parliamentary Committee for Spain
included the Duchess of Atholl (Conservative), Megan Lloyd
George (Liberal), Eleanor Rathbone, Ellen Wilkinson and
Dr Edith Summerskill. In May 1937, 3840 Basque children were
evacuated from Bilbao to Britain. Leah Manning, leader of the
National Union of Teachers and later a Labour MP, headed
the massive task of overseeing the shipping of the children to
Southampton.[115] Altogether, Spanish aid was one of the most

important grass-roots social movements of the twentieth century and one in which women played a very important part. Opponents of totalitarian regimes viewed the fight against the military uprising in Spain as a prelude to a general struggle against fascism, and it is to this wider conflict that we now turn.

4

'WE CAN DO IT!':
THE SECOND WORLD WAR
1939–1945

The Second World War marks a definitive moment in British history. Never before or since has British society been so massively affected by warfare. The enormous mobilization of resources, scale of government intervention and extent of civilian involvement made this even more of a 'total war' than the First World War. Sometimes referred to as 'the people's war', the Second World War was certainly a more 'popular' war than the first, although much of the population was war weary towards the end of the six long years.[1] Many contemporary and early historical accounts of the war maintained that social divisions were lessened, but more recent work has failed to substantiate this.[2] Events such as the Blitz have also been subjected to the revisionist treatment.[3]

We are fortunate in that many more detailed first-hand accounts by ordinary women are available than there were in the 1914–18 war. *Nella Last's War, Mrs Milburn's Diaries* and the edited collection *War Wives* give us an unprecedented insight into the Englishwoman at war.[4] We also benefit from the huge volume of Mass Observation (MO) material that is available for this period.[5] Early work, particularly by Arthur Marwick, followed many contemporary accounts in arguing that the war had had an emancipatory effect and that these changes endured.[6] Penny Summerfield produced a more realistic analysis of women in the war and immediately after.[7] However, as Summerfield herself states, her study focused on government policy and industrial women, and a comprehensive social history of women in the Second World War would require a much broader remit.[8] Harold Smith has taken the revisionist path one stage further in arguing that the main effect of the war was to reinforce traditional roles.[9] Summerfield has responded that, although the war did not 'liberate' women in any simple sense, that does not mean that important changes did not occur.[10] Moreover, oral evidence does suggest that many women did feel that their lives had been profoundly changed by the war, as we shall see below. As women during the war were by no means an homogenous group (as indeed they never are), it is essential to examine the ways in which class, age, occupation, marital status and other factors mediated their experiences and this is a guiding theme for the chapter.

Although the origins of the post-war social reforms lie in the war, they were not implemented until 1945, so discussion of these initiatives has been left until the following chapter.

Paid Work (1)

The outbreak of the war produced conflicting tendencies as regards women's labour. A wave of conservative nostalgia swept the country and many enlisted men felt that a wife at home symbolized what the struggle was all about.[11] Many women, on the other hand, realized that the war might give them increased opportunities and were keen to take advantage of this. There was also the practical question that separation allowances for men in the forces with dependants were woefully inadequate. In 1940 the allowance for a private in the army with a wife and two children was £1 13s, which was considerably below what most men were earning and provided a powerful incentive for many housewives to return to work.[12] There is some evidence to indicate that in the first year of the war women's unemployment rose as consumer industries traditionally employing women, such as textiles, suffered a fall-off in demand.[13] In the early months the government were very much inclined towards the former view and did little to encourage more women into paid employment. But, as labour shortages in the war industries mounted, the Ministry of Labour (MoL) began to look seriously at methods of recruiting women. Propaganda campaigns were launched, but attracted only a small fraction of the women required. Women cited domestic commitments as the major reason, but they were also wary of the vague appeal which was being made to them, with little information on pay and other important aspects of the work.[14]

Reluctantly, the government came around to the view that an element of compulsion was necessary. As Summerfield has shown, this immediately produced a tension within the state over conflicting views of women's role in society – as mothers and nurturers and as workers, or, as she puts it, between the capitalist and patriarchal modes of production.[15] If large numbers of married women were to be recruited into industry, collective provision would have to be made for childcare, meals and many other functions of the full-time wife and mother. This could produce a potentially radical transformation. Consequently, the legislation which was introduced was framed in such a way as to retain the primacy of women's domestic role. This in turn meant that women's unequal position in the workforce was perpetuated and given official sanction.

From March 1941 all women aged 19 to 40 had to register at employment exchanges. This was progressively increased, so that by 1943 50-year-olds were included. On the basis of this, women could be directed into specific jobs. Under the Essential Work Order (1941) employees lost the facility to change jobs without permission from the local Labour Exchange and employers also lost the power to dismiss workers and had to take whoever the Labour Exchange sent them. The only military conscription of women came in December 1941 with the call-up of women aged 20 to 24, who could officially choose between the women's services, civil defence or the munitions industries. In reality, almost all were channelled into the ATS (Auxiliary Territorial Service) or industry. Although these provisions appear somewhat draconian, in practice this was far from the case. Mothers of children under 14 living at home were exempt, although they were, of course, welcomed on a voluntary basis. Women were classified as either 'mobile' or 'immobile'. Single women without dependants were mobile and could, therefore, be directed to work anywhere they were needed. Married women were regarded as immobile and had to be found work locally. This category applied to a very large number of women, including those without children, those who had domestic help at home and those whose husbands were in the forces. This latter group were officially allowed to take a week's holiday if their husbands were home on leave.

Continuing the pre-war feminist tradition, women in Parliament had been active from the start in pressing for women to make gains from the increased demand for their labour. There was much dissatisfaction from this quarter when the government did little to promote women, especially as many educated married women were eager to take up positions of responsibility which had been denied to them in the very different circumstances of the inter-war years. As a result, the group coalesced into a cross-party parliamentary caucus which, in May 1940, took the name of the Woman-Power Committee, with members such as Edith Summerskill (Labour) and Irene Ward (Conservative).[16] This group was represented on the Women's Consultative Committee, which advised the MoL on aspects of women's employment. Summerskill in particular pressed for conscription of women to include provision for equal pay. This was to no avail, although by the end of 1943 the forces pressing for equal pay had combined to form an Equal Pay Campaign Committee.[17] This group succeeded in making equal pay for teachers a provision of the 1944 Education Act.[18] Further gains were stemmed, however, by the government's shrewd decision to set up a Royal Commission on Equal Pay. By refusing to set a time limit for the report, the government effectively shelved the issue until after the war.[19]

As we have seen, the percentage of women in the labour force was showing an upward trend in the 1930s. The war greatly accelerated this movement. The participation rates for married women show an increase from 16 per cent in 1931 to 43 per cent in 1943.[20] By September, 1943 there were seven and a quarter million women in some form of national service. A wave of literature appeared, such as J.B. Priestley's *British Women Go to War* (1943), which cast factory women as heroic patriots cheerfully giving their all to the war effort, seemingly untroubled by problems of childcare, shopping, etc. In reality, this mobilization of women was not achieved without both the state and employers becoming directly involved in the tension between the competing demands of home and work. Absentee rates among women were considerably higher than those of men and this was particularly so for married women. Hours varied, but the standard 54-hour week was usually supplemented by overtime which could not easily be refused. With a 12-hour day a fairly common practice, younger women complained that they had no time for a social life and mothers of young children found combining work and family virtually impossible. Edith had two small children and although her sister cared for them well while she was at work, she decided to leave after a few weeks.

> I know she does everything for them, but I never seem to see my babies now. I miss it, dressing them and feeding them, and I sort of feel they'll forget I'm their Mummy ... Starting at six in the morning and getting back at nine, all I see of them is when they're asleep.[21]

Many women were keen to work on a part-time basis, but the MoL was slow to recognize this. This could be attributed to an inability to understand the needs of working women and also to a fear of a slippage from women already working full-time to part-time. Gradually, during 1943, a variety of part-time schemes were to be introduced for women in industrial production, so by 1944 900 000 women were working part-time.[22] It was soon noticed that the productivity of part-time women workers was higher than of those working full time. Part-time work certainly suited many women but, as Summerfield has written, it confirmed women as low-status workers and 'did nothing to change the centrality of women in the home'.[23]

Although women with dependent children were not directed into war work, in fact there were, as we have seen, many factors compelling them into work, Denise Riley estimates that there were approximately three-quarters of a million women in industry with children under 14.[24] For women with children under five, nurseries were an obvious solution and there is quite a lot of evidence, from MO and other sources, to show the demand for nurseries. There was a conflict, however, between the Ministries of Health and Labour. The former, whose customary role included care of infants, opposed nurseries, tried to insist that there was little demand for them and generally acted in an obstructive manner. During 1941 the MoL took up the idea of local authority provision, having rejected workplace nurseries as being too vulnerable to precision bombing. Grants were forthcoming and by 1944 there were over 1500 nurseries, the great majority of which were run by local authorities.[25] The MoL also supported minding schemes, which were more favoured by the Ministry of Health. When it funded nurseries, the MoL always made it clear that it was doing so to assist war production and not as a social service. Useful though they were, we should not overplay the importance of nurseries. Less than a quarter of under-fives were in nurseries with the great majority being cared for by relatives or neighbours.

Shopping was another big problem. Of the large number of women interviewed in *People in Production* for MO about half were responsible for their own shopping and nearly all of them found shopping difficult.[26] Lack of supplies late in the day, long queues and other problems made women very anxious: 'some women are almost desperate in conversation about it'.[27] The high rates of absenteeism convinced employers and government that some sort of help was needed, although no one seems to have suggested that male workers should take any responsibility. Predictably, the preferred option was to try to persuade other women to do it on a voluntary basis. One or two local schemes did operate, but it was officially frowned upon by the voluntary services as not appropriate for voluntary work as the women concerned were in paid employment.[28] Retailers were asked to give factory women priority, but that created resentment amongst other women who were also, in their own way, doing valuable war work. Some factories experimented with 'professional shoppers', but women's own preference was for time off. Women activists in the labour movement took up this issue and many factories conceded demands for a 'shopping hour' or an extended lunch break on a regular basis. The high proportion of women working meant that both childminders and casual help with events such as shopping crises were increasingly difficult to find. Many families were saved by girls of 12 or 13 who kept the household going by taking on these tasks, as well as helping out with the housework and caring for younger siblings after school.

The Essential Work Order made it obligatory for large factories doing munitions work to establish works canteens.[29] By the end of the war over 10 000 works canteens were in operation, although only a minority of workers actually used them. This was all part of a more welfare-orientated approach to factory work, which was promised alongside the provisions for conscription. In 1940 the BBC introduced two daily half-hour sessions of 'Music While You Work', which proved popular, as did the occasional lunch-time entertainment in the canteen by ENSA (Entertainments, National Services Association) and other groups. Toilets and washrooms were upgraded. Medical facilities were introduced, with many large factories providing a sick-bay employing medical and nursing staff. Not all women workers appreciated all this extra attention to their mental and physical well-being. One woman interviewed in the MO Study explained why she left the Midlands factory where she previously worked, which was known for its welfare policy: 'You couldn't call your soul your own, they welfared you to death.'[30]

The People in Production study by MO involved 20 investigators and 500 voluntary observers in industry between October 1941 and March 1942. One significant fact which emerged was that, 'not one single woman was encountered in a senior position'.[31] The role of welfare manager appears to be the only area of management which women had penetrated. The great majority of women in industry were employed in what was officially termed 'women's work' – low-status, repetitive work such as machine operator, simple assembly and packing. In fact the majority of the 'new labour' had experience of industrial work already, predominantly before marriage in the 1930s. That what most of the women did was regarded as unskilled is readily apparent from their earnings. The MoL census of war industries in July 1941 revealed the average earnings, including bonuses etc., of adult women to be £2 4s 2d, with men earning £4 19s 3d.[32] It was quite common for women to have to work at monotonous, routine work for up to four and a half hours without a break. Understandably, boredom became a feature of the work. The MO study *War Factory* reported that clock-watching and various forms of slacking off were commonplace.[33] Despite the drawbacks, women were fairly satisfied with their work on the whole, according to MO.[34] It appears that, for most women, putting up with low pay and dull, undemanding work was outweighed by a measure of economic independence and the company of other women. Although many skilled occupations were officially 'reserved', there was still a serious shortage of skilled labour. This gave further impetus to the already existing tendency to break down skilled work into shorter, unskilled or semi-skilled tasks. The MoL set up training centres where basic training in engineering was given and some women did gain acceptance on these courses, which varied in length from a few weeks to several months. Rosemary Moonen gave up hairdressing and graduated from a training centre with a semi-skilled fitter's certificate. She met with this response when she was sent to her first job.

> I was sent with a group of die-hards (men) to report to a certain foreman. He surveyed us all grimly, gave each one a job to do, with the exception of yours truly. No doubt I looked nervous and scared. He ignored me, and as he turned to walk away, I said, 'What shall I do?' He turned towards me, sneered, 'Oh yes! We've forgotten sunshine here! What shall you do – Here!', indicating a broom, 'And sod around!' – With that he threw the broom at me and walked off. I was stung to humiliation.[35]

In time Rosemary found grudging acceptance. Like many women from training centres she could do the work extremely well. There were numerous cases of women being removed for surpassing male work rates to an embarrassing degree. As with the 1914–18 war, the whole issue of female dilution was a fraught one. By 1944 all the major unions had secured dilution agreements. As before, the skilled unions sought arrangements that ensured that the use of female labour on skilled work should be regarded as strictly temporary. On a more general level, the Extended Employment of Women agreement (1940) gave women doing 'men's work' without assistance or extra supervision the right to graduate towards the male rate over a period of time, but it also made clear that women were to be regarded as temporary workers. The Restoration of Pre-War Practices Act (1942) guaranteed their removal at the end of the war. In any case, male resistance was so strong that women rarely achieved

anything approaching equal pay. Summerfield cites the example
of Rootes in Coventry, where management and shop stewards
colluded in a secret agreement which prevented women dilutees
from proceeding beyond 75 per cent of the male rate.[36]

The war provided a great stimulus to women's membership
of trade unions, which climbed from just over half a million in
1939 to one and a third million in 1945.[37] Until 1943 women
could only join the general unions, but after a ballot in 1942
the engineering union (AEU) admitted women. Many women
became shop stewards and the Women's TUC actively campaigned on nurseries, shopping, equal pay and other issues
related to women. Both government and management promoted
the recruitment of women into the labour movement. The
motives behind this newfound enthusiasm for trade unions
centre mainly around questions of discipline, particularly the
controlling of absenteeism. Arthur Exell worked at Morris Motors
near Oxford and was a leading trade union activist in the plant.
A lot of young women were sent from London as 'mobile labour',
but many were unhappy and frequently took time off. The
manager made it clear to Exell that he favoured the recruitment
of these women as he hoped that the shop stewards would have
some leverage with them over the issue of absenteeism.[38]

Although industrial action was officially banned under the
emergency powers regulations, strikes did break out from time
to time, particularly in the area of the grading of work. It was, of
course, in the employers' interests that as much work as possible
was graded as 'women's work'. In a situation when many
workers were new and work processes were themselves in a fluid
state, disputes could easily arise over insensitive grading. Such
was the case at the Rolls Royce plant in Hillingdon near Glasgow,
in November 1943, which involved a large number of women
workers.[39] Management sparked off the strike by reducing the
piece rate for a particular process. Although an official enquiry
was held and a regrading of 'women's work' was carried out, the
dispute dragged on and gave impetus to the movement for
the removal of sex-typing in jobs. This came to be the official
position of the AEU, the electrical trades union and the general
unions. At Rolls, the dispute eventually reached a conclusion
when every machine in the factory was named and a rate fixed
for working it. Such arrangements appeared to favour women,

but in practice the work that women did was almost invariably put at the bottom of the gradings ladder, restricting them yet again to low pay and low status.

Paid Work (2)

So far the emphasis of this chapter has been on factory work but, of course, women were occupied in a huge range of employment during the war. The post office took on several thousand postwomen. The number of women in white-collar occupations expanded by half a million during the war.[40] The civil service in particular recruited large numbers of women clerks and typists for its ever increasing government departments. Although women white-collar workers no longer fell foul of the marriage bar, they still had unequal pay and were often excluded from some of the privileges of male workers. As we saw above, only women teachers managed to secure an equal-pay agreement. Women once more took over positions from their husbands or other relatives on an informal basis, as in the previous war. Many jobs were war-related in some way or another. About one-sixth of the country's Air Raid Wardens were women. They were paid on the same terms as men, but very few positions were full-time and women wardens were most likely to be working long hours for only a few shillings a week.

The female bus and tram conductress became a familiar sight throughout the country. Some buses were run by husband and wife teams, although the 'motormen' always kept their privileged position as drivers. As Braybon and Summerfield point out, this was the only area of manual employment in which women enjoyed equal pay and, as a result, women conductors were among the highest women earners during the war.[41] In 1945 women in transport were on average weekly earnings of £4 1s 8d, which put them at the top of the league of women earners.[42] Thelma Katin was a botany graduate who married soon after graduating and was unable to find employment. When 'called up' 18 years later she volunteered for transport in preference to factory work. After training as a 'clippie' she found herself on the job: 'I was exhilarated and proud because I was able to do it – at 40. The trams had rejuvenated me.'[43] Even so after a few months she found that she could no longer cope with the long hours and constant shift work. She was granted permission to go part-time and work a four-day week.

Nearly half a million women were in the women's armed services by 1945: the WRNS (Women's Royal Naval Service), the WAAF (Women's Auxiliary Air Force), the ATS and some smaller groups, such as the FANYs (First Aid Nursing Yeomanry) who concentrated on driving. As Dorothy Sheridan has indicated, women in the military have been neglected both in popular memory and by academic historians.[44] Although the Wrens had a reputation for recruiting from the middle classes, the women's services as a whole recruited from a wide variety of backgrounds. They were not lavishly paid, but they did not have to pay out for board and lodging and were kept rather better than the rations at home would allow. The strict regime of service life with its endless drills, kit inspections and petty rules could be very trying, but for many it was an escape from a narrow and restrictive family home. As the official role of the women's services was to 'assist' the men, many of these women found that they were doing similar work to what they had done before. Although the bulk of service women were engaged in rather traditional tasks, the overall range of employment in the women's services in this war was considerably broader than before. Training courses for service women appear to have been taken rather more seriously than in civilian industry. For some women this meant new horizons opened up. Mrs Johnson was a 19-year-old cashier in a butcher's shop in Twickenham before signing up for the WAAF with a friend in 1942. Neither of them knew how to drive, but they requested driving jobs and were given a ten-week course of instruction, which included maintenance as well as driving.[45] Women 'spotters' sat on top of tall buildings and in isolated locations with binoculars looking for enemy planes; women worked at the top secret code-breaking headquarters at Bletchley; there were women flight mechanics and women stang the enormous barrage balloons which were aimed to deter enemy aircraft. One of the most engaging works of the artist Laura Knight is her painting 'A Balloon Site', depicting a team of WAAF women in Coventry hoisting a barrage balloon into the air.[46] The work performed by the women's services overlapped a great deal. All of them had cooks, typists, clerks and so on and all of them became involved in some sort of anti-aircraft activity. Using radar, Wrens would plot the progress of enemy aircraft over the sea and the ATS would constitute over half the personnel in mixed Anti-Aircraft Batteries, which aimed to intercept and shoot at enemy aeroplanes before they could drop any bombs.

Despite this progress towards integrated work, a distinction was always maintained between men and women. As M. and P. Higgonet have argued, the work women performed may have altered in content but its status vis à vis 'men's work' was still subordinate.[47] For example, women ferry pilots (civilians, the WAAF would not train women pilots) could transport aircraft from one location to another, but were not allowed to carry passengers. Also, it remained fundamental to official policy that women were not to be armed and would offer no resistance if actually faced with the enemy. Sometimes the distinction between combat and non-combatant was not a very meaningful one. As Sheridan points out, women in mixed 'Ack-Ack' batteries could make all the calculations and manoeuvres associated with aiming the guns, but were not allowed to fire them.[48]

In fact, there are examples of women taking on active military roles on the same basis as men, particularly in intelligence work. WAAF Squadron Officer Diana Rowden, a fluent French speaker, volunteered for undercover work in occupied France. Unaware that the resistance unit she was to join had already been betrayed, she was sent to France in 1943 and was arrested within a few weeks. After refusing to be interrogated in Paris, she was sent to Germany and executed along with six other British women agents who were all in their early twenties.[49] Pearl Withington, a British woman living in France, became involved in the resistance and eventually took control of a unit of 3500 men which played a key role in bringing about the disintegration of German forces in south-west France in 1944. In recognition of her services she was recommended for the Military Cross. The British military command, however, did not recognize women as capable of performing in a military capacity and awarded her a civilian medal instead. Pearl sent it back with an explanation that there was nothing civil in what she had done.[50]

Over 80 000 women responded to the call to 'Lend a hand on the land'. The women of the Women's Land Army worked

alongside Italian and German prisoners of war (POWs), conscientious objectors and older farm hands, who were often
resentful of their presence. As Raynes Minns has written,
government propaganda at the time portrayed images of land
girls as a 'romantic band of happy volunteers tossing bales of hay
lightly onto carts'.[51] In reality, they worked long hours in all
weathers for very low pay. Mrs Allen wrote of her time in the
Land Army in Kent, stating that in her group of 30 they all
suffered from 'aching backs, sore feet, cuts, bruises ... frost-
bite ... getting soaked to the skin, became part and parcel of the
daily routine'.[52] Living conditions were often primitive and their
work carried such low status that, until they protested, they were
placed behind Boy Scouts on parades.

Women moved into all branches of agricultural work, including dairying, fencing, ploughing, harvesting, care of livestock and
tractor driving. It was often very physically demanding. Anne
Hall remembered the morning the farm manager

> said he wanted us to unload the sacks of potatoes from a trailer
> and carry them up a ladder to the loft over the granary [which]
> had us all laughing. We really thought that this was his idea of
> a joke. He somewhat testily reminded us we were employed to
> replace farm men and that involved doing men's work.[53]

Of course, these women never received anything like men's
wages. The Women's Timber Corps was a special section of
the Women's Land Army. At first it was thought that their
use would be limited as much of this work was regarded as very
skilled, but women soon took over all the aspects of the work –
felling, clearing, measuring, driving tractors and lorries, etc.[54]
Altogether, the Women's Land Army performed a very important role on the home front. Not least of their achievements was
their contribution to the doubling of Britain's food output
during the war.

The war greatly increased the demand for nurses (state
registered, auxiliaries and VADS) to work for both the civilian
and military populations. Those working in a hospital environment were subjected to harsh discipline and were expected to
give total commitment to the job. The Blitz necessitated nurses
working in all kinds of outposts, rendering immediate assistance

to the wounded. Amy Briggs, a Leeds nurse and mother of two, worked night shifts in a local first aid post. She recorded in her MO diary in October, 1941 that 'Everyone tired at work, therefore grumpy'.[55] At times medical services were strained beyond the limit. Coventry experienced heavy bombing in late 1940 and early 1941. Several nurses died trying to protect patients when the hospital was destroyed by a direct hit.

Large numbers of nurses were posted abroad with the forces. Many in the Far East, along with Australian and New Zealand nurses, were captured by the Japanese and endured terrible ordeals in POW camps. Others served in Europe. Brenda McBryde, from Northumberland, qualified as a state registered nurse in 1943 and joined the Queen Alexandra's Imperial Military Nursing Reserve. She followed the allied troops into Normandy with the 'D Day' landings and was immediately inundated with casualties.

> Most of their proud uniform, stiff with blood and caked with mud, had to be cut from them. We sliced the tough boots with razors to release shattered feet. The stretcher bearers came again and again until every trestle was occupied and the floor crammed so that there was barely room to put a foot or kneel between the stretchers.[56]

Women Organize

There is no doubt that women volunteers were the backbone of the war effort on the home front. The Women's Voluntary Service (WVS) played a particularly valuable role. Set up by the Home Office in 1938 and headed by Lady Reading, its official role was to assist in promoting women into civil defence. Its guiding principle was that women should give of 'their muscle, their sweat, and their thought' rather than their purse.[57] Its growth was phenomenal. Nearly a million women became involved in WVS activities during the war. Mrs Appleby is perhaps a typical example of a WVS worker. In 1939 she answered a call for voluntary workers to staff a canteen at York railway station. She worked from midnight until eight in the morning once a week, serving hot drinks, pies and sandwiches.

Sometimes they had only half an hour to serve 500 men. The
canteen on Platform Eight never closed its doors for the duration
of the war.[58]
The range of WVS activities was staggering: they assisted with
the evacuation of children; helped to establish new nurseries; ran
clothing exchanges; distributed goods from abroad; provided
vegetable hampers for sailors; made camouflage nets; collected
salvage for recycling. It was in the Blitz that WVS women really
pitched in. As Minns has written, 'there were no cups of tea or
mobile canteens, no facilities to wash soot-soaked clothes and
bodies, no advice centres or enquiry posts and no future for the
blitzed, until the women's voluntary groups organized them'.[59]
Following an incident, WVS women could set up an Incident
Enquiry Point in less than ten minutes, which would co-ordinate
vital information to rescue services about who was likely to
be buried where. Mobile Emergency Feeding Units would be
rushed in. In Coventry after the raid of 14 November 1940,
15 000 snack meals a day were served from mobile canteens for
over a week.[60] Mobile laundries and baths were also available.
Rest Centres would take in those in need of temporary shelter.
This work could be emotionally as well as physically demanding,
as this incident at a WVS centre reveals.

The next arrival was a boy of twelve who approached the
woman in charge of the bureau with an anxious look on his
face. He said: 'Please miss, could you get me off going to school
tomorrow?' 'You are a naughty boy, just trying to play hookey
because of the air-raids.' 'No, miss; Mum said that if anything
happened to her I was to come to you to get leave off school
and look after the other kids. You see, she was killed last night
so I have come to you.'[61]

Of course, the WVS was not the only women's organization to be
doing war work. Women's Institutes (WI), Townswomen's
Guilds, Girl Guides and other groups dug collective allotments,
made blankets, helped out in British Restaurants and mobile
canteens and performed hundreds of other tasks. In 1940 the
WI secured government approval for the release of sugar for
collective jam-making and as a result over 17 tons of jam was

produced from villages all over the country.[62] At the time when the threat of invasion loomed, many women became keen to acquire weapons training for self-defence. As the Home Guard would not admit women, except as 'auxiliaries' to the men, the Women's Home Defence was founded by Edith Summerskill and others. Summerskill recalled in her memoirs that official channels were not at all sympathetic. When she attempted to approach Sir James Grigg, Secretary for War, he snapped, 'I don't want to hear any more about your bloody women.'[63] Despite this, Women's Home Defence groups formed all over the country and many ex-servicemen stepped in to provide the expertise for training sessions.

Many women, particularly in rural areas, found themselves involved in a whole range of voluntary activities. Clara Milburn was a middle-aged housewife of some means living near Coventry. Although women of her class have always been expected to do philanthropic work, it is clear in her diary that wartime circumstances dictated that this role be extended. She acted as a supervisor for local Land Army girls and would from time to time host social evenings at her house for them. She was secretary of the local WI and also collected for the Red Cross and items for salvage. She helped with the evacuation of children and transported blood donors. Much of this work involved driving. As petrol coupons were no longer distributed for personal consumption, voluntary work was the only way that she could keep her car in use. As she wrote after she volunteered it for the WVS car pool, 'Anything to get a legitimate run in the car these days!'[64]

It is apparent that, although it is true that women of different backgrounds often worked together harmoniously, class divisions remained as significant as ever. Both Clara Milburn and Nella Last retained domestic help, although neither had dependent children. Mrs Trowbridge was a middle-aged housewife in Bradford who sent in information for MO. She undertook various voluntary duties for the WVS, including canteen work. In October, 1941, she hinted that some WVS canteen women were motivated more by a desire to avoid conscription than by a genuine voluntary spirit. At the same time, she recalled the recent experience of her sister-in-law at a feeding centre in the south:

The non-titled ladies went early to prepare the vegetables and do the cooking – the 'titles' arrived with the cooked dinner, passed the plates to the children with a profuse sprinkling of 'darlings', and disappeared in their cars when dinner was over, while the non-titled continued with the washing up, etc.[65]

The war brought with it something of a renewed interest in feminist issues. In 1940 a London Women's Parliament was organized by Mary Corsellis.[66] This and other women's parliaments campaigned on issues such as nurseries, reduced working hours and provision of canteens. In Parliament, the small number of women MPs acted more like a cross-party 'women's lobby' than ever before. Mavis Tate, Eleanor Rathbone, Edith Summerskill and Thelma Cazalet-Keir were among those who worked from 'The Boudoir', as 'the lady member's room' at the Commons was unsympathetically referred to by some male MPs. We have already seen how their attempts to push through equal pay were thwarted. The abolition of the marriage bar in teaching and the introduction of family allowances could be construed as feminist victories, but in fact both have quite complex causalities, which only partly involved feminist motivations. Another of the great feminist causes of the war was the iniquity in government compensation payments paid to victims of air raids. The 7s a week difference between men and women incensed feminists, who organized a petition which was submitted by Edith Summerskill in April 1942. The government responded by setting up a Select Committee, which resulted in a new ruling that henceforth male and female civilian war victims would be compensated at the same rate.[67] In many respects wartime conditions were favourable for feminists to promote women's issues, but the attempt to push through a comprehensive bill which would outlaw all forms of discrimination did not succeed. This measure, which arose from the Six Point Group during discussions about conscription of women, did not win widespread support, even within feminist circles.[68]

Feminist pacifism was not an issue in the Second World War as it had been in the First, although many women were unhappy about conscription for war-related work. Over a thousand women registered as conscientious objectors and refused to do war work, but very few of them were imprisoned. The novelist

Ethel Mannin was among those who refused. The first to be given a custodial sentence (of one month) was Constance Bolan, a housemaid, who announced to the court that 'she disagreed with war in any shape or form'.[69] Vera Brittain continued her pacifist work and was one of the most outspoken campaigners against the saturation bombing of civilian targets in Germany.[70]

Domestic Life

The war led to perhaps the greatest disturbance in domestic life that Britain had ever known. One of the most significant areas of upheaval was population movement. The country was divided into three categories according to probable risk – evacuation areas, reception areas and neutral areas. No one was to be subject to compulsory evacuation against their will, but billeting officers in reception areas had powers to make householders take in evacuees. On the first three days of September 1939, one and a quarter million people were evacuated, including 735 000 unaccompanied children, in a highly organized exercise on a grand scale.[71]

Inèvitably, such a massive movement could not be accomplished without a few failures. In one Norfolk village, a trainload of mothers and children arrived from east London when unaccompanied children had been expected. Such chaotic conditions meant that journeys often took longer than expected and children arrived exhausted and hungry, as well as bewildered and sad. It was much easier to place unaccompanied children than it was to place family groups. One woman wrote about an experience in Dunstable: 'We arrived (at 5 p.m. Saturday) at a skating rink and then were picked out so you can guess what some poor devils were like who had four or five children. They were still there on Sunday afternoon.'[72] Some writers have stressed the 'cocktail shaker' effect of these massive social changes during the war, but as far as evacuation was concerned it was the affluent middle classes with space in their homes who were often the least willing to take in evacuees. Angus Calder quotes a regional administrator for the WVS: 'We find over and over again that it is the really poor people

who are willing to take evacuees and that the bridge-playing
set who live at such places as Chorley Wood are terribly difficult
about it all.'[73]

The problems of adjustment were enormous. Many of the
children arrived undernourished, poorly clad and suffering from
various skin disorders. Some had never used a bed or a toilet
before. So many complaints were made about bed-wetting and
soiling that a special allowance of 3s 6d had to be added to the
billeting allowance of 10s 6d.[74] The country women made allegations about the slovenly behaviour and poor management of
their guests, but the evacuated mothers had many complaints
of their own. They missed the fish and chip shops and other
urban facilities to buy prepared food and were unused to
country-range cooking. They were often only allowed access to
the kitchen at restricted times, barred completely from the living
room and sometimes had to resort to walking the streets for hours
on end. Ethnic differences also led to tensions as inner city and
seaport towns were much more cosmopolitan than country areas.
Black, Jewish or Chinese evacuees were often met with suspicion
or outright hostility by narrow-minded host populations.[75]

The 'phoney war' circumstances in the early months induced
the great majority of evacuees to return home within three
months. When the bombing began the exodus started up again,
but this time it was on a more *ad hoc* basis. Although the majority
of those eligible for evacuation did not go, there were plenty of
cases of terrified people in blitzed areas fleeing to wherever they
thought they might find someone to take them in. By far the
most preferred form of evacuation was to stay with relatives in
the country.

With food supplies declining, the government introduced
rationing early in 1940. Ration books were issued which varied
according to status: general adult; heavy manual worker; infant;
pregnant woman, etc. It was generally a woman in each household who was responsible for food shopping. She would have to
register with a particular grocer and surrender coupons in order
to receive basic supplies of 2 oz tea, 2 oz butter and so on per
week per person. During 1941–2 another system was introduced
for certain other non-perishable foods, such as canned and dried
goods, soap and biscuits. Ration-book holders were entitled to a
certain number of points for each four-week period which could

then be expended on goods which had a points value. The desired goods would not necessarily be available; generally women had to take what they could get.[76] Although rationing was extremely popular with women as it was manifestly fairer than the free market, its operation was not without difficulties. The problems of the housewife who was also a full-time worker have already been raised. Queuing became an inescapable part of daily life, especially when unrationed goods such as fresh fish made a rare appearance. Women were sometimes so desperate that even an air-raid warning did not shift a queue if some highly valued commodity had just come in. Shop keepers complained about all the extra work that rationing entailed and were apt to keep back scarce goods for favoured customers, such as Mrs Milburn, who would sometimes find a couple of lemons or tomatoes placed in her bag.

Rationing soon surpassed the weather as the most popular topic of conversation as everyone did their best to eke out their rations. Meat was a particular problem as 1s 2d worth a week did not go far. Amy Briggs, the nurse from Leeds, had her husband home on leave when she recorded in her diary: 'Burns his dinner which includes 1 person's meat ration for a week. Go to work heartbroken.'[77] Nella Last took great satisfaction in making the meat ration go a long way and could make a tasty casserole for two out of a quarter of beef cut up into small pieces and cooked slowly with vegetables, potatoes and pulses. The Ministry of Food bombarded housewives with leaflets on how to cook nourishing meals without meat, eggs or fat. Although these were sometimes read out at women's meetings, there is little evidence that housewives actually took much notice. Women managed as best they could. Ration swaps were organized in order to suit individual requirements. Works canteens and British Restaurants provided meals without depleting precious rations, but families could not afford to eat regularly at the latter even though they were relatively low cost. Many households kept chickens or joined in with others to keep a pig. Allotments provided much needed vegetables and fruit. Cicely Bower helped in a WVS canteen run for an RAF base. She helped to organize a wedding from her house for a service couple: 'How we conjured up the dresses, the cake and the eats, I'll never know.' The wedding dress was borrowed and the bridesmaid was in uniform. Dried apples and bottled blackberries were used to make tarts for the reception which was served on bedsheets acting as tablecloths. The wedding cake was made from whatever anyone at the canteen could contribute in the way of dried fruit, dried milk, a few precious eggs and 'a bit of this and a bit of that'.[78]

Unlike the 1914–18 war, the Second World War resulted in a high number of civilian casualties in Britain. Although the much feared gas attacks did not happen, bombing from the air resulted in 60 000 deaths and many more seriously injured.[79] In the bombing campaign of 1940–1, Britain was 'blitzed' by the Luftwaffe. At its height, several hundred people died every night. Later, in 1944, the V-1 and V-2 flying bombs created more havoc, but this campaign never reached the intensity of the earlier bombing. In all, nearly a quarter of a million homes were either totally destroyed or rendered unusable. Only a minority of the population had any kind of domestic shelter, either in the garden (Anderson) or in the house (Morrison). For most people it was a question of finding space in some kind of public shelter. Refuge was sought in any dry underground space. At first, the government tried to prevent people using the London underground platforms, but it was forced to concede to overwhelming public pressure. With massive overcrowding and no provision for sanitation or ventilation, conditions quickly became almost unbearable. Only slowly did the government, from March 1941, respond to the need to improve conditions. For mothers with young children the air raids created huge problems. Feeding and settling babies in such conditions result-ed in exhausted, nervy mothers who were sometimes unable to breastfeed their infants.

Death and destruction became an unavoidable part of daily life. Alfreda Pickles came out of a London shelter one morning and found that, 'so many houses had gone that the street was almost unrecognizable, and there were parts of bodies – people's arms and legs – hanging from the telephone wires'.[80] For mothers of large families, such as Kathleen Benn of Kent who had five children, it was especially difficult to keep track of their children during raids. Like other residents of Dover she took refuge in the deep caves; 'my little Jimmy, aged four years and ten months, ran out of the cave and was killed by the blast of a shell. Nobody saw him go out. It was terrible.'[81] Those who survived but were made homeless by the raids were taken in by neighbours or arrived dazed, shocked and filthy at the rest centres. Nella Last remembered her 'odd sensations' after a bomb blew out the windows of her house, brought down the ceilings and cracked the walls: 'one a calm acceptance of "the end", the other a feeling of regret that I'd not opened a tin of fruit salad for tea – and now it was too late!'[82]

With over a third of a million men in the forces and the merchant navy killed, many women had to face up to bad news from overseas – husbands, fathers, sons and brothers who would never be coming home. For women whose husbands had died, financial considerations very soon became paramount. Mabel Terry of York had two young sons when her Sergeant wireless operator husband was killed:

> When I got my pittance of a pension, on which we could not live, I had to get a job. But first I had to get Malcolm into a nursery school, which I did. I then got a job as an assistant cook at a nearby school.[83]

There is no doubt that stress and fatigue among women was very high. In addition to the air raids, rationing and constant uncertainty about loved ones, women had to contend with the blackout and financial problems. The responsibility of bringing up children and managing a household alone was a heavy one to bear. Many women became lonely and depressed, listless and war-weary. However, on the whole, morale held up remarkably well. Possibly the key to this is the fact that some women certainly felt that the stresses and challenges of war had actually changed them for the better. This change was not necessarily linked to paid employment. It is interesting that Nella Last, whose diary provides the most insightful of all the wartime women's testimony, felt herself to be liberated by the war. After she had been working at the WVS centre for a few months, her husband noted that she was 'not so sweet' as she used to be. This was because he was no longer the centre of her universe: 'He never realizes – and never could – that the years when I had to sit quiet and always do everything he liked, and never the things he did not, were slavery years of mind and body.'[84] She became more

assertive towards him and also started to cut down on the
housework, regarding many of her previously routine tasks, such
as turning and airing beds, as no longer quite so essential. She
hoped that this change, undergone by her and other women,
would be permanent; 'I cannot see women settling to trivial
ways – women who have done worthwhile things.'[85] Although
Smith is right to argue that we cannot generalize from this one
woman's experience, Summerfield is equally right in asserting
that testimony such as this should not be ignored.[86]

Sexuality

As with the First World War, the dominant ideology regarding
gender roles in the 1939–45 war emphasized that, despite the
changes demanded of both men and women, traditional gender
distinctions were preserved. Social observers were at pains to
demonstrate that women war workers could serve the war effort
without any loss of femininity. Munition workers were referred
to as 'Bevin Beauties'. Theodora Benson wrote of WAAF
sparking-plug testers, 'The first thing that struck me was how
pretty they all were.'[87] In contrast to earlier wars, however,
sexuality became much more overt. There is no doubt that the
Second World War was a very romantic war. Although there
were many reasons for this, two seem to be most significant. First,
there was the presence in Britain of large numbers of overseas
troops, particularly American GIs, who had far more money in
their pockets than British soldiers. Second, the inter-war period
had ushered in the age of mass entertainment. Cinemas and
dance halls provided the ideal territory for romantic encounters.

   About two million American soldiers were stationed in Britain
at some time during the war (as well as many thousands of other
overseas troops and POWs). British girls were thrilled to be
taken out to dances, treated to restaurant meals and for an evening removed from the grey weariness of wartime Britain. Dance
halls, with their craze for chain dances such the conga, created a
party atmosphere in which many British women fell for the
charms of the American GI. For some 70 000 British women
such encounters changed their lives for ever, as they were later
to cross the Atlantic as 'GI brides'. With the American army

enforcing a strict colour bar, the presence of black soldiers became a source of tension. Many British women ignored the American army ruling that they should not associate with black GIs, which did not receive official British government support. It has been estimated that about fifteen hundred babies were born to black American servicemen during the war.[88]

Not all the liaisons between British women and overseas troops went smoothly. American troops were particularly forward and were sometimes apt to think that their generosity gave them a right to sexual favours. Charges of rape and sexual molestation were not uncommon, although this problem was not restricted to American soldiers. Mary Clayton, mother of a small son and with a POW husband, had her life made 'something of a nightmare, fending off advances from lonely soldiers' in the forces canteen where she worked.[89] There were reports from WAAF girls that whilst on night duty soldiers attempted to rape them when they had to go out to use the toilets.[90] WAAFs at a Warwickshire base were instructed to refrain from saluting Czechoslovak officers in nearby Leamington 'as the gesture was likely to be misconstrued'.[91] Land army girls, who were often in isolated and vulnerable locations, were also prone to become victims of sexual harassment from lecherous farmers.

The war produced much comment from social observers regarding a supposed loosening of moral standards. The rise in the birthrate from women not married to the father caused particular concern. By 1945 this accounted for over 9 per cent of all births, which represented a doubling of the pre-war rate.[92] At the height of the blitz, something of a moral panic arose over allegations of supposed immorality in the women's services, particularly the ATS. It reached such a pitch that the government launched an enquiry, which was set up under the chairmanship of the lawyer, Miss Violet Markham. The Markham Committee spent six months touring 123 military camps and then duly announced that, although there might have been one or two lapses, there was no case for the generalized charge of immorality.[93] Edith Summerskill, who was a member of the committee, was very sceptical about the whole exercise:

I never quite understood how, by paying a visit to an officers' mess at lunch-time and making a cursory tour of a camp one bright summer day, one could discover anything adverse about the sex life of the girls.[94]

For lesbians, the war probably created more opportunities than ever before, particularly for those who left home for the forces or the Land Army. 'Eleanor' worked as a dairy and poultry maid at a farm in Suffolk where she met the woman who was to be her lover for five years. They lived together and were left alone: 'I don't think the owners of the farm thought anything of it. They didn't say. I don't suppose we cared really. We lived our own life together.'[95]

Women whose husbands were posted overseas endured years of sexual deprivation. Such women were constantly warned that troop morale depended on complete fidelity. Many contemporary songs reflected the perennial concern of the soldier to ensure that his sweetheart remained faithful. The enlisted man, however, was permitted a few indiscretions. Wives were expected to understand 'a soldier's needs in wartime'. Some women found the temptations too great. Women's magazines of the time were deluged with letters from women asking for advice about situations such as this:

My husband is a prisoner of war, and I was dreadfully depressed and lonely until I met two allied officers who were very sweet to me. Now I realize that I am going to have a baby, and I don't know which is the father. My husband is shortly to be repatriated, and I don't know how to tell him.[96]

Wartime marriages, often made in haste, were difficult to sustain when often neither partner had the necessary writing skills to really communicate through letters. When husbands did return both partners had a lot of adjusting to do. Reintegrating husbands into families was an urgent problem for the post-war era, to which we now turn.

5

FROM AUSTERITY TO PROSPERITY AND THE PILL: THE POST-WAR YEARS, 1945–*c*.1968

Britain emerged from the war elated but exhausted. The enormous personal prestige of Winston Churchill had done much to disguise the country's declining world status. Overtaken by the superpowers of the USA and the Soviet Union, who were now locked into the Cold War, Britain would never again be a major player on the world stage. The haste to relinquish the nation's remaining imperial possessions is but one symptom of these changed times. At home, the hardships were not over as rationing and shortages continued, with the winter of 1947–8 being worse than anything experienced during the war. Despite the deprivations, the mood was optimistic and there was a determination to build a new consensus to overcome the old divisions of the past. The 1945, first ever majority Labour government's commitment to a comprehensive plan for social reform was a major aspect of this. By the end of the 1940s, exhortations to duty and sacrifice were wearing thin and the British people were more than ready for the benefits of consumerism which sustained economic growth would soon bestow on them. As austerity gradually gave way to affluence, cars, fridges, vacuum cleaners and many other consumer goods became part of everyday life for increasing numbers of the population.

An essential aspect of this new consumer culture was the emergence of a distinctive youth culture, based on teenagers who had more money in their pockets than ever before and who largely looked to the USA for inspiration. The boom of the post-war years took place despite acute labour shortages, which were only overcome by the importation of nearly a third of a million British citizens from the Caribbean. Rather than reaping the benefits of the new consumer society, West Indians in Britain met with hostility and resentment, depriving them of equal access to jobs, education and housing. In this age of population movement others were leaving to seek a better life abroad, starting with the war brides of US and Canadian servicemen and later emigrants to the ex-colonies, particularly the 'Ten Pound Pommies' who went to Australia in the 1950s and 1960s.

By the early 1960s, the long boom was drawing to a close and the higher growth rates of Britain's European competitors were adding further to its relative economic decline. As the economy began to falter, unemployment once again began a menacing advance. The unbroken 13 years of Conservative rule from 1951 gave way to a new Labour administration pledged to take advantage of the 'white heat of the technological revolution' and to address the problems of poverty and inequality which were still all too apparent. This was the setting for the emergence of the 'Swinging Sixties', which had British fashion and pop music at its heart. Soon the simple pop melodies of the early Mersey sound gave way to the more haunting lyrics of social protest and a counterculture. This flowering of youth reached its peak with the student protests of 1968.

The progressive vision of the New Britain of 1945 was flawed by a fundamentally conservative view of women. Fears about the falling birthrate and juvenile crime and the need to reassure returning soldiers that their wives would be at home waiting for them combined to reinforce the idea of women at the heart of the family, which was to be the heart of the New Britain. In reality, the problems of readjustment were often painful. Many women though were happy to retreat into domesticity to bear the children postponed by the war. By the early 1950s, popularization of the theories of 'maternal deprivation' helped to create a climate in which mothers of small children feared public condemnation if they worked. In spite of this, the numbers of married women at work never sank back to their pre-war levels and continued to rise, slowly but steadily, throughout this period. This trend was in great part brought about by the spread of part-time work. Although many individual feminists were active in various women's pressure groups these years were, on the whole, at a low ebb as far as the feminist movement is concerned. Women did, however, benefit from one very important advance in the 1960s. The introduction of the female contraceptive pill must rank as of the most significant events for women in twentieth-century Britain.

The post-1945 era is only just opening up for historians. Although we already have several texts on women covering this period, there has been little time as yet for the generation of historiographical debate compared to earlier years.[1] There are, however, masses of primary sources relating to women. Many of these are from sociological investigations, particularly those concerning the family. From the women's point of view, these sources must be treated with caution.

Paid Work and Education

The victory celebrations during the summer of 1945 were accompanied by a general expectation, aided by the national media, that large numbers of women would soon be leaving paid employment. The craft unions in particular emphasized that women's work in industry had only been 'for the duration'. Women who had undertaken work on dilution schemes were made to feel that they should make way for returning soldiers. The Labour Party's programme for 1945 contained no commitment to women workers and this is underlined in its attitude to the Report of the Royal Commission on Equal Pay. Set up in 1944 at a time when wartime needs had begun to challenge the whole notion of 'women's work' and 'men's work', the Report came out in 1946 when production needs were no longer paramount and the climate was running against any fundamental challenge to the gendering of work. The Commission made an argument for 'equal pay for commensurate work' but only found this to be applicable to lower grades in teaching, the civil service and local government. Women in industry and commerce were generally found to have a lower productivity than men. (The three women on the committee, Miss Nettlefold, Janet Vaughan and Ann Loughlin issued a minority report which made stronger recommendations.)[2] There were fears that if women's wage levels were raised, they would be replaced by men. Also lurking in the background was the feeling that, if women's wages were raised significantly, women would not view motherhood and unpaid work at home as sufficiently attractive for the much awaited boost to Britain's ailing birthrate. Even the Commission's very limited support for equal pay was rejected by the Labour government on the grounds that it was inflationary.

By 1947 nearly two million women had left work.[3] During the six years of war many women had postponed childbirth, so it was inevitable that peace and returning husbands would mean women would want to start families. What was not inevitable was that they should withdraw from the labour force, but in practice this proved to be the case. The example of Glynis Baker of south London is perhaps typical. She worked at a south London factory during the war and welded sten guns. She married in 1945 and had a daughter in 1946. Her husband earned what was regarded as a good wage in 'fruit and veg'. She missed the company of work, 'I wanted to go back to work, but my husband wouldn't hear of it, until she was about ten I think, then he relented, I went to work part-time.'[4] There is evidence that many women wanted to stay on. An engineering union survey undertaken 1944–5 concluded that 66 per cent of the women in engineering wanted to stay on after the war.[5] For women with small children, the obstacles to working were formidable, not least of these was the practical side. State funding of nurseries was wound up very quickly. In 1945 the annual grant to local authorities for nursery subsidies was cut in half and in 1946 it was abolished altogether. As most councils could not afford to meet the subsidy and they knew that passing on the cost to the parents would be prohibitive, there was no alternative to closure. As Denise Riley has written, nursery closures were driven by administrative and financial factors rather than arguments about 'maternal deprivation' of small children.[6] Riley goes on to argue that given the enormous burden of domestic labour which fell to women at this time (exacerbated by rationing, queues, etc.) it is perhaps not rational to expect married women in these circumstances, particularly those with small children, to want to continue working.[7] Despite the fallout of women from paid employment, there were actually more women working at the end of 1947 than there had been in mid-1939.[8] In contrast to the previous war, there was no wholesale removal of women workers in 1945. Those who were replaced by returning soldiers were usually found 'women's work' elsewhere. With the economy broken by the burden of the war, there was a desperate need to rebuild export industries to pay for essential imports and post-war reconstruction. Even with the higher levels of women's employment, the labour shortage was acute and was aggravated by the raising of the school-leaving age in April 1947. With a labour deficit of over a million workers, the government was forced to launch a national campaign in June 1947 to bring some of the 'drop-outs' back into industry.[9] Observers have argued that this campaign indicates the contradictory stance of the state at this time: it promoted women in the home but implored them to return to work.[10] In fact it was very selectively aimed at areas of shortage, especially textiles (women themselves were preferring to work in the secretarial sector or newer consumer industries). It also targeted older married women aged from 35 to 50 rather than mothers of young children. Even so, it is significant that the campaign had little effect, with only 31 000 extra women being taken on.[11] In the main, the state was not offering any practical assistance to enable women to return to work. It expected women to shoulder all the responsibilities of running a home which, even with older children, were still very great and to take on paid work outside the home. It is hardly surprising that many women rejected the double burden. The fact that women were not able to use their power as workers to push through changes to the sexual division of labour by making demands of the state, employers and their husbands, underlines the limited nature of the gains for women in the war.[12]

By 1950 the longer term trends of women's employments had reasserted themselves, the greatest expansion being in the tertiary sector and the new industries of the interwar years. The most common outlets for female school-leavers were now secretarial or factory work. Domestic service, once so prevalent, was now firmly rejected by young women who had other

ities. In contrast to earlier years, virtually all young
men were at work; working-class girls no longer stayed
to 'help' with younger brothers and sisters and middle-
c... ls no longer made a career out of looking for a husband.
At the end of the war, women were still only earning just
over half of male earnings and there is no evidence that this
differential changed much during these years.[13] They were overwhelmingly in sex-segregated, low-skill occupations. The expla-
nations for this are very complex, as Jane Lewis has skilfully
described, with many interrelating factors contributing to
women's inferiority in the workplace.[14] Of crucial importance
though was the general expectation that the lives of all women
would centre around motherhood and that this was their central
responsibility in life. May Hobbs provides a vivid example of
this in her account of an interview with the youth employment
officer in East London in 1953:

> A right old git, he was. His advice was, don't think of making a
> career out of anything because you'll only give it up to get
> married and have kids. Either be a secretary, he said, or, better
> still, go into a factory ... Seeing that all the other girls were
> busy saying they were going to be secretaries, I told the
> employment officer that was what I wanted.[15]

The employment officer did not mention to May that almost
certainly she would resume employment in her married life.
Census returns reveal that the biggest change in women's
employment in the post-war years was the growth in numbers of
married women workers; in 1931 the proportion of married
women recorded at work was 10 per cent, by 1951 it was 21 per
cent and in 1972 it was 47 per cent.[16] Lewis cautions us that the
figures for the interwar years may well be underestimates as
many women would not have declared their earnings in official
returns.[17] It does seem the case, however, that many more
poorer married women who were previously in unrecognized
work, casual labour outside the home (charring, street-selling,
etc.), and within the home (taking in lodgers, sewing, washing, etc.) were now within the realms of official statistics.
Elizabeth Roberts, for example, tells us in her survey of three

northern towns in the post-war years that there was a drastic decline in paid work within the home of the type described above in these years.[18]

Observers noted that women's employment was increasingly 'bi-modal', or phased; working lives were interrupted for child-rearing years and resumed when children were deemed to be no longer dependent on a housebound mother. With smaller families, it was likely that women would only spend about a third of their adult lives in active childrearing. The idea that mothers of small children should be full-time carers was rarely challenged. The argument emanating from child psychologist John Bowlby that young children deprived of full-time maternal care would be psychologically damaged was very influential in the 1950s, although by the 1960s it was received more critically.[19] In any case, unsupported mothers (widows, abandoned wives, etc.) and mothers of low-earning husbands continued to work, as they had always done, as they had no alternative. Also, as ever, regional and occupational differences are extremely important. Viola Klein reports, for example, in her survey of employers in 1960, that there was a jute factory (presumably in Dundee) which had a nursery for children from three months to five years and a school nursery for those of five to nine years.[20]

The increase in married women's employment was almost entirely accounted for by the growth of part-time work. Klein's study, *Britain's Married Women Workers*, states that roughly one third of married women were in gainful employment.[21] Of these, just over half were in part-time work. Whilst the most pre-dominant occupation for single women was some form of office work, for married women it was domestic work, followed by factory work. It appears that although more married women were in employment, it was mostly unskilled work. It is difficult not to conclude that married women were disadvantaged as workers by considerable loss of skill, status and pay. Employers' attitudes to married women workers, particularly part-timers, back this up. Many would not consider promoting married women; they were excluded from sick pay provision and pension schemes and generally were not considered as reliable and committed as other employees.[22] It is clear from this that employers only took on married women part-timers reluctantly when no other form of labour was available. Full employment and labour shortages made it possible for married women to work part-time, but they did so on very inferior terms. Despite all these drawbacks there is much evidence that married women were keen to work part-time. Given that they were not able to relinquish any domestic responsibilities, combined with their eagerness to grasp the new opportunities to raise living standards, part-time work was usually the only solution. Beryl Sutherland, mother of two school-age children and married to a decorator, started work in a radio factory in 1955 in Surrey:

> She [her daughter] wanted to go on a school trip to Switzerland, and we didn't have the money. My husband didn't agree with me working, but I paid for her to go, and she loved it. So I could pay for those sort of things, because we didn't get much money in those days, you know.[23]

Beryl stayed on for 19 years. Many women regarded work in the same way as did Beryl: to earn money for extras – clothes, furniture, a holiday, a car – never challenging the breadwinning role of their husbands, and fitting in their work around other commitments. Factories experimented with different shift systems. Barbara worked afternoons: 'I liked to do my housework and get my dinner ready for my husband, I wouldn't dare put him out.' The most popular shift was evening work, usually about 6–10 p.m. According to Roberts, grandmothers were much less willing to sit for daughters, either during the day or evening, than they had been previously.[24] Perhaps this accounts for the popularity of the evening shift when fathers could take over childcare. It also meant minimum disruption to the household. By being housewives and full-time mothers all day and preparing the evening meal (and often clearing up) before leaving, the greater part of the time spent away from home was achieved by sacrificing their own leisure and relaxation time. Besides financial considerations, married women also felt the need to overcome the social isolation of the home and valued the companionship of work. On the whole, women part-timers do not seem to have resented their inferior status compared to male workers, or even to full-time single women workers. Constrained by their primary role as mothers, and happy to be in congenial company for a few hours a day, they had little expectation that life could be any different. For the new settlers in London and the Midlands from the Caribbean and elsewhere, life was different.[25] It was considerably worse. Although West Indian women came to be economically active, they were immediately caught up in the patriarchal ideology which regarded them as a secondary labour force, working for extras or pin money.[26] On top of this, they suffered race discrimination which directed them into areas of employment which the indigenous population didn't want as economic growth had given them better opportunities elsewhere. This meant demeaning jobs in unsocial hours as nursing auxiliaries, hospital cleaners, catering and low-paid factory work. This was made clear to Cecilia Wade soon after her arrival from Montserrat in 1956 when she went to register at the labour exchange in east London:

> I took my references from home saying I was a teacher. This woman at the counter said, 'Oh you were a teacher back home, were you? Well, you won't get teaching here!' I said, 'Well, what have you got to offer?' 'Nothing at the moment. Come back next week.' The following Monday I went and she looked me up and down again and said, 'All I have to offer you is Lyon's Tea Shops or there is a job going at a hospital in Clapton. Which would you prefer?' I said, 'I don't know much about Lyon's Tea Shop because, as I said, I was a teacher and I'm looking for clerical work.' 'Oh! You won't get clerical work here.' She was positive.[27]

Cecilia ended up operating an electric sewing machine in a rundown factory. Despite their reluctance to accept West Indian women such as Cecilia Wade, the female-dominated professions of teaching, nursing and social work were actually experiencing a growing labour shortage. It was estimated that four out of five women teachers were lost to the profession due to child-rearing.[28] Public disapproval of working mothers, combined with the near impossible task of obtaining adequate domestic help, condemned many well-educated women to a life at home after childbirth. This problem of wasted talent, experience and skill was addressed by Alva Myrdal and Viola Klein in 1956 in their book, *Women's Two Roles, Home and Work*.[29] As Lewis has pointed out, Myrdal and Klein couched their arguments in terms of what was good for 'society' and 'the economy' rather than feminist demands, but nevertheless this text does represent an advance for women.[30] The authors, who were primarily addressing professional women, did not challenge the notion of women with small children at home full-time, but they argued forcefully for much greater acceptance of the bi-modal pattern of employment for women. This would include re-educating schoolgirls to expect them to train for a working life rather than a few years before marriage and childbirth, extended maternity leave and more emphasis on retraining older women. In fact, by the 1960s, many more professional women were returning to work, although they were still failing to make significant inroads into the traditionally male-dominated professions, and they were not expected to be interested in career advancement. In 1968 Marghanita Laski complained that in a recent television programme involving four successful women, the interviewer questioned them in a hostile fashion, 'implying there must be something wrong, something essentially unfeminine, about all of them'.[31]

Women union activists in teaching and the civil service, such as Miss Jones of the Civil Service Clerical Association (CSCA), carried on their agitation for equal pay and this finally bore fruit, starting in 1952 when the London County Council (LCC) agreed to introduce equal pay for all its women employees in its 'common classes', which included teachers, clerical workers and nurses.[32] Following this, equal pay was phased in between 1954 and 1962 in teaching and the civil service nationally and this proved to be a considerable spur to non-professional women. There was still the problem, however, of all-female occupations such as typing and the related issue of the domination of women in the lower end of the pay structures.

The difficulty of establishing equal pay in sex-segregated areas came up in the Ford's strike at Dagenham, north London, in 1968 when 183 women car-seat machinists came out for recognition as skilled workers in order to achieve a pay increase. The media were fascinated by the women machinists who were threatening to bring down the giant car plant and gave the dispute a great deal of attention. The strike leader, Rose Boland, became something of a celebrity for her forceful style. In one interview, Rose was asked about Harold Wilson's leadership of the country and she replied that she would like 'to get hold of him myself and shake the liver out of him'.[33] During the strike, it transpired that there were men doing the same work in the plant but graded at a higher rate. The media then transformed it into an equal pay dispute, which induced Ford to offer an increase to reduce the differential to within 8 per cent of the male rate. Militant trade union activity by women was not common. Female union membership in general was at a peak at the end of the war, with over a million women members for the first time since 1918, representing one in four of the female work force.[34] But this level of activity fell away in the post-war years and by the mid-1950s unions were resorting to fashion shows to try to attract women recruits.[35] In truth, male union leaders often paid only lip service to the needs of women members, and in practice ignored them, holding branch meetings in the evenings or even on Sunday mornings. As Sheila Lewenhak points out, they often colluded with employers in encouraging the idea of women workers as being only temporarily in the labour force, as this made it easier for male members to obtain promotion.[36]

It will already be obvious that the majority of girls were brought up to have very limited horizons and the education system was largely geared to this outlook. State policy promoted the view that the education of girls was primarily for citizenship rather than work, and by this they meant motherhood. Right into the 1950s, educationalists such as John Newsom were arguing for increased attention to the 'domestic arts' for less academic girls.[37] As Mirium David and others have pointed out, the tripartite system of secondary education (grammar, technical and secondary modern schools) which came in after the war was designed with boys in mind.[38] The only kind of technical training girls were likely to get was shorthand and typing. They might get on the job training in apprenticeships in hairdressing or dressmaking, but these were low-pay ghettos. The younger age of marriage and the increased school-leaving age added further fuel to the prevalent view that girls should be educated to think of work as something to do for a few years between school and marriage, and to this end local education authorities spent less on girls than boys, even in the grammar schools.[39] During the 1950s, the class injustices of the tripartite system came under systematic attack and in 1965 the Labour administration began to introduce the new comprehensive schools for all abilities. But it was not until second-wave feminism in the 1970s that gender inequalities were really addressed in the education system. For almost all of this period, grammar (and independent) schools catered for the education of the academically able. Even though fees were abolished in 1944, working-class girls who did make it, against the odds, still had a tough time. Mary Evans' description of the vast list of school uniform and kit required for her entry to grammar school in 1956, which could *only* be bought at a central London department store 40 miles from the school, must have been truly daunting for working-class parents.[40] Within this protected, pressurized and status-conscious environment, academic success was expected. Achievements in literature-based subjects such as English, French and History were the most highly prized; the 'hard sciences', maths and technology were regarded as inferior forms of learning. Evans argues that the girls' grammar schools cannot be regarded as straightforwardly sexist in that they were, at least outwardly, competing with boys' selective schools and fostering aspirations to higher education and professional careers.[41] This was in fact only one aspect of their double (and conflicting) identity, the other side of which was the model of the 'well behaved middle-class woman who knows how to defer to and respect the authority of men'.[42] Only a minority of grammar-school girls actually went on to university or teacher training. Motherhood was held up as a valuable and rewarding occupation to which they need not feel any shame in committing themselves. By the 1960s, however, the differential between girls and boys entering higher education was narrowing fast. With the growth of the new universities and the polytechnics and the provision of maintenance grants from 1963, many more (mainly middle-class) girls began to study for degrees. Predictably, they overwhelmingly chose liberal arts or the new social science courses.

The State, the Family and Marriage

On Victory in Europe (VE) Day, 8 May 1945, Mrs Milburn, who we met in the previous chapter, wrote in her diary that, 'we rejoiced at our deliverance'. Soon a telegram arrived from her son Alan, who had been a prisoner of war for five and a half years, announcing that he would soon be home, 'I nearly leapt to the ceiling ... all three of us shed a tear or two. We were living again, after five and a half years.'[43] Soon after Alan's homecoming, Mrs Milburn and Alan took a walk through the village which turned into a sort of 'triumphal procession, shaking hands with people we met ... everybody smiling and looking pleased'.[44] This example illustrates the public face of the end of the war. In reality, homecomings were often much more complex and traumatic. Children who had been evacuated were not always pleased to be reunited with by now unfamiliar parents. Parents who had adjusted to being single had to reacquaint themselves with the routines and constraints of parenthood. Fathers came home to children with whom they had no shared experience and who wanted to know 'why was Mummy sleeping with this strange man?'

The biggest problems, however, came from reconstituting marriages after years of separation. Husbands were not keen to accept marital infidelity after years of absence, but expected wives to be understanding about their own amorous adventures. Many couples found that they just couldn't live together again, they had drifted too far apart. Undoubtedly, years of economic independence and self-reliance had changed many women who were no longer willing to be subservient to their husbands. It is hardly surprising then that the divorce rate in 1945 was five times higher than it had been in 1939 and was to climb even further to a peak in 1947.[45] This, combined with the falling birthrate and the alarming rise in juvenile crime during the war, created much public anxiety about the family. In 1945, with the birth rate running at below replacement level, the government were caught up in the tide of panic and created a Royal Commission to look into the apparent population decline. By the time the Commission reported in 1949, public anxiety had been allayed by the post-war baby boom.

Nevertheless, the mood in 1945 was that stable families were crucial to post-war reconstruction and women, in spite of all their wartime work, must be at home to ensure that stability. This was the context for the Beveridge Report and the subsequent reforms of the welfare system. Beveridge, the civil servant charged by the wartime government with formulating plans for post-war welfare, believed firmly in the 'equal but different' principle. Therefore, the 1946 National Insurance Act embodied the idea that men and women occupy different, but equal roles in society. However, by treating husband and wife as a single economic unit, Beveridge denied any independent rights to income maintenance to the wife.[46] Beveridge argued that married women could not expect to regard paid work on the same basis as men as their duty, above all, was to be mothers and service providers for the male breadwinners. Second-wave feminist writers, notably Elizabeth Wilson (and feminists at the time), emphasized the enforced dependency of the wife in the new welfare system.[47] But, as Lewis has written more recently, the situation was rather more complex. Although Beveridge condemned motherhood outside marriage, the new system did allow single mothers to claim through the social security net (rather than national insurance). Since the rise of the single-parent family in the 1970s and 1980s, right-wing theorists have criticized the post-war welfare system for undermining men's position in the family by enabling women to bring up children without fathers.[48]

Other elements in the 1946 Act were more straightforwardly discriminatory. For example, on marriage women were to receive 25 per cent less sickness and unemployment benefit regardless of their contributions, and their pension rights were reduced.[49] The pro-natalists, including Beveridge, did ensure that one feminist demand was fulfilled at this time. The cause of family endowment (now called allowances), to which Eleanor Rathbone dedicated much of her life, was finally translated into legislation and the first payments were made in 1946. The allowances, which were only paid for second and subsequent children and at much lower rates than both Beveridge and Rathbone had hoped for, were seen as a necessary step to provide a much needed boost to the unpaid worker in the home. Even so, it was at first planned to make the payments to fathers until a howl of protest from the feminist voices in Parliament induced the government to back down and pay the allowances directly to the mother.

By the early 1950s, much of the anxiety about the family had subsided. After the post-war baby boom the birthrate settled down and the small family became a permanent feature of

British society. Peace, rising living standards, the security of full employment and the youthful enthusiasm of the young Queen Elizabeth for nation and family all helped to create a feeling of optimism. Marriage was more popular than ever before and the age of marriage continued to fall so that the typical pattern for a woman was to marry in her early twenties and finish childrearing before the age of thirty. Although Bowlby (and his popularizers) was not the only influence in the area of childcare, his theory of maternal deprivation was increasingly dominant. Middle-class women were particularly prone to the idea that mothers would cause psychological harm to their children if they were not constantly with them in the early years. In fact, evidence for this was based on children in residential care and it was never proved that working mothers caused any harm whatsoever to their offspring. As we saw above, part-time work for married women of school-age children was now accepted, but childcare 'experts' railed against the perils of 'latch-key children', so that attempts by mothers to work beyond school hours, even with adequate care, often met with public disapproval. Educationalists urged mothers to encourage discovery, creativity and child-centred learning rather than the more laid-back approach of previous years, especially in large families. All this meant that the relationship between mother and child was more intense than had ever previously been known, resulting at times in a bond which many women found claustrophobic and restricting.

The trend towards a more individualistic style of life continued, particularly for those families who benefited from the housebuilding programme which was part of post-war reconstruction. This often meant that the assistance and support of the extended family was no longer available and neighbours now tended to 'keep themselves to themselves'. The new consumerism encouraged people to seek satisfaction in buying gadgets for the home and for spending on the expanding leisure industry. Television became widespread and reinforced the new home-centred existence. Women were crucial factors in this new force as they were the main agents behind buying. Jackie Stacey has written about the way in which the consumerism associated with Hollywood stars had a major role to play in creating a new feminine identity at this time.[50] Hollywood stars promoted images of femininity which had enormous influence over British women. During the 1940s, austerity conditions meant that fans mostly used the cinema for escapism, but by the 1950s it became possible to directly emulate Hollywood stars in dress, make-up, hair, etc. As Elizabeth Wilson has noted, there was a major shift from the powerful and intelligent female heroes of the 1940s, such as Joan Crawford and Lauren Bacall, to the 'femmes enfants' of the 1950s and 1960s, notably Marilyn Monroe and 'sex kitten' Brigitte Bardot.[51] Stacey points out that the female stars of Hollywood films were always white; glamour was associated with whiteness, hence racist ideology was perpetuated.[52]

Helped by the new gadgetry, economic security and benefiting from higher standards of housing, the 1950s housewife had been released from some of the worst drudgery of the past. But how much had sexual divisions been transformed in this new Britain? Certainly, many influential sociological surveys at the time argued that fundamental change had occurred. Willmot and Young's investigation into family life in Bethnal Green and 'Greenleigh' in Essex in the mid-1950s is an illustration of the liberal optimism of the time.[53] In this study of the impact of new housing, Wilmott and Young argued enthusiastically that the brutal, self-centred and remote figure of the inter-war male was a thing of the past. Dads could now be seen wheeling prams up the Bethnal Green Road or playing with their children in the park.[54] In what they describe as 'one of the great transformations of our time' the authors state that they discovered 'a new kind of companionship between man and woman'.[55] In a later study, Ronald Fletcher also argued that fathers had become far more involved in family life and that there was much greater comradeship and equality between husband and wife.[56] It was argued that the family had become 'symmetrical' with both husband and wife involved in paid work and unpaid labour in the home. These writings support the idea of the prevalence of 'companionate marriage', but as Finch and Summerfield have noted, this term, which we first mentioned in the inter-war chapter, covers a wide range of behaviour.[57] Although it has been associated with increased teamwork and sharing within marriage, there was still an assumption that the husband was the breadwinner and what he did in the home was 'helping'. Men probably did do a little more at home but this was still a long way short of any concept of equality. Finch and Summerfield have also asked how far can we take this idea of companionate marriage, given the dominance of childcare manuals which impelled mothers to be in continuous and constant contact with their children for their normal mental development and which apparently gave little weight to the father?[58]

It appears that what was really meant by companionate marriage was not a greater degree of equality in the home, but more consideration on the part of the husband towards the burdens of childcare and running a home.[59] Even then, there is little evidence that husbands were really willing to accommodate themselves to the needs of their wives. There are other contemporary studies which do not support the views of the liberal optimists. Dennis, Henriques and Slaughter's investigation into life in a Yorkshire mining town in the 1950s portrays a horrific picture involving abuse, deceit and public humiliation of women.[60] In 'Ashton', boys and girls were gradually drawn into different worlds. Men who expressed too much interest in 'women's affairs' were accused of being 'cissy' and fathers expressed little interest in their daughters, accusing them of 'moaning' if they sought attention whilst father and son were playing.[61] Husbands, far from viewing marriage as a co-operative partnership, regarded it as a contract for labour and sexual services, in which there was a 'never-ending tussle for advantage' between husband and wife.[62]

Whilst the Dennis *et al.* study of the mining town in the 1950s provided evidence of continuation of the 'darker' times of the past, Hannah Gavron's work on housebound mothers in London in the 1960s pointed to the more depressing aspects of recent social changes, particularly the decline in community life and extended family networks.[63] Although she notes that many of the wives remarked that their husbands (particularly 'skilled manuals') were more helpful than their own fathers had been, Gavron does not see this as hugely significant in the way that Willmot and Young and Fletcher did. Dividing her sample by class, Gavron found that the middle-class women, who still expected to keep up outside contacts and interests, were happier. The working-class housewives were far more likely to be isolated and resentful. The great majority had no contacts at all with neighbours and contact with friends appeared very limited for many. Over a third of this group felt that they had married too young and a third also expressed regret that they had not had training to equip them for work later in life.[64] According to Gavron, working-class girls were brought up to view marriage as 'a marvellous event' and not really encouraged to think about the reality of life at home with the 'relentless boredom of scrubbing floors and ironing shirts' which inevitably followed.[65] They were ill prepared for what married life had to offer them and consequently many felt trapped and depressed by unrelieved childcare and domestic drudgery.

More recent studies have also supported a less optimistic view. Roberts' survey does not support the argument for companionate marriage in general but she does illustrate how complex this issue is, with many geographical and occupational variations and models operating at any one time.[66] The Lancashire weavers, for example, could be said to have had companionate marriages from the late nineteenth century! In addition, Roberts opens up another possibility – that the post-war changes have actually undermined the position of the married woman.[67] She argues that the heroic, struggling, working-class mother of the interwar years won much respect and admiration for her ability to manage on a tight budget, to make meals and clothes 'out of nothing', and her ability to keep the family together in times of great adversity. Now, more prosperous times had made her job easier, but she was no longer held in awe as being the essential linchpin of family survival in the way she had been previously. Fathers (and children) demanded more say in decision-making but rarely took responsibility. Housework was much less stressful, but children were now more indulged than previously and no longer expected to help in the way that they had before. Roberts concludes that the married woman had lost status at home and this had not been compensated for by her increased economic activity outside the home as this was largely, as we saw above, in low-pay and low-status occupations which reinforced her inferior status.[68]

Sexuality, Youth and the Permissive Movement

Integral to the idea of the companionate marriage was the importance of achieving satisfying sexual relationships. It was the duty of the husband to ensure that his wife was sexually fulfilled, and it was the wife's responsibility to be as 'sexy' as possible for her man. The Marriage Guidance Council was founded just before the war and its huge expansion in the post-war years illustrates the fact that couples felt that if marriage wasn't working they should seek help to achieve a more reward-ing sexual life. The Kinsey Reports, published in 1948 and 1953, with their matter-of-fact descriptions of sexual behaviour helped to create a climate in which sexual activity was demystified and women's enjoyment of sex more openly recognized.[69] Slowly, signs of a liberalization of attitudes regarding sex were appearing. A survey conducted in 1956 revealed that two-fifths of first sexual intercourse was occurring before marriage.[70] Following on from this was the expansion in the use of contra-ceptives, particularly the sheath. This became more widely available during the war, although it was by no means reliable. Diaphragms were disliked by British women and only a small minority made use of them. As Hera Cook argues, the fact that birth control literature at this time was couched in discourses of family planning detracts from the fact that more and more couples were disassociating sex from reproduction and family structures entirely.[71] There is evidence that, by the end of the 1950s, couples who previously might have held back from sexual activity were increasingly deciding to become sexually active. The old moral and religious dictums about the importance of confining sex to marriage were breaking down among the younger generation.

To understand the sexual activity of these young people it is necessary to turn briefly to the emergence of the 'teenager' in these years. Adult wages were rising in the 1950s but adolescent wages were rising twice as fast.[72] The rapidly expanding con-sumer industries lost no time in producing goods specifically aimed at the new teenage market – clothes, records, cosmetics, etc. The leisure market also opened up to young people with films and dance halls geared to teenagers. In her survey, Roberts found that the youth of the post-war years were indulged as never before.[73] Parents who had been through the war and possibly endured separation, bombing and post-war austerity, sought, above all, to achieve a happy life for their children. They were noticeably less strict about enforcing discipline, although they did not abandon standards altogether. The youth of the

1950s and 1960s were more self-aware and self-centred than any previous generation of young people. Partially released from parental authority and with the freedom that money allows, they began to form distinct subcultures. Influenced by the rock scene in the USA, 'teddy boys' emerged in the 1950s, and were later superseded by the 'mods and rockers' of the early 1960s and the hippie and 'flower power' generation of the later 1960s. As Angela McRobbie has noted, there has been much interest among sociologists in youth cultures, but this has been almost entirely from a male point of view.[74] Consequently, we know very little of the behaviour of teenage girls at this time. Elizabeth Wilson argues that rebellion in young women was associated with sexuality: 'for girls their sexuality was a crime'.[75] Among the youth of the 1950s, gender differences appear to be very marked, as would fit in with general ideas about femininity described above. Male and female youth of the 1960s were far more visually alike, but there is little evidence that gender behaviour had markedly changed.

By the late 1960s youth culture had developed a strong counter-cultural element. The Profumo affair in 1963, in which it was revealed that a government minister lied to Parliament in an attempt to cover up the fact that he was involved with a prostitute, laid open the hypocrisy of the 'establishment' and the older generation. Youth began to attack the values of the consumer society which had spawned them. 'Dropping out' became the 'in' thing to do. The revolt of the younger generation reached a peak with the student rebellions of 1968 in Europe and the USA. Many of the women activists of the student movement were soon to question gender divisions in society and to build a new feminist movement (which is covered in the following chapter).

The 1960s have rapidly become enshrined in popular memory as the 'swinging sixties'. Despite its declining economic status, Britain, and particularly London, became a cultural mecca at this time. In the fashion world the new geometric shapes of designers such as Mary Quant had a huge impact. The music of the Beatles and the other Mersey groups took the world by storm. The 'groovy', 'trendy' and 'hip' younger generation were the heart of the 'swinging sixties', although Sarah Maitland in her quest for testimony on 'the 1960s' found that almost every woman she spoke to felt that 'the sixties were really happening just over there'.[76] This feeling, which was even shared by sixties icon Julie Christie, suggests that perhaps the notion of the swinging sixties is in fact a myth. Nevertheless, it has been a very potent myth and an essential part of it has been the idea that the sixties was a time of sexual revolution for the young. Was there ever any truth in it?

Writers such as Jeffrey Weeks and Jane Lewis acknowledge that change was taking place but they argue, citing surveys conducted at the time, that fundamentally British youth were conservative in sexual matters during the sixties.[77] This view is supported by Roberts who writes that the idea of the swinging sixties has been 'overworked' and that pre-marital sex was still widely condemned.[78] Certainly, marriage was more popular than ever and weddings were becoming increasingly elaborate. However, there is much evidence that, despite what people were saying in interviews with social scientists, their actual sexual behaviour was increasingly radical, particularly in the late 1960s. Evidence for this can be seen in the usage of the female contraceptive pill, which was introduced into Britain in 1961. By 1964 half a million women were on the pill.[79] As a result, the birthrate, which had risen in the early 1960s (arguably on account of increased sexual activity with less than foolproof methods) fell. Illegitimacy was also rising at this time, indicating again that sexual activity was on the increase, and this trend was not halted by the introduction of the pill. Starting with the Brook Clinic in London in 1964, contraceptive advice was gradually made available to unmarried women.[80] Leah Manning, the ex-Labour MP, started an independent clinic for unmarried women in Harlow in 1964 following the Family Planning Association's refusal (it was retracted a couple of years later) to allow access for the unmarried. Within a year it was given premises consisting of five rooms and much back-up support from the local authority.[81] Although unmarried women found that access to the pill was difficult, there is evidence that they were increasingly keen to have it. The National Survey of Health and Development, which tracked a sample of all births in England, Scotland and Wales in the first week of March 1946, revealed the cumulative use of the pill. By 1969, when the females in the survey were 23, nearly half had used the pill and the usage rates continued to rise sharply.[82]

Women quickly learned that, as long as they said that they were
planning to marry, they could get the pill. 'Georgina', a student
in Manchester in 1965, is a case in point. Although fairly new to a
relationship with 'Dave', they decided quite early on that they
wanted to have sex. She went to see a woman GP whom she had
heard would prescribe the pill to unmarried women students:

> you had to say you were going to get married after you'd both
> graduated! I learnt to fantasize a bit then about Dave. You
> always do for family planning doctors. What I really wanted to
> tell her was, 'Look, this is a very exciting day. Here I am making
> a conscious decision to lose my virginity, because I'm crazy
> about him. And I feel really randy and I'm desperate to lose it.
> I don't care whether he and I get married so much as when he
> and I are going to be able to get it off together. And I'm
> getting an extra kick out of the fact that I'm taking control
> over my own body, being responsible, and no, I don't equate
> sex with babies.' She gave me the tablets.[83]

Up until the introduction of the pill, birth control had mostly
been the province of men, with the sheath and withdrawal the
most common methods. The pill revolutionized contraception
for women by giving them a totally reliable method which
involved no messy jells or rubber and which left them in control.
Millions of women, both married and unmarried, enjoyed these
benefits. It soon became apparent, however, that the pill posed
health risks to certain groups of women and this issue was later
raised by feminists in the seventies. Increasingly, sex outside
marriage was condoned between couples who showed any commitment to each other. Sex became a recreational activity with
couples completely separating their sexual lives from any notions
of family planning. Of course, there was a downside. The pill
enabled casual sex without risk or consequences. Men, who could
be as predatory as ever, undoubtedly exploited the introduction
of the pill to persuade women to make themselves sexually
available. The pill revolutionized women's control over their own
fertility, but that in itself could not transform power relationships
between men and women. It may, however, have contributed to
the growing feminist consciousness in the late sixties and helped

to create a feeling among women that they must seek control over other aspects of their lives. Other elements of the 'permissive movement' need to be considered, albeit briefly. In 1967, the abortion movement finally won a victory when legal abortions became available to women if they had the consent of two doctors. The figures for abortions rose dramatically after 1967, but their accuracy must be questioned as undoubtedly there were also many thousands of illegal back-street abortions, at grave danger to women's health, before the act. Unmarried mothers were no longer stigmatized as they had been in previous years and, increasingly, women who bore a child out of wedlock were deciding to keep it rather than hand it over to an adoption agency.[84] The Divorce Reform Act of 1969 removed the idea of 'matrimonial offence', and therefore moral blame, and introduced the notion of 'irreconcilable breakdown' of marriage. It cannot be denied that the wave of progressive legislation from the late 1950s onwards points to a new interest in the individual and a desire to end suffering. But it is also true that this movement was associated with a growing 'eroticisation of many aspects of social life', which meant increasing use of sexually explicit films, magazines and other material.[85] Sex had become commercialized more than ever before. Visual imagery using women's bodies for male titillation became universally available.

Following the Wolfenden Report in 1957, state regulation of male homosexuality took on a markedly more liberal stance. As lesbianism had never been recognized within British law, the situation remained as before; lesbianism was largely invisible, therefore gay women were forced to lead double lives. A small lesbian sub-culture was slowly emerging, however. In 1963 a group of five women formed the Minorities Research Group for lesbians to help them deal with 'the difficulties of guilt, isolation and loneliness and to encourage them to come to terms with themselves'.[86] It organized a lesbian counselling service and the first ever lesbian publication, *Arena 3*. Elizabeth Wilson worked in psychiatric social work in London at this time: 'at work I was a silent demure little girl in my mini-skirts'.[87] Out of the workplace, she lived with her lover and frequented the Gateways Club in Chelsea which had been exclusively lesbian since the late 1950s. At 'the Gates', as it was known, and other lesbian clubs,

1 and femme stereotyping was strictly adhered to. Pat James
was a butch lesbian in her twenties who went to bed with a
woman whom she took to be a femme:

> Then I was shocked to find that she was making love to me.
> And I didn't mind, I rather liked it and it turned out very well
> with two active people making love. But I was petrified and
> told her not to tell anyone, which shows the atmosphere of
> the time.[88]

It was not until the emergence of the women's liberation
movement in the 1970s that lesbians really began to question
these roles.

Feminism and Women in Public Life

The feminist impetus provided by the war, which had coalesced
women inside and outside Parliament, was undermined in the
post-war years. The sudden death of Eleanor Rathbone, in
January 1946, contributed to the erosion of a women's lobby
inside Westminster. With the ending of the wartime coalition,
party loyalty came to take precedence over women's interests.
Women's organizations, such as the Women's Co-operative
Guild, complained vigorously about the enforced dependency
inherent in Beveridge's proposals for post-war welfare. But apart
from the reversal over family allowances shown above, they were
met with an unyielding government. The new Labour administration came to power in the summer of 1945, a time of mass
jubilation and the long awaited peace. It was not long, however,
before grass-roots discontent began to swell up, particularly in
the areas of food supply and housing.

Mass bombing had destroyed or made uninhabitable nearly
half a million homes, with many others severely damaged.
Angry with continued military control of buildings which
could be used for housing and the continued high priority for
defence spending, squatters began occupying empty army huts.
By August 1946 there were nearly 40 000 people occupying
army accommodation.[89] The squatters movement, supported

by the Communist Party, also took over empty blocks of flats and large houses, particularly opulent mansions which had been standing empty for some time. This was a spontaneous, grass-roots movement, in which working people achieved a remarkable degree of co-operation. Women activists were an integral part and often acted to ensure that women's interests were addressed. Dr Joan McMichael was a Communist councillor in Westminster. She arrived at the squat at Fountain Court just as people were handing babies and prams over the railings. An official from the council came and 'laid down all the threats about writs ... and about breaking the law and so on'.[90] After allowing the official to put forward the council's case, the squatters resolved to continue with the squat:

Then we got down to practical details. We elected a team for Red Cross if necessary, a group to run a crèche so that women could go to work the next day, guards for the door so that the door was covered for twenty-four hours, and cooks – we had two volunteer army cooks who said they would cook for all the squatters.[91]

Gradually, as the rebuilding and repair programme took hold, local authorities were able to rehouse squatting families and the movement, including its grass-roots women's activism, ebbed away. There was, however, women's activity of a different kind on the issue of food supply and the perceived threat of totalitarian control. After the victory celebrations, Britain's long-suffering housewives eagerly anticipated an end to queues and rationing in the not too distant future. The government, however, felt compelled to continue rationing and strict controls as the severe balance-of-payments deficit meant that increased food imports could not be paid for. In 1946 the situation actually got worse, with rations cuts in February and bread rationing introduced for the first time in July. Bewildered and outraged, many women turned to a variety of protest organizations. The one which proved to be of most importance was the British Housewives League. James Hinton argues that it was the only significant organization to oppose the view that post-war reconstruction necessitated the continued suspension of the free market into the immediate post-war period.[92] Set up by Irene Lovelock and

Alfreda Landau soon after the end of the war, it had little momentum until the unexpected ration reductions. Contrary to previous opinion, it was not a Conservative front but sought to be non-partisan.[93] There is little evidence for strong working-class support, but it certainly seems to have struck a chord amongst middle-class housewives, especially in the London suburbs and the home counties. Early in 1947, Dorothy Crisp became chairman of the League and led the organization to disaster by promoting militant action and attempting to turn it into a political party. In the autumn of 1947 its official membership was 80 000, but this is likely to have been an exaggeration.[94] It was, in fact, in steep decline and continued from 1948 on a very small scale with negligible influence.

By the end of the forties, grass-roots activity amongst women, from either the left or the right, was at a low point. There were a number of active women's groups such as the Married Women's Association, but overall there was a decline in women's organizations. After equal pay had been achieved for professional women, both the National Union of Women Teachers and the National Association of Women Civil Servants decided to disband. The Women's Co-operative Guild was faced with an ageing and declining membership. Within the Labour Party, there was little enthusiasm for the annual Labour Women's Conference. Much to the dismay of the now elderly suffrage campaigners, women had still only made very limited gains in Parliament. In the 1966 General Election there were only 80 women candidates (out of ten million adult women voters) as against 1627 men.[95] Only 21 of these were elected. It was very rare for a woman to get anywhere near a safe seat, especially for the Conservatives. With the ascension of a woman to the throne in 1952 it became impossible to continue to defend an all-male House of Lords. After several failed attempts, the Life Peerages Act, allowing for the creation of both female and male life peers, was finally passed in 1957. Four women peers, the first being Lady Reading who had led the Women's Voluntary Service during the war, took their seats in 1958.[96] Although there was no women's lobby as such in Parliament, there were individual women who pursued feminist aims. Edith Summerskill is one notable example. During the fifties in the Commons and from 1961 as a life peer, she vigorously fought many feminist causes including maintenance for deserted wives, the right of women to a share of household savings and recognition of single women as carers. There were active Tory women also, such as Pat Hornbsy-Smith and Irene Ward, the latter being a prominent force in the equal pay campaign.

Margaret Roberts, later Thatcher, searched for a safe Tory seat during the 1950s. As Martin Pugh points out, during the early fifties she was willing to address meetings of the Six Point Group and defend the right of mothers to work.[97] Eventually, she was selected for the safe seat of Finchley and returned in the 1959 election. During the 1960s Margaret Thatcher became a key figure in the New Right.[98] Part of its appeal to women was the reaction against the liberalization of sexual behaviour in the 1960s and the undermining of the 'sanctity of marriage'. This appeal for a return to 'family values' was also shared by Mary Whitehouse, who became an international figure for her public opposition to sex education in schools without moral guidance and for her 'Clean Up TV Campaign'.[99] The latter became the National Viewers and Listeners' Association and had a membership of 10 000.[100] It opposed sexually explicit material in the media and claimed to speak for the 'moral majority'.

Whilst the New Right women fell in with cold-war ideology, there were other women grass-roots activists who questioned the spiralling arms expenditure and the arms race. The National Assembly of Women, a Communist Party-inspired organization dating from 1952, soon came to focus its activities primarily around the peace issue.[101] The realization of the effects of radiation in the mid-fifties was an important impetus for the peace movement. Vera Leff, Marion Clayton and Agnes Simpson began actively campaigning against the bomb after reading about the effects of radiation. Jill Liddington has written how these three north London women of the Golders Green Women's Co-operative Guild decided that 'we should do something' and set up a public meeting to form a group opposed to nuclear weapons.[102] Other women, such as Gertrude Fishwick, an ex-suffragette, set up similar groups. In 1957, these local groups merged to form the National Council for the Abolition of Nuclear Weapons Tests, which was the forerunner of the Campaign for Nuclear Disarmament.[103] In 1958, Dora Russell organized a Women's Peace Caravan and with 15 women toured east and west Europe for a year. She was disappointed, however, with how little support she received, probably due to the dominance of cold-war ideology and the decline in women's groups generally. Around the same time, Jacquetta Hawkes founded the Women's Committee of CND. Women were very prominent within CND, Peggy Duff and Pat Arrowsmith particularly, although many of the CND women activists were not acting from specifically feminist impulses. As Josephine Eglin has written, it is not surprising that at a time when the feminist movement was weak, those that did organize as women pacifists did so as mothers.[104] This was the primary concern of Judith Cook who wrote to *The Guardian* at the time of the Berlin crisis in 1961 and was overwhelmed by a thousand letters of support within a few days, prompting her to start a new women's peace group, Voice of Women.[105]

As the Afro-Caribbean population of this country grew during the early 1950s, the extent of racist hostility and discrimination became apparent. In response, the black community began to organize itself, particularly in west London, which was a major area of settlement. Within this community there were several important women organizers, such as Pearl Prescod and Amy Ashwood-Garvey. The most prominent black woman's voice, however, was that of Claudia Jones. a Communist, who was deported to London in 1955 after many years of organizing for both black and women's emancipation in the Harlem district of New York.[106] Within a couple of years Jones founded and edited *The West Indian Gazette*, which became an important focus for the Afro-Caribbean community in Britain. *The Gazette*'s coverage linked the struggles of Afro-Caribbeans in Britain with nationalist and colonial movements internationally. Jones's editorials included in-depth analysis of the 1962 Immigration Act and how it could be opposed.[107] In addition, she involved herself with community life and worked alongside Pearl Prescod, Corrie Skinner and Nadia Cattouse to co-ordinate the first West Indian carnival in Britain in 1958.[108] Sadly, this active life was cut short by death from heart disease in 1964 at the age of 49. She is buried in Highgate cemetery next to the grave of Karl Marx. In a book published in 1985 on the lives of black women in Britain, one of the respondents remembered Claudia Jones affectionately.

I first met Claudia in the early sixties. I had not long been in this country, and was experiencing the worst of British hospitality. I was in the launderette, and she must have noticed me sitting there alone, depressed and on the verge of tears ... she put her book to one side and came over to talk to me. I told her about the problems I was having over accommodation – I was living with my three very young children in one room on hardly any money. She was very sympathetic. She showed me where she was living in the next street, and I remember her telling me that all Black people throughout the world were going through the same kind of experiences. Then she helped me to claim Social Security, which I hadn't known about. She could talk to you in political terms, and explain things very clearly, but she was also there with practical help, too. After that, she came to visit me quite often ... She stopped me from going around thinking that what was happening to me here was my fault.[109]

Finally, returning to the mainstream feminist movement, it is clear from the above that feminism survived, but it was fragmented and weak. It operated under a separate-spheres ideology according to which equality had been achieved and all that was necessary was for women to add a humanizing element.[110] Feminists in these years did not challenge the fundamental gender divisions in society and remained on the margins, chipping away at the system, largely through single-issue pressure groups, and raising women's issues in other campaigns. Feminist ideology was largely obscured by the general view that women were now freed from the drudgery and oppression of the past and basked in 'equality in difference'. As Wilson wrote, 'the idea that women had "choice" repressed but did not resolve the conflicts that surround the position of women'.[111] Although veteran feminist Hazel Hunkins-Hallinan despaired that 1960s women did not even seem to realize that they were oppressed, there were, in fact, signs that feminist consciousness was on the move.[112] Simone De Beauvoir's epic analysis of women, *The Second Sex*, was issued in English in 1961 and went through 14 paperback reprints in one year.[113] In 1963 in the USA, Betty Friedan published *The Feminine Mystique* which attempted to bring out into the open the 'problem with no name' – that millions of American women were leading dull, unfulfilled lives and felt trapped and isolated by domesticity. These stirrings would soon combine with the growing equal-pay lobby in the labour movement and erupt into a new mass feminist consciousness at the end of the decade.

6

SECOND-WAVE FEMINISM AND BEYOND: THE PERSONAL IS POLITICAL, c.1969–1999

Britain's declining economy, particularly its manufacturing base, is a key feature of the background for this period. It was primarily an attempt to reverse its poor economic performance in relation to its European counterparts which led to the UK's entry to the European Economic Community in 1973. The apparent failure of Keynesian economic policies and the rapidly escalating costs of the welfare state led to a revival of economic liberalism and a desire to reduce the role of the state in the economy and society. The election of the Conservative government under Margaret Thatcher in 1979 brought these policies to power. In 1982, success in the Falklands War gave Thatcherism increased confidence at home and abroad, deepening its mission to put a final end to the post-war consensus. Thatcher's authoritarian populism politicized the family as never before in its attempt to restore so-called 'family values' and reverse the progressive tide, particularly equality for women and the growth of the single-parent family. Thatcherite economic policies accelerated the decline of Britain's manufacturing base but other sectors, particularly services, experienced a minor boom in the eighties. Thatcher lost power in 1992, although it was not until 1997 that a Labour government was returned to power. There are several other significant features of this period. Economically, increasingly Britain was (and still is) being locked into the global economy. This process has been aided by the introduction

147

of computer technology which has brought about an 'information revolution'. Immigration, although increasingly restricted, continued and the arrival of the Asians expelled from Uganda in 1972 led to an resurgence of racist activity, fuelled by the National Front and other far-right groups. By the 1980s immigration had virtually ceased.

In contrast to previous chapters, we have to start this one with feminism, because without a knowledge of the women's liberation movement and its impact, the rest of this period would be almost impossible to comprehend. Although perhaps not recognized at the time, it is clear now that 'second-wave feminism' had a profound influence on British society. In many ways, this period is the hardest to write about as it covers the largest chronological time period and the volume of sources available is overwhelming. This contemporary era has yet to be digested and 'dusted over' by historians. What follows therefore can only be an initial sketching out of major developments concerning women during these years.

Feminism; 'Women's Liberation' and Beyond

There is little doubt that the explosion of feminist activity in the USA in the late 1960s had a major impact on Britain. New feminist 'bibles' such as Kate Millet's *Sexual Politics* (1969) and Shulamith Firestone's *Dialectic of Sex* (1970) were rapidly disseminated in Britain. American women's liberation did not create the movement here however, but merely helped to kindle a flame that was already alight. The movement took off at the end of the sixties, largely due to a combination of two factors. The first was that the student movement and the growth of the New Left had politicized large numbers of women, who were now turning their new political consciousness to their own situation and asking, 'Why do we stand for it?'[1] Olive Banks has drawn attention to the fact that the New Left in these years developed an aggressive form of masculinity which had a 'contempt for women that reduced them to servants and camp followers'.[2] When Audrey Battersby applied to join the local north London branch of the Socialist Labour League she was interviewed by the Chairman who told her, 'Learn to type and learn to drive a car, and we'll have you.'!³ Feelings of gathering rage amongst these women were fused with the second element: the growing militancy amongst women in the labour movement on the issue of equal pay. This movement coalesced into the National Joint Action Campaign Committee for Women's Equal Rights, which held a national demonstration in central London in May 1969 that has been hailed as the first major event of second-wave feminism in Britain.⁴ Supporting this Committee were the vestiges of the old suffrage organizations and traditional liberal feminist groups.⁵ The fiftieth anniversary of the granting of the vote to women in 1968 appears to have produced a last flowering of the old suffrage movement spirit and a determination to pass on to younger feminists the message that there was still a long way to go.

During 1969, 'women's liberation' groups started to spring up spontaneously. Some were formed by women in left-wing groups, particularly the International Socialists and the International Marxist Group. Others began when groups of women just started talking to each other about their situation. The Peckham Rye group from south-east London started from women based at home who attended a 'One O'Clock Club' with their small children. History Workshop was a movement of radical historians very much associated with the New Left. When Sheila Rowbotham stood up at a meeting in Ruskin College in November 1969 and tried to get together with other History Workshop women who were interested in women's history 'there was a great guffaw from the floor' from men who thought that the whole idea of women's history was a joke.⁶ Out from this incident came the idea for a women's history conference at Ruskin. As the applications flooded in for the meeting in early 1970 it soon became clear that this would not be a history conference. Nearly six hundred women attended the conference and it is this event more than any other which is fixed in popular memory as the real beginning of the women's liberation movement (WLM) in Britain. The conference adopted four basic demands: equal pay; equal education and opportunity; 24-hour nurseries; and free contraception and abortion on demand. Most of the women who attended felt that it had changed their lives for ever. Sheila Rowbotham wrote, 'you had the amazing feeling of your whole being completely opened … we were heart and soul in it, we had created it, and we loved it'.⁷

The British movement was accompanied by an array of new feminist literature. *Shrew, Women's Report, The Women's Newspaper* and various other early journals were joined by the first commercially successful feminist magazine, *Spare Rib*, in 1972. The first in-depth piece was Juliet Mitchell's article 'Women, The Longest Revolution' in *New Left Review* in 1966 which was enlarged and issued in book form in 1971. Like Rowbotham's pamphlet, *Women's Liberation and the New Politics* (1969), Mitchell located her analysis firmly within a socialist framework. Germaine Greer's more individualist *The Female Eunuch* (1970) received more media attention but it did not strike the same resonance in the movement as had Rowbotham and Mitchell. The British movement was always more socialist-feminist orientated than its American counterpart. The movement did not have a single unifying ideology but at its heart was a powerful attack on the sexual division of labour in society. By resisting sex-role stereotyping and bringing gender oppression from the home (and elsewhere) into the public domain, they were asserting that 'the personal is political'. The words 'sexism' and 'male chauvinist' sprang into popular use. The Peckham Rye group gave a paper at the Ruskin Conference in which they attacked the enforced domesticity of mothers: 'Our window on the world is looked through with our hands in the sink and we've begun to hate that sink and all it implies – so begins our consciousness.'[8] The early WLM resisted domination by Maoist and other left-wing influences and grew as an autonomous movement of self-directing groups with little overall co-ordination.

Fundamental to the movement's ethos was the idea of 'consciousness-raising' – small groups of women discussing their lives and connecting their own personal feelings of oppression to a wider context. Gill Philpott wrote that through consciousness-raising came the realization that 'what you are voicing is no longer anger at yourself and what you took to be personal failings, but rather at a society which continues to oppress us all as women in it'.[9] Many groups took up the issue of sexuality and the American pamphlet *The Myth of the Vaginal Orgasm* (1970) by Anna Koedt was widely disseminated. As well as consciousness-raising, WLM groups became involved in local campaigns – for nurseries, accessible health care, assisting lone mothers to make social security claims, refuges for battered women, etc. Some women (and their men) tried to live collectively and to set up shared childcare regimes. Direct action was very much a feature of the movement. Here I have to declare an interest. Whilst a student, I took part in the disruption of the 1970 Miss World competition. I also remember joining in a raiding party to Imperial College to storm a men-only bar and marching down Oxford Street and chanting, 'mothercare out, fathercare in!' as we passed the Mothercare store. The movement for women's liberation was paralleled by Gay Liberation which drew in many lesbian activists, although as Jeffrey Weeks acknowledges, their position within the Gay Liberation Front was always problematic.[10] These women quickly saw the attractions of working within an all-female movement and promptly deserted the GLF early in 1972.

Following the Ruskin Conference there were several other national conferences, but the early feelings of optimism and euphoria faded. Women became weary with heavy theoretical debates about domestic labour and the arguments for and against 'wages for housework'. Those who were attempting shared childcare discovered just how difficult it was to either share one's own biological children or to fully engage with other peoples'. Many realized that it was going to take more than individual acts of will to change women's lives in any fundamental sense. Also, the all-embracing unity of 'sisterhood' was being overwhelmed by internal divisions. The most basic was between radical feminists and socialist feminists. The former saw hegemonic male power, organized into a system of patriarchy, as the primary explanation for their oppression. Socialist feminists wanted to unite a class and race analysis with feminism to build a broader movement of oppressed peoples. Lesbians within the movement succeeded in pushing through an additional demand for 'an end to all discrimination against lesbians and a woman's right to freely determine her own sexuality'. Following this, radical feminists developed the idea of 'political lesbianism' and became very antagonistic to women who defined themselves as heterosexual. The national conferences of 1977 and 1978 were dominated by the split between heterosexual women and lesbians. The seventh and final demand, for an end to male dominance and violence against women, was only passed in 1978 after much bitter wrangling and created such a terrible atmosphere that no more national conferences were held.[11]

In fact, trying to hold it all together was a pretty pointless exercise as from the mid-seventies there was no single unified movement. The emphasis had shifted from local, all-purpose women's liberation groups to work on specific issues, which was often nationally co-ordinated. Regrettably, there is only space here to give some indication of the campaigns of the 1970s. Agitation on equal pay and fighting sexism in education are both referred to in later sections rather than here. The adoption of the fifth demand in 1975, for financial and legal independence, was followed by the 'Why Be a Wife?' campaign which fought against the legal subordination of married women within the tax and social security systems.[12] Other issues were also taken up, such as the rights of single parents and lesbian mothers. Black women decided early on that they needed to organize separately, as racism forced them to have different priorities from white feminists. For them,

> what Samora Machel had to say about women's emancipation made a lot more sense than what Germaine Greer and other middle-class white feminists were saying. It just didn't make any sense for us to be talking about changing life styles and attitudes, when we were dealing with issues of survival, like housing, education and police brutality.[13]

A Black Women's Group was formed in Brixton, south London, in 1973 which developed its own journal, *Speak Out*. A national organization of black women, The Organization of Women of Asian and African Descent (OWAAD) was formed in 1978. Besides fighting specific campaigns it actively promoted black culture.

The National Abortion Campaign was founded in 1975 to defend the 1967 Abortion Act and 'a woman's right to choose'. The campaign gained a large groundswell of support, including that of trade unions and MPs. Several attempts to restrict access to abortion and thereby undermine the 1967 Act were vigorously resisted. The 'pro-choice' march sponsored by the Trade Union Congress (TUC) in 1978 mustered over 100 000 supporters.[14] Overall, it was probably the most successful of all the feminist campaigns of the time. It was the only one which encouraged the participation of men, both on demonstrations and in local groups. Women's Aid also had male supporters, although they tended very much to work on the periphery in supportive roles. In 1975 the National Women's Aid Federation was formed of 35 local groups. Erin Pizzey's rather individualist style prevented her from working within this network, but her refuge in Chiswick caught media attention and many desperate women flocked there. In 1977 Chiswick Women's Aid took in 1122 mothers and children from all over Britain.[15] Whereas previously police, social workers, lawyers, etc. had consistently refused to recognize the problem of domestic violence, the women's aid movement brought the whole question out into the open. The same could be said of Rape Crisis Centres, which sprang up in many major cities in the late 1970s.

By this time many radical feminists were calling themselves revolutionary feminists and calling for feminists to adopt a separatist lifestyle. Many of these women became involved in Women Against Violence Against Women (WAVAW) which linked male domination with rape and other violence against women. Angered by the advice of the police for women to stay in at night for fear of attack, WAVAW held colourful 'Reclaim the Night' marches through the red-light districts of major cities.[16] Leeds revolutionary feminists were particularly active during the time of the 'Ripper' murders, which terrorized millions of women in Yorkshire over a period of several years.

By the end of the seventies women who opposed revolutionary feminism, separatism and the idea of 'political lesbianism' were forced to admit that the attempt to forge a synthesis of socialism and feminism had failed. In a new initiative, Sheila Rowbotham, Lynne Segal and Hilary Wainright argued in *Beyond the Fragments* (1979) for women to bring their feminist commitment and methods of organization into the broader progressive movement, to transform the left. In the same year, the new Tory government began its regime of cuts in public services, erosion of welfare rights, deregulation of industry and attacks on vulnerable groups of workers. Although the Labour administration under Callaghan had already drifted to the right, the scale of the Thatcher onslaught took everyone by surprise. In this new and frightening context, the hopes of the authors of *Beyond the Fragments* appeared overly optimistic.

Progressive elements of all types were in a state of shock in the
early eighties as the New Right vigorously pushed through their
agenda. Second-wave feminism as a mass movement was already
declining before Thatcher came to power, but the burst of anti-
nuclear protest from women at the US air base at Greenham
Common was to be a last flowering of mass feminist activism.
After a comparative lull, the anti-nuclear movement in Britain
began to take off at the end of the seventies. The decision to site
Cruise and Pershing II nuclear missiles at US bases in Britain led
to widespread opposition. *Spare Rib* started referring to 'feminists
against nuclear power'.[17] At the end of August 1981, Ann Pettitt
organized a march of 'Women for Life on Earth'. Forty women,
four men and some children marched from Cardiff to RAF
Greenham Common, which was to be a site for the new weapons.
At the end of the march it was decided to make a permanent
camp. Early in February 1982, women at Greenham voted to
make the camp women only. There was no formal organization,
no structure, no 'officers', no hierarchies. It became a women
only space which attracted large numbers of women, many
leaving jobs and families behind to stay for a few weeks or
months, years in some cases. Unlike the early 1970s 'women's
liberation' activities, it attracted a fair number of older women.
They lived in appalling conditions and had only flimsy plastic
sheeting to protect them from the rain and the cold.[18]

Despite the fact that even making a cup of tea required near
miraculous powers, the women at Greenham devised some
extraordinarily imaginative tactics. After issuing a rallying call for
help, 30 000 women arrived on 12 December 1982 to 'embrace
the base', many pinning baby clothes and other symbols of life
to the 16 miles of perimeter fence.[19] They persistently blockaded
and invaded the base, on one occasion with a $4\frac{1}{2}$-mile serpent tail
that had been sewn by 2000 women. They dressed as snakes,
painted aeroplanes with peace symbols and wove a giant web
to float over the base with helium balloons. On Nagasaki Day
(9 August 1984), women covered their naked bodies with ashes
and blockaded the main gate. Their likeness to real bomb victims
disturbed personnel at the base, who were only persuaded to
remove the women by demanding that they were allowed the use
of protective clothing.[20] Numerous attempts were made to evict
them from the base. At a court hearing in February, 1982,

'Catriona' was asked if she would be bound over 'to keep the peace'. She replied:

> I will not be bound over to keep your peace. I am already keeping my peace. I will not take punishment, or recant, or admit guilt. I am responsible for this – for seeing the war machine grinding on, building silos arming the arsenals of the world with death and using all the non-violent means I can to stop it. I am asking you to keep the peace. We are not on trial, you are.[21]

Events at Greenham struck a chord with women who had no previous connection to activism. They even won sympathizers among Conservative women.[22] The government were rattled by the degree of support for the anti-nuclear protest. Pacifist feminism did not meet with universal approval within the movement, however. A minority of radical feminists objected to the hijacking of the women's movement by what they viewed as a 'diversion'.[23] Socialist-feminists have also criticized the maternalist feminism of Greenham and elsewhere, which associated women with nurturing, peace and mysticism and men with technology, warfare and violence in a reductionist manner. As Jill Liddington has written, this ideology rejected equal-rights feminism in favour of an anti-patriarchal maternalist separatism.[24] Lynne Segal's *Is the Future Female?* (1987) offered a trenchant critique of this essentialist form of feminism, which harks back to biological difference and hence 'separate spheres' arguments. Following the lead from American feminists such as Andrea Dworkin and Robin Morgan, British revolutionary feminists of the 1980s in WAVAW took up the issue of pornography, taking the view that 'pornography is the theory and rape is the practice' and initiated direct action attacks on porn shops and cinemas. As Segal and others have pointed out, the connection between pornography and sexual violence is by no means proven and, even if pornography were banned, it would not do a great deal to alleviate the oppression of women, which has complex causes across the public and private domains.[25]

Whilst many feminist groups declined to extinction during the early 1980s, black feminism found new self-confidence and vigour. Following the first OWAAD national conference in 1979 many more local groups were established, some succeeding in obtaining public funding for black women's centres. Black women were at the forefront of community struggles against racist provisions in education and health care, against deportations and police violence. Unlike white feminists, they did not attack the family as they viewed it as a vital source of strength against racist attack from the often hostile world outside it. Neither were they keen to speak out publicly against their men for fear that it would play into the hands of racists in the police and the judicial system.[26] The different perspectives of black feminists, argued forcefully by women such as Valerie Amos and Pratibha Parmar, were eventually recognized by socialist-feminists who came to realize that many of the generalizations they had arrived at in the 1970s were in fact specific only to white women.[27] The increasing presence of black feminism can be seen in publications such as *The Heart of the Race, Black Women's Lives in Britain* (1985), by Beverley Bryan, Stella Dadzie and Suzanne Scafe, which reveals the depths of anger and bitterness of black women in Britain.

Another group of women who fought against Thatcherite policies were the women in mining communities. During the miners' strike of 1984–5, women in these areas began organizing communal feeding, distribution of donated food and fund-raising. These are very traditional activities for miners' wives but, on this occasion, they proved to be the catalyst for a remarkable transformation in many of the women involved. The awakening of consciousness and activism in one Welsh mining village, Abertillery, is graphically depicted in J. Miller's *You Can't Kill the Spirit, Women in a Welsh Mining Valley* (1986). The early weeks of the strike were grim. Several women stated in Jill Miller's book that when the first of the three £10 (a small sum in shopping terms) vouchers came from the council, they found that they couldn't spend it all at once:

> spending ten pounds in one go when you have been so broke has to be one of the most difficult things in the world ... suddenly we could buy something special like a quarter of ham that we hadn't tasted in months.[28]

After an initial request from the men for communal feeding of miners coming off the picket lines, the women formed the

Abertillery Women's Support Group. It was soon providing a cooked meal for between 120 and 150 people a day. They also organized fund-raising for a Christmas party and presents for all the children. Women who had previously been depressed and isolated immediately felt lifted by the great spirit amongst the women. As more women were drawn in and the communal feeding could be easily covered, the support group began to branch out and send representatives to political meetings and rallies. This proved to be a class awakening; 'it hit us women, and like a ton of bricks, the greatest realisation that what we had entered was the class war'.[29] The women of Abertillery undoubtedly felt that what they were fighting was a class war and they were with their men a hundred per cent. But they had also discovered female solidarity and their own political strength. As Nita put it:

> Our group will go on, and stay together. It would be silly to let such a good thing go. We can't and won't give up. We will never be destroyed; we have a fighting spirit that will last forever. We are tough, we are proud, we are resourceful, and now we are out in force. Look out world, here we come![30]

It was a similar story in other coalfields, particularly in Yorkshire. A national network of 'Women Against Pit Closures' was formed. In July 1985 this group applied for associate membership of the National Union of Mineworkers. Although the NUM leadership backed the women's application it was turned down by the rank and file, reflecting their obvious unease about the newly found confidence of their women in the public domain.[31] Before the strike ended, a Kent miner made a 'half-joking, half-earnest' request at a meeting, 'Please, Mr Chair, when the strike is over, can I have my wife back? Not this one, the one I had before.'[32] But as Nita said to Jill Miller, 'I could never go back to my knitting and the kitchen sink now.'[33]

Finally, this section should reflect briefly on the development of feminist theoretical writing in these years, much of which has emanated from the USA or France. Starting with Juliet Mitchell in 1974, feminists have been drawn to the world of psychoanalysis and have devoted their efforts to developing the works of Freud and Lacan to analyse women's inner psyche to understand the internal mental processes associated with women's oppression.[34] Other writers focused on the attempt to create a large-scale synthesis of Marxist and feminist thought, explaining the connections between patriarchy and capitalism. [35] These attempts have now largely been abandoned. More recently, feminist theory has been greatly influenced by the 'linguistic turn' in philosophy.[36] Ideas of reason and certainty, trying to make feminism fit into and develop from either liberalism or Marxism, have become outmoded. Post-modernist feminists write about knowledge, language and power and the oppressive way in which the dominant patriarchal ideology has defined femininity. Language and meaning are seen as the site of political struggle, and writings are analysed in terms of 'discourse theory'. This has the advantage of leading us away from previous simplistic certainties and apparent universal truths, which were in fact based on a white middle-class perspective. It has also problematized masculinity and drawn attention to its changing forms just as femininity is constantly being reformulated and renegotiated. But too little attention has been paid to real material factors – institutional and economic structures which are just as important to women's oppression as language and ideology.

Law and the Political System

Between 1970 and 1977 there was a wave of legislation favourable to women. A key factor behind this was the commitment amongst Labour women MPs and the influence of the WLM on the Labour Party generally. Pressure for equal-pay legislation was given a boost when Barbara Castle became Secretary of State for Employment in the Labour government of Harold Wilson. Castle was able to find a compromise between the conflicting views of the employers and the TUC over how equal pay should be defined in law.[37] The result was the Equal Pay Act of 1970, which allowed for 'equal pay for the same or similar work or for work that had been rated as equivalent under an evaluation scheme'.[38] The Sex Discrimination Act (SDA) of 1975 made it illegal for a woman to be treated less favourably than a man, because she was a woman, in the areas of housing, employment, education and training and the provision of goods and services.

The Equal Opportunities Commission (EOC) was established under the terms of the SDA. Its role is to oversee the SDA and the Equal Pay Act by promoting equal opportunities and fighting cases of discrimination.

There have been a number of interesting cases resulting from the SDA. Belinda Price was a single mother of two who had spent some time at home with her young children. She wanted to enter the executive grade of the Civil Service, but found that she was barred from entry as, although she had the necessary qualifications, she was older than the stipulated age limit of 28. Her claim of discrimination was upheld as she had successfully proved that the age limit unfairly discriminated against women who had stayed at home to care for young children.[39] As a result of this case the Civil Service raised its age restriction to 45. There have been other gains, particularly in the area of women's access to credit, but overall the interventions of the EOC on both equal pay and sex discrimination have been disappointing, particularly in view of its relatively generous funding. [40] Clearly, the Equal Pay Act and the Sex Discrimination Act and the Equal Opportunities Commission could not, by themselves, create large-scale social change. But their existence did help to create a climate in which women could make advances. The Equal Pay Act, for instance, was deeply flawed in a variety of respects and resulted in very few successful claims. Nevertheless, it has been an invaluable tool for feminist trade unionists who have made a sustained attack on family wage ideology in wage bargaining since the late seventies and, as we see below, this has reaped real rewards. The SDA was treated as a joke in much of the popular media in the 1970s but, 20-odd years on, direct and overt discrimination on grounds of sex usually brings public disapproval.

The Employment Protection Act of 1975 gave women workers the right to six weeks paid maternity leave and extended leave up to 29 weeks. Also in 1975, changes to the state pension scheme gave women increased pension rights by making new provisions for people who had stayed out of employment because of domestic responsibilities. The introduction of Child Benefit as a universal cash payment made direct to mothers was also an important advance. The first two phases of the 'Social Contract' of the mid-seventies between government, employers and trade unions, made a commitment to narrow wage differentials between low-paid women workers and other groups. Taken together, this legislation represents a new approach to women by the Labour administration.[41] This radicalism appears to have disintegrated in the later seventies under Callaghan when Labour swung back to representing its more traditional interests, particularly those of skilled male workers. Margaret Thatcher came to power in May 1979 as the first woman prime minister in Britain's history. Any pro-feminist leanings she might have had in her youth were certainly not in evidence during her 11 years in office. By deregulation of industry and the promotion of low-paid, part-time jobs for vulnerable women workers, she actively worked against the interests of working-class women. For several years the Thatcher government resisted the European Commission ruling on 'equal pay for equal value' until, in 1984, it ran out of excuses and reluctantly pushed the necessary measure through Parliament. As a result, the Equal Pay Act has been strengthened and it is now considerably easier for women to argue equal pay claims.[42]

As part of its equal opportunities strategy, the European Commission issued a Directive on Parental Leave in 1996. This allows for three months statutory leave for men and women when they become parents, and can be taken on a flexible basis any time up until the child's eighth birthday. The British government is committed to implementing this directive by December 1999.[43] At the time of writing, full details have yet to be finalized. The indications are that the government will opt for the weakest possible interpretation of the directive and will not commit the UK to parental leave on a paid basis.[44]

The local state was also influenced by the feminist movement. In many areas, local authorities in the late seventies and early eighties gave new life to flagging feminist activism by funding projects covering nurseries, employment promotion, training opportunities, women's aid, rape crisis centres and many other feminist schemes. By far the most ambitious and wide reaching authority was the Greater London Council (GLC) under Ken Livingstone, elected in 1981. As part of its commitment to cater for, and bring into the democratic process, groups which had previously been excluded it set up a Women's Committee. By its fourth and final year in 1986 it had a budget of £90 million and 96 employees.[45] Its grants funded hundreds of projects, including black women's centres in Southall and Brixton and it enabled 3000 nursery places to be created.[46] The Committee's consultative meetings drew in over 500 women, stretching out to groups of disabled women, housebound mothers (whose child care expenses were paid or a crêche provided) and other disadvantaged groups. It also worked closely with other departments of the GLC, such as planning and education, to promote this feminist ethos. Not surprisingly, all this was too much for the Thatcher government which passed legislation for its abrupt abolition in 1986, thus ending perhaps the greatest experiment in 'municipal feminism' in modern times.

The WLM of the 1970s did not make promoting the increased involvement of women in the institutions of state a priority. But, by the 1980s, there was serious pressure for increased representation of women, particularly within the Labour Party. In the 1987 General Election the number of women elected climbed above 5 per cent for the first time, to 6.3 per cent, making a total of 41 women MPs.[47] It was still, however, extremely difficult for a woman to be selected for a winnable seat. For a brief period in the early nineties, the Labour Party adopted a policy of targeting specific seats for 'women only' short lists. It proved to be a very divisive issue for the Labour Party, but it did result in a startling rise in the number of women MPs to 120, constituting 18.2 per cent of the total.[48] Many of these new Labour women members are pressing for changes to how Parliament is run (for a crêche, for changes to its working hours, etc.) and for an end to the notion that an MP must be seen to be a workaholic to be viewed as good at the job. How successful these efforts will be still remains to be seen. In 1992 Betty Boothroyd became the first woman Speaker of the House of Commons. There have also been a number of significant 'firsts' in public life for women from ethnic minorities in these years. In 1987 Diane Abbott, whose family were originally from the West Indies, was elected to a safe Labour seat in London. Shreela Flather immersed herself in community work and local politics soon after her arrival from India in 1968. She became a magistrate in 1971 and a councillor in 1976, making her the first woman councillor from an ethnic minority. She was Lady Mayor for Windsor and Maidenhead in 1986.[49] Flather has been subjected to racist hate mail and abusive phone calls. In 1982 she had a metal bar thrown through her kitchen window and was told by one of the investigating police officers that it was 'only a prank'.[50] Although a talented, hardworking and ambitious Conservative, the party failed to express any interest in offering her a winnable seat and she has now taken a life peerage and sits in the Lords as the first Asian woman peer.[51]

Aristocratic and royal women have not featured to any great extent so far in this text. An exception is made for the case of Lady Diana Spencer, daughter of Earl Spencer, whose life, wrote June Purvis, 'laid painfully bare many of the contradictions and complexities that women face in the late twentieth century'.[52] In 1981 at the age of 19 she married Charles, Prince of Wales and heir to the throne, who was 32. It appears that she was chosen by Charles after a long search for a suitable young woman without a 'past', as this was seen as an essential pre-requisite. Over the next few years the couple had two sons, but the marriage was not a happy one and in 1993 they officially separated and later divorced. By all previous royal protocol, it would be expected that in such circumstances the ex-wife would retreat into obscurity. Instead, Diana continued to lead a very public life in charity work and as an international celebrity. She was particularly known for her association with vulnerable groups (Aids patients, the homeless, etc.) and for her tactile (some would say feminine) approach to meeting the public, in contrast to the remote and formal stance of the rest of the royal family. The Palace's 'war of attrition' against her continuing high profile wore her down, and in November 1995 she gave an interview to the BBC to give her side of the story. In this interview she publicly called Charles to account for his long-standing adultery with Camilla Parker Bowles.[53] The monarchy, which has traditionally tolerated royal mistresses, had never seen anything like this and had still not come to terms with the 'loose cannon' of Diana, Princess of Wales, when she was suddenly killed in a car crash in August 1997. The nation mourned for Diana in a way that it had never mourned for any other individual, royals included.[54] Diana Spencer's unprecedented determination to stand up for herself and to take on her husband, and therefore the monarchy, revealed not only great strength of character but also the infiltration of feminist ideas into the British upper class. Still stunned by the unmistakable truth of Diana's huge popularity, the senior royals, and Charles in particular, have been making efforts to give the monarchy a much needed overhaul as it approaches the millennium.

Work and the Labour Movement

During these years, the participation rate of women in the labour force continued to increase. Between 1975 and 1996 it increased from 60 per cent of women of working age to 71 per cent.[55] These are, of course, averages as there are many variations within the female population. Older women and single parents are less likely to work, the latter partly on account of the 'poverty trap' which makes employment unviable unless they can earn substantially above the benefit levels.[56] During the same period, male economic activity rates have declined. By 2000 it is expected that women will constitute a majority of the workforce – they already do in Liverpool, Glasgow, Bristol and Sheffield.[57] The greatest growth rate has been recorded amongst women with children under five. In a guidebook for working mothers published in 1975, Barbara Toner wrote, 'if you dare to return to work before the child is at school for reasons which appear indulgent – to pursue your career – you are somehow regarded as an unfit parent'.[58] Toner herself discouraged women with pre-school children from working full-time. After explaining about rushing to and from childminders 'as well as coping with shopping, cooking and washing', she concludes that 'the likelihood is that both you and the child will suffer'.[59] By the mid-1990s the social pressures against women with small children resuming employment had considerably lessened and two out of three women were returning to work within 11 months of giving birth.[60] Part-time work has increased, and although a small proportion of men are now working part-time it is still predominantly a women's activity. During the 1980s, as the manufacturing sector shrunk, relatively well-paid 'men's jobs' declined and there was a big growth in 'non-standard' employment. The government actively pursued a low wages strategy and the creation of a 'flexible labour force'. Thus, many of the new jobs created were low-paid, unskilled, part-time and temporary. This accounts for a considerable proportion of the rise in women's employment during these years.

Horizontal gender segregation in employment has been considerably reduced since the seventies by women breaking into a range of occupations which were previously male monopolies. There are now women bus drivers, train drivers and fire fighters.[61] Women police officers are no longer restricted to 'women's duties' and are integrated into the main police force. But the number of women who have succeeded in breaking into traditionally male preserves is still very small. Women workers are still concentrated in the low-paid sectors of secretarial/clerical jobs, retail, catering, cleaning, nursing and hairdressing. Sylvia Walby argues that, although most occupations are still dominated by one or other sex, 'there has been a marked reduction in the extent of segregation'.[62] According to Walby, 'women have increasingly entered top positions, especially those managerial, administrative and professional jobs for which University degrees are the effective entry qualification, during a period in which these posts increased as a proportion of all jobs'.[63] These gains are not entirely what they seem, however, as can be seen in the case of medicine. Twenty-nine per cent of all doctors are now women, but they are not spread evenly across the medical profession.[64] Only 17 per cent of consultants are women and very few of these are in prestigious specialities such as surgery.[65] Vertical gender integration has meant that more women are now in management, but as Rosemary Crompton had indicated in the case of banking, they have tended to move into female niches in management which are 'skill' and 'expertise' posts rather than into directly controlling the workforce, unless it is supervising other women.[66] In any case, the recent increase of women in banking can be mostly attributed to their entry not to management but into the lower levels of the new telebanking services where women are recruited as basic operators and not expected to progress. A recent survey published by the EOC showed that at all levels of qualifications 'women were less likely than men to receive training, and to receive significant internal promotion'.[67] Moreover, this tendency was more marked amongst women from ethnic minorities, revealing the existence of both sex and race discrimination.

Over the last 30 years there has been a narrowing of the pay gap between men and women in full-time work. In 1996, women who were working full-time earned 80 per cent of the male average hourly earnings.[68] Significantly, the pay gap for part-time women workers has not narrowed whilst this area of work has increased. The pattern established in the post-war years of an association between part-time work and downward occupational mobility has continued. Related to this, older women workers, who are more likely to be part-time, tend to be on much lower pay than men. It appears that it is young, well-qualified women who have made the greatest gains. This leads Crompton to write of the growing divide between 'work-rich' households where both partners are in full-time work and 'work-poor' households where there is no one in official paid work.[69] Caught in the poverty trap, women who are on benefit fall prey to super-exploitive, casual, 'cash-in-hand' jobs. This type of work includes homeworkers, who still occupy the 'shadowlands' of the employment spectrum. A survey by the Low Pay Unit in 1983 revealed that three-quarters of homeworkers were earning less than a pound an hour, when low pay was officially defined as being less than £2 25 an hour.[70] Almost all homeworkers are women, many of whom come from Pakistani or Bangladeshi households where it is not accepted that women work outside the home. It is probably the case that many of these women, who are officially housewives, in reality make a vital contribution to the family economy. There is also a new and different breed of home-workers, both men and women, who are choosing to work at home via the use of computer modems, fax machines, etc. These 'remote workers' are usually well-paid professionals who share their work time between home and office. Whilst many women might find this form of work less stressful than being away from home full-time, it has obvious drawbacks as other members of the household tend to make demands which they would not otherwise make.

The narrowing of the pay gap and the lessening of gender segregation suggests that gender convergence is increasing in employment. It is necessary, however, to guard against sweeping generalizations. These changes are very specific to particular age and occupational groups and still leave many women in disadvantaged positions. Patriarchal discourses still

operate in many workplaces to ensure continued male dominance. Formal barriers to women have virtually disappeared,
but other forms of control, such as sexual harassment and
assumed lack of commitment, are still in evidence, although
increasingly challenged. In addition, due to continued inequality
in the home, women do not enter the labour market on the same
terms as men. There is evidence that the priority given by
women workers to childcare commitments is directly linked to
low pay.[71] Also, as we see below, men are doing more domestic
labour, but this is still seen as overwhelmingly a woman's
responsibility even if she is in full-time work.[72] When Cherie
Blair came to Downing Street as the first working wife of a
British Prime Minister, Tony Blair revealed in interviews that he
regarded the home and their three children as primarily her
responsibility. 'She's got her practice and she's got the family to
manage,' Blair said of his wife, who is a QC in one of the
country's top law firms.[73] Britain has the lowest proportion of
publicly funded childcare in Europe. The preference of many
women for part-time work has to be seen against the lack of
affordable childcare.[74] Although informal childcare arrangements are still important, through family, neighbours, etc.,
professional childcare using nannies, childminders and nurseries
is increasing. Women are having to meet this cost directly
through their own earnings and usually bear the brunt of
grappling with the stress of liaising with carers, transporting the
child/children, making back-up arrangements for sickness, etc.
There are signs that women in work-rich households would like
more parenting to be undertaken by their male partners and for
there to be a less stressful workaholic culture, but there is little
evidence that men are exerting any pressure for this.[75]

For an explanation which goes beyond the traditional patriarchal assumptions which men have in the home, it is necessary
to look at changing discourses of masculinity. The boom of
the eighties created a more aggressive form of masculinity in the
growth sectors. Crompton, for example, shows that in banking
the regime of the paternalistic and bureaucratic male bank
manager has given way to a more competitive, selling culture.[76]
The whole pace of work has shifted upwards and become more
stressful. Men (and women) who wish to keep their jobs often
have little choice but to work long hours and struggle to meet

unrealistic demands from employers who view family commitments as distractions from whole-hearted dedication to work.
It can be seen, therefore, that women have not made advances in
an otherwise static landscape. Discourses of both masculinity and
femininity are dynamic over time and operate in conjunction
with economic pressures. The changes of recent years have
simultaneously operated both to the advantage and disadvantage
of women. To some extent, women have made their advances
towards equality entirely on male terms.

Turning to the organized labour movement, patriarchal
discourses have often acted against the interests of women.
During the 1970s, male trade unions often fought to try and
maintain sex-monopolies. Bus drivers and male postal workers,
for instance, strongly resisted the entry of women, but were
eventually worn down by pressure from women seeking entry.
Where women were attempting to organize and make collective
demands of employers, trade union officials were often unhelp-
ful. In an assessment of the early 1970s night-cleaners' campaign
for better pay and conditions for London's super-exploited army
of office cleaners, Sally Alexander wrote,

> the officer responsible in the T and G [Transport and General
> Workers' Union] for the night cleaners was very elusive. He
> seldom replied to letters or telephone calls, twice did not turn
> up for meetings and specific requests for help on issues such as
> victimisation, unhealthy conditions etc. were ignored.[77]

In these circumstances it is not surprising that many feminists
of the 1970s, particularly radical feminists, gave up completely on
the formal institutions of the labour movement. Selma James, for
instance, argued that women should withdraw from trade unions
as they did not represent the interests of women.[78] But there
were other women, more socialist-feminist inclined, who were
fighting within the unions, forcing them to take their interests
seriously and to take on the employers on their behalf. We have
seen above how feminists within the trade union movement
succeeded in winning mass trade union support in defence of
abortion rights.

There are several memorable examples of grass-roots militancy among women during the 1970s. The women workers at

the Trico car component factory in Brentford, West London, came out for equal pay in 1976. Despite having rather less than full support from the men at the plant, the women mounted 24-hour pickets and attracted widespread support, culminating in a victorious settlement.[79] Several strikes, such as the one at Grunwick photoprocessing plant in north-west London, made male trade unionists in traditional sectors realize that the labour force was changing and that Asian and black women were very much part of this new scene. The sight of the diminutive Jayaben Desai standing up to the mass police ranks on the Grunwick picket line is one of the unforgettable images of the 1970s.[80] Within the movement, however, women were still disadvantaged by having little access to formal union power. Meetings held in the evenings effectively cut off most married women from access to participation in their union. Some unions, such as the NUPE and the AUEW began to hold women-only meetings and day schools and began to think about organizing child-care, but there were many others that remained indifferent or even hostile.

In the 1980s there is still plenty of evidence of male-orientated trade unions' undervaluing of women's skills and abilities. Sallie Westwood's detailed study of a hosiery firm 'StichCo' in the Midlands, where almost a third of the women workers were Asian, paints a dismal picture of union involvement with the women on the shop floor.[81] The women observed the 'cosy accommodation' between management and union, and the union priority given to the male knitters, and drew their own conclusions: 'The union, the management, they are all the same.'[82] A union official told Westwood, who worked at the factory for a year, that the wages at StitchCo were 'good for women', when they were earning considerably less than the average weekly earnings for women in Britain at that time.[83] Despite (perhaps because of?) their lack of status and outside support, the women at StitchCo forged a unique shopfloor culture which succeeded in forcing the management to write off time and resources. Integral to this manipulation of the management by the women was the use of the symbols of femininity, especially weddings and pregnancies, to devise elaborate shopfloor rituals which took women away from their benches for extended periods of time and used company materials.[84]

Westwood's study was carried out in 1981. By the late eighties, under the onslaught of Thatcherism, with traditional areas of union power declining fast within the manufacturing sector, there are signs that the more forward thinking unions were beginning to take women's issues much more seriously. It began to dawn on them that the survival of unions might well depend on their ability to adapt to the new feminised workforce. An early example of this new approach was a speech made by John Edmonds when he took over as leader of Britain's second largest trade union, GMBATU, in 1986. He argued that the old-style bureaucratic union dealing with skilled, relatively privileged workers was a thing of the past, and that unions had to adapt to what he termed the new 'servant' economy with millions of highly exploited, often part-time, women workers in the service industries.[85] A study published in 1992 revealed a 10 per cent difference in union density between women and men (32 per cent compared to 42 per cent).[86] Early in 1998, the TUC launched a new American-style 'Organising Academy' for would-be full-time union organizers. Two-thirds of its first cohort of 36 trainees were young women in their twenties.[87] As Beatrix Campbell, long-time feminist critic of the unions, points out, it's not just a question of rejigging demands to accommodate women: 'the real challenge for the unions is to create a new culture which is comfortable for women'.[88]

Education

In the early 1970s, boys were outperforming girls across the range of educational qualifications and feminists pointed the finger at sexism within the education system to explain the relative under-peformance of girls. These early critiques were later developed by Dale Spender, whose research in the classroom showed that, when observed by cameras, teachers systematically gave boys more attention than girls, even when they professed in interviews to give equality of treatment.[89] Boys were expected to be assertive in the classroom and this behaviour was met with respect and rewards but, when girls acted in the same demanding way, they were punished or rebuked.[90] Evidence for gender stereotyping in the classroom was overwhelming. The 'hidden curriculum' operated to ensure that girls understood that marriage and motherhood was their vocation in life and that education was of minor significance.[91] Although working-class girls were probably the most affected by this undervaluing of girls, it was also prevalent in other sections of society. Lady Diana Spencer was a prime example of this, leaving school at 16 in 1977 after an expensive private education without a single qualification, whilst her brother went to Oxford.

Bob Dixon's survey of reading schemes showed that male characters appeared much more frequently than female characters and were more often seen in leading roles. Boys appeared in active physical roles whilst girls were usually seen in much less adventurous situations, often not straying from mum at home.[92] The 'tomboy who is made to conform' was an enduring feature of the girls' fiction surveyed by Dixon.[93] When Annmarie Turnbull, Jan Pollock and Sue Bruley looked at school history teaching, they found a similar picture.[94] Women were largely peripheral to the main historical actors in these texts; 'a merchant and his family' ... 'ancient Egyptians and their wives' ... 'everyone enjoyed himself on Mayday', etc.[95] The modern nuclear family was not viewed historically, but as a universal 'natural' institution, unchanging throughout human history. Sexism in the education system was formalized by the enforced segregation for 'boys' subjects' (then called woodwork, metalwork and technical drawing) and 'girls subjects' (then called needlework and home economics or domestic science). In the rest of the curriculum, sex-role stereotyping applied: maths and hard sciences being 'boys' subjects' and arts, humanities and biology being 'girls' subjects'. Not surprisingly, the under-performance of girls in maths, hard science and technology was dramatic.

The feminist critique of education also reached into higher education which was scrutinized for male bias. Ann Oakley attacked sociologists for their preoccupation with men and work whilst paying almost no attention to women's working lives, particularly unpaid work in the home.[96] Oakley's books, such as *Sex, Gender and Society* (1972), along with the work of other feminist sociologists, began to transform sociology in the 1970s. History, as we have seen, was intimately connected to the birth of 'second-wave feminism'. Leonore Davidoff, Marion Kozak and others started a London Feminist History Group in 1973 which gave an invaluable platform for young feminist scholars (from both inside and outside academia) to develop their work and challenge the dominant patriarchal discourses within academic history. Books such as Sheila Rowbotham's *Hidden From History* (1973) helped to change the whole orientation of social history and made it impossible for historians to continue to ignore gender divisions in history. Other subject areas developed feminist groups, in economics, science, geography, literature, etc. Gradually, university and polytechnic syllabuses were adapted and many colleges began offering 'women's studies' courses. Feminist academics stressed that they did not want feminist perspectives merely 'tagged on' in the form of optional courses, but that feminists' insights should also be integrated into core courses. Further education colleges also started offering 'Return to Study' courses, with built-in childcare via a college crèche, aimed primarily at mature women who had missed out on education at school. For many women this proved to be a turning point. One of the women interviewed by Bryan, Dadzie and Scafe put it this way:

> after about a term, I began to feel a lot more confident about my own abilities, and that made me see the other subjects differently. I realised I didn't have to stop at RSA Typing because there are other things in life that I can do, if I put my mind to it. I suppose this was because I woke up to the fact that it wasn't just me who was in that boat. All the women on that course were struggling to bring up kids and to make a life for themselves, and I figured we couldn't all be failures. There has to be something wrong with the system.[97]

Change also occurred lower down the system. The SDA made it illegal to operate on the basis of 'boys' subjects' and 'girls' subjects'. Change was slow to occur, however, and many schools pleaded lack of suitable staff, resources, buildings, etc. to avoid adapting to a non-sexist curriculum. It was not until the 1980s that schools really took this on board. Overt gender bias is now avoided, with domestic science relabelled 'food technology' and needlework replaced by 'textiles'. Usually, younger secondary-school pupils undertake a range of different technical subjects before deciding which ones they will proceed with to the higher level, but gender bias is still very much in evidence with girls and boys leaning towards what they still perceive as their traditional subject areas.

Since the 1970s a remarkable transformation has occurred in the relative performances of girls and boys at school. The figures for 1997 show that 50 per cent of girls achieved five or more GCSE grades A–C compared with 40.5 per cent of boys.[98] At all levels of school examinations, girls are now performing better than boys. In a complete turnaround, concern is now being expressed about the relative under-performance of boys in the education system. This is undoubtedly a great success story for girls, but their advance still shows evidence of the traditional gender bias. 'A' Level subject choices reveal that girls are still opting predominantly for arts subjects and boys for maths and non-biological sciences.[99] There are signs, however, that gender specialization at GCSE and 'A' Level is declining.[100] It is a similar story in further and higher education. During the period of great expansion in higher education in the 1970s and 1980s, the number of female undergraduates more than doubled whereas male undergraduates only increased by a third.[101] Chinese women, along with other Far Eastern females in Britain, have done particularly well in higher education in recent years. [102] The bulk of the new women students have been taking arts and humanities degrees.[103] Many of the more vocational subjects, engineering for example, are the most sex-segregated and these are often associated with greater earnings as graduates. Walby is optimistic, however, asserting that although gender specialization in higher education is still important, there has been a significant decline in recent years.[104]

Marriage, Families and Households

In the early 1970s it was commonly assumed that the small, privatized, nuclear family, consisting of a breadwinning adult husband, a domesticated wife and dependent children, was a 'natural' institution and an indispensable part of western society. The assumption that adult women take responsibility for child-care and the running of the home was a fundamental cause of the inequality between the sexes. These different expectations of men and women meant that employment made little difference and neither did the absence of children. Adult women living in partnership with adult men were assumed to be responsible for servicing their material needs: cooking meals, washing, ironing, cleaning, etc. Ann Oakley's *Housewife* used data from a selection of housewives who were interviewed in 1971. The women in the study commonly had a very restricted range of experience before marriage and after marriage became victims of 'a circle of learnt deprivation and induced subjugation'.[105] Being forced to view housework as a major commitment they must not fail to discharge, women such as Patricia Andrews became psychologically dependent on a demanding daily routine:

> I'm a fanatic for housework. I dust, go round with the carpet sweeper [she had no vacuum cleaner], and wash these two floors every day. The only thing I don't do the same is I don't do the stairs and I don't polish properly on a Saturday and a Sunday, because he's home and he don't like it ... When he's here I try to leave it but I do keep looking at it and wishing I could get up and do it.[106]

As we have seen above, a challenge to this female conditioning was the very basis of the women's liberation movement which made a devastating critique of the sexual division of labour in society and brought out into the open the dissatisfaction which many women felt with their lives. This and other social forces have undoubtedly brought about many changes between the 1970s and the 1990s, but has marriage, the family and the whole area of private life changed that much?

The nuclear family described above, as the central institution for rearing the next generation, has been challenged as never before. Marriage is seen as optional rather than essential as the trend towards cohabiting couples has increased. It is no longer a social stigma for couples or lone women to bear children out of wedlock. The rise of the single-parent family has continued. Between 1975 and 1995 the percentage of families containing a lone mother increased from 9 to 20 per cent.[107] Lone fathers are still comparatively rare. Many single-parent families are created through divorce, which has continued to rise, but increasingly children are born into this situation. Professional women with financial independence are now in a position to bring up children without a male partner, if they choose. But, more often, lone mothers are in poverty as women's earnings are still lower than men's and women without recognized skills or qualifications are caught in the poverty trap if they attempt to work rather than claim benefit. Although it is not common, there are lesbian mothers who are bringing up children jointly with 'two mums'. Women who became lesbians after becoming mothers have had to face court battles over custody as lesbians are seen as 'unfit mothers', but this area of discrimination has lessened in recent years.[108]

It was noted in the section on employment that the rate of women's participation in the labour force has continued to rise, so that the dual-income household has become the norm. Even women with small children, who bore the brunt of the post-war assault on working mothers, are no longer expected to be fully occupied at home. Mothers in the 1950s and 1960s were made to feel guilty about going to work, but now they are much more likely to feel guilty if they want to stay at home. Statistics for 1997, gathered by the British Household Panel Study at Essex University for the Economic and Social Research Council, showed that only 15 per cent of households now have a husband in full-time work and a full-time housewife at home.[109] But the demise of the full-time wife and mother did not necessarily mean a transformation to the sexual division of labour in the home. The same study showed that where both partners are in full-time work, on average the man does five hours housework a week, whilst the woman does 14. It is still predominantly the wife who prepares the main meal and organizes the washing and cleaning.[110] Men are still likely to take responsibility for household repairs. It has been suggested that the higher the wife's employment status, the more likely the husband is to engage in housework.[111] Younger people no longer automatically assume that housework and childcare are the woman's sole responsibility, but this is still a long way from equality. Change has been very slow and the early optimism of sociologists of the 1970s about gender convergence has not been realized. As yet, women's increased financial independence has not relieved them of their domestic commitments.

Fertility has fallen as more women choose not to have children. It is predicted that one in five women born in 1967 will be childless at 40.[112] There are concerns about age imbalance in the population in future years as fertility is well below replacement level. Although young women from disadvantaged backgrounds with little education are likely to see pregnancy as a route to social status, more educated women (and there are now a lot more of them) are increasingly renouncing motherhood. With almost no state financial or institutional help (nurseries, etc.) and the non-appearance of the 'new man' to co-parent, it is not surprising that many women feel that the rewards of motherhood are out-weighed by its burdens. These women are ambitious and rightly perceive that motherhood is often associated with downward occupational mobility. To professional women, motherhood is a threat to status and hard-won financial and personal independence. The British Household Panel Study for 1998 revealed a boom in single-person households and connected this to the rise in women living alone.[113] Within the last generation, women have been able to obtain mortgages and credit on the same terms as men. Rising incomes have given them real lifestyle choices for the first time. Increasingly, women are seeing motherhood as a trap they can avoid. Claire Gallagher and her mother and grandmother talked to *The Guardian* in 1995 about the changes women had experienced over these three generations. The older two women did not receive higher education. Claire, on the other hand, had just graduated and was about to undertake a post-graduate teaching course. She seemed keen to avoid any suggestion that she might aspire to becoming a 'supermum' and was all too aware of the limitations of working motherhood: 'Two perfect children, nice home, good job, and still there for your husband when he comes home; but I think I'm too independent for that.' Claire told her mother at her graduation ceremony: 'You'd better enjoy this, because its the nearest thing you'll get to a wedding from me.'[114]

Post-war immigration transformed Britain into a multi-cultural society. Different ethnic groups of immigrants brought with them different family structures and traditions. These ethnic communities are also in transition, especially with new genera-tions born in the UK. The West Indian population had never absorbed the ethos of the male breadwinner. Under colonial rule, the slave master took responsibility for meeting material needs, rather than individual male slaves.[115] Later, the extended family, including grannies, aunts and cousins, cared for children to enable mothers to work. Many West Indian women left their children in the care of relatives when they first came to work in Britain. West Indian women who bore children in Britain have missed out on the support of relatives at home and have tried, not always successfully, to force their men to take more responsibility.

Pakistani and Bangladeshi households, on the other hand, tend to contain extended family groups rather than nuclear or single-parent families, and their higher birthrate means that these households are likely to contain much larger numbers of children than in the mainstream British population.[116] Amrit Wilson described the situation of Asian women in Britain in the 1970s in *Finding a Voice, Asian Women in Britain*.[117] Post-war Asian immigration came mainly from the Punjab, Gujerat and Bangladesh in response to the demands for male labour. Ironically, tightening immigration laws in the 1960s increased immigration as men sent for their wives while they could still get them in, with a view to settling rather than working for a few years and returning which was the initial approach. Asians who had settled in Uganda came to Britain in 1972 after their expulsion from East Africa. The Asian population in Britain originates from a wide variety of backgrounds. For example, the Bangladeshis are usually Muslim and were originally poor farmers whilst the Gujerati and East African Asians are more often Hindu and more likely to be urban and educated. Traditionally, an Asian woman went to live with her husband's joint family on marriage and resources were pooled. This system carried over to Britain amongst poorer Asians, but is less common today. The joint-family system had both advantages and disadvantages. Both the oldest male and the mother-in-law could be tyrannical to a new wife, restricting her outside life and making her do the most menial jobs at home. Economic independence was impossible as wages would have to be handed over. On the other hand, women were never isolated with small children, as childcare, as well as cooking and cleaning, was done collectively. If the sisters-in-law got on well together, a great sense of female solidarity and affection was generated.

Family honour has always been an extremely important force in the Asian community and this remains so today. This entails very strict control of young girls who must be kept 'pure' and away from corrupting influences. This is especially true of Muslim families, which are explicitly patriarchal. Muslim women are expected to be demure, dutiful and submissive and to keep away from strange men. Consequently, they are much less likely than Hindu women to work outside the home after marriage. Asian girls of the 1990s who have been born in Britain, educated here and subjected to the cultural influences of the wider society, often see themselves as belonging to two cultures and struggling to find a compromise between the two. Shaheena Begum Mossabir, a law student, wrote about this in *Telling It Like It Is, Young Asian Women Talk*:

> The hard part about living in Britain for me – as I'm sure it is for many Asian women – is that I feel torn between two cultures. While on the one hand, I want to be loyal and maintain the culture my parents have brought me up in, with its sense of family security, the respect it gives to its elders and the air of magic it spins during social gatherings, I also want to embrace the good parts of the one I see around me in Britain. This includes the respect that British culture gives to women, allowing them to be more independent. I take for granted being allowed to walk around in public, unchaperoned, which would be unheard-of in Bangladesh ... I am also envious of women who reach the age of twenty-five without feeling the threat of marriage lurking around them ... To incorporate British culture into the Bengali community is easier said than done.[118]

It will be several years into the new century before we will know whether young Asian women such as Shaheena have succeeded in creating a genuinely new Anglo-Asian feminine identity.

Conclusion

Transforming Femininity, Transforming Masculinity

This survey of femininity over the last hundred years has revealed very significant shifts in female identity. Much of this has been positive. Many of the goals of nineteenth-century feminism are now accepted features of our society.[1] Sexual segregation has been dramatically reduced. Almost all the formal barriers to gender equality have been removed and women enjoy full citizenship. Women's right to employment and educational opportunities is taken for granted. In education, the performance of girls is surpassing that of boys at almost every stage. Women have made inroads into many previously all-male occupations. Women's average earnings in relation to men have risen from about 40 per cent to 80 per cent. These and other gains have led to allegations that gender equality has arrived and that there is no longer any need for a feminist movement.

This new form of anti-feminism ignores the major disadvantages which women still face. At the end of the twentieth century, the 'forward march of women' is still flawed and incomplete. Women have gained formal rights but very little power. The home and childcare is still seen as primarily women's responsibility, but now they are expected to work as well. Many working mothers are disillusioned and exhausted. Higher-earning women buy their way out by paying other women to take over these roles. It is common for women to experience downward occupational mobility when they become mothers, as a way of easing the 'double burden'. This does not happen to men when they become fathers. Gains in educational performance have often not been translated into employment. Female labour is still concentrated in low-skill and low-status occupations. Women are much more likely than men to be living in poverty. Those who have made it into management and the professions still encounter a 'glass ceiling' which restricts them to 'feminine' roles. The narrowing of the pay differential has mainly affected younger women in full-time employment. Older women, particularly if they work part-time, have not advanced and few women have pensions which are comparable to those of men. Women's right to sexual pleasure has been recognized, but sexual behaviour is still largely male-orientated. The number of women employed in the 'sex industry' is actually increasing. Pornography, rape and other forms of sexual violence continue to degrade and oppress women.

Whilst agreeing then that some degree of gender convergence has occurred, it is important not to over-emphasize these changes as, fundamentally, we still have a gender system in which men are dominant. At present, what passes for equality is often assimilation of femininity into a male norm.[2] An example of this is the growing trend for pregnant women with no medical complications to arrive at ante-natal appointments with their diaries and asking for elective caesareans to be performed in order to fit in with work commitments. Is this what we should be aiming for? As we saw in the last chapter, increasingly women are avoiding these conflicts by choosing to remain childless.

Feminists are divided on the way forward for the twenty-first century. Both radical and maternalist feminists see a need to assert female values. The latter are loath to let go of the idea that women's biological role in reproduction and lactation gives them a special relationship to their children which fathers and other carers cannot share. Very recent feminist writing, such as that of Melissa Benn and Kate Figes, has swung against equal rights feminism and is instead reasserting the value of the 'maternal tradition'.[3] This can perhaps be viewed as a reaction to the 1980s advances described above which have resulted in a crop of burnt-out supermums.[4] It could also be argued that whilst the public domain continues to be male-dominated, the home, especially care of babies and small children, is one area where women have at least some degree of control and are therefore reluctant to relinquish, especially as increased equality at home would not necessarily bring great power in wider society. But if 'female' characteristics are linked to biological females, where does this leave men? We cannot change the gender system without challenging and undermining tradition-ally held masculine values and that must mean, in part, accepting that men can adopt the so-called female qualities of nurturing and caring. Radical feminists who will not engage with men on these questions cannot hope to transform the gender system and will remain politically isolated and weak.[5]

Another strategy, which is more associated with socialist-feminism, is for feminism to empower women to reconstruct masculinity along non-oppressive lines.[6] This would mean accepting that neither gender roles are attached to any sort of biological essence. It means overcoming the processes whereby 'difference' becomes 'disadvantage', and creating masculine and feminine identities which are genuinely non-hierarchical.[7] Ultimately, it may mean forging new unisex identities, along with a range of sexual identities. The feminist aim of eliminating any disadvantage created by sex-specific differences is still relevant. It will not come about, however, unless women retain a sense of their own collective (socially constructed) identity and power as men will not give up their dominant position spontaneously. Women need to organize against men to undermine patriarchal values and privileges, both inside the home and in wider society. But, at the same time, they also need to work with men as allies in a wider struggle against all forms of oppression.

Whilst affirming the relevance of feminism for the twenty-first century, it is also important to reassert the notion of difference within the movement, particularly class and ethnic divisions. If feminism is to be anything other than white and middle class it must address other forms of domination. Ultimately, feminism must be linked to (but not assimilated by) wider movements for radical social change. Here, it must be admitted that, writing in the winter of 1998–9, the situation does not look hopeful. Large-scale social change would require a much more interventionist state and this does not look remotely likely in Britain, or indeed in any other western state. Even gains which appear consolidated can be challenged. The ground is always shifting. The examples of both world wars show that dominant notions of femininity can be temporarily manipulated to meet the requirements of the state when it is in a situation of total war. The ageing of the population could result in women becoming more tied to the home than before, caring for elderly parents rather than young children.[8] Caroline Ramazanoglu argues that western states, which have long been stabilized as capitalist, male-dominated and individualist, are least likely to enact major change.[9] Third-world countries which are less stable and more obviously in transition seem more likely candidates for feminist advance. Even then, progress in these societies is likely to be uneven, as we have seen with the resurgence of an extreme form of patriarchal ideology and sexual segregation in the form of Muslim funda-mentalism in many states. This phenomenon is also growing in influence among some ethnic communities in Britain, although here there are many opposing trends.

Even though the present outlook in Britain is not encourag-ing, feminists have little option but to continue to struggle against gender domination, making the best of whatever opportunities present themselves. One of the aims of this book in mapping out a record of changing femininity in the twentieth century is to reaffirm women's collective identity by making women conscious of their past. On this a future can be built, in which femininity will not imply disadvantage in any sphere of social life. One of the book's features has been to provide examples and illustrations from individual lives to illuminate the major themes. In the introduction I introduced a personal element by outlining the different lives of my grandmother Daisy and her great granddaughter, my daughter Charlotte, as these two women have come to maturity at either end of the century. We do not know what future awaits Charlotte's great-grand-daughter (if she has one) at the end of the twenty-first century. But it is my hope that whatever her life chances are they will no longer be restricted by gender in the way that so many of her predecessors' have been.

NOTES AND REFERENCES

Introduction

1. J. Scott, *Gender and the Politics of History* (New York: Columbia, 1988). D. Riley, *'Am I That Name?' Feminism and the Category of 'Women' in History* (London: Macmillan, 1988).
2. S. Rowbotham, *A Century of Women: The History of Women in Britain and the United States* (London: Viking Penguin, 1997).

Chapter 1: The Bitter Cry of Outcast Women, 1900–1914

1. Lady Bell, *At the Works: A Study of a Manufacturing Town* (London: Edward Arnold, 1907; Virago edition, London: 1985). M.P. Reeves, *Round About a Pound a Week* (London: G. Bell, 1913; Virago edition, 1979).
2. A. Mearns, *The Bitter Cry of Outcast London, An Enquiry into the Condition of the Abject Poor* (London, 1883).
3. M. Llewelyn Davies (ed.), *Life As We Have Known It, by Co-operative Working Women* (London: Hogarth Press, 1931; Virago edition, 1977). M. Llewelyn Davies (ed.), *Maternity, Letters from Working Women, Collected by the Women's Co-operative Guild* (London: G. Bell, 1915; Virago edition, 1978).
4. M. Vicinus, 'Male Space and Women's Bodies: The Suffragette Movement', in *Independent Women, Work and Community for Single Women 1850–1920* (London: Virago, 1985) p. 263. L. Bland, *Banishing the Beast: English Feminism and Sexual Morality 1885–1914* (London: Penguin, 1995) pp. 91 and 48. S. Kingsley Kent, *Sex and Suffrage in Britain 1860–1914* (Princeton: Princeton University Press, 1990) p. 32.
5. E. Ross, *Love and Toil, Motherhood in Outcast London 1870–1918* (Oxford: Oxford University Press, 1993) p. 34.
6. M.L. Davies (1915) p. 143.
7. A.S. Jasper, *A Hoxton Childhood* (London: Centerprise, 1969) p. 40.
8. M. Stocks, *My Commonplace Book* (London: Peter Davies, 1970) p. 6.
9. Lady Bell (1907) p. 171.

182

10. M. Toole, *Mrs. Bessie Braddock MP, A Biography* (London: Robert Hale, 1957) p. 11.
11. Lady Bell (1907) p. 202.
12. M.L. Davies (1915) p. 53.
13. M.L. Davies (1915) p. 31.
14. M.L. Davies (1915) p. 128.
15. M.L. Davies (1915) p. 100.
16. M.L. Davies (1915) p. 45.
17. E. Ross (1993) pp. 102–5.
18. A. Davin, 'Imperialism and Motherhood', *History Workshop Journal*, no. 5, Spring 1978, p. 44.
19. J. Gaffin and D. Thoms, *Caring and Sharing, The Centenary History of the Co-operative Women's Guild* (Manchester: Holyoake Books, 1983) p. 48.
20. J. Lewis, *The Politics of Motherhood: Child and Maternal Welfare, 1900–1939* (London: Croom Helm, 1980) p. 166 using material from the *Co-op News*.
21. J. Lewis (1980) p. 19.
22. E. Ross (1993) p. 217.
23. L. Davidoff and C. Hall, *Family Fortunes, Men and Women of the English Middle Class, 1780–1850* (London: Hutchinson, 1987).
24. L. Bland (1995) p. 91.
25. S. Kingsley Kent (1990) p. 32.
26. L. Bland (1995) p. 69.
27. C. Hamilton, *Marriage as a Trade* (London 1912: Women's Press edition, 1981) p. 48.
28. C. Hamilton (1981) p. 50.
29. L. Bland (1995) p. 60.
30. *The Freewoman*, 22 February and 21 March, 1912.
31. *The Freewoman*, 25 July, 1912.
32. Widely quoted, see L. Bland (1995) p. 265.
33. C. Pankhurst, *The Great Scourge and How to End It* (London: Utopia Press, 1913) passim, but see particularly pp. 17, 48, 95 and 181.
34. J. Weeks, *Coming Out, Homosexual Politics in Britain from the Nineteenth Century to the Present* (London: Quartet, 1977) p. 104.
35. S. Jeffreys, *The Spinster and Her Enemies, Feminism and Sexuality 1880–1930* (London: Pandora, 1985).
36. L. Bland (1995) p. 257.
37. D. Russell, *The Tamarisk Tree, My Quest for Liberty and Love* (London: Virago, 1977 (first published Elek Books, 1975)) p. 23.
38. M. Stocks (1970) p. 8.
39. A. Davin, *Growing Up Poor: Home, School and Street in London 1870–1914* (London: Rivers Oram, 1996) p. 101.
40. A. Nield Chew, 'The Problem of the Married Working Woman', *Common Cause*, 6 March 1914, reproduced in D. Nield Chew (ed.), *The Life and Writings of Ada Nield Chew* (London: Virago, 1982) p. 232.

41. J. Purvis, *A History of Women's Education in England* (Milton Keynes: Open University Press, 1991) p. 83.
42. B. Vernon, *Ellen Wilkinson* (London: Croom Helm, 1982) pp. 7–28.
43. J. Purvis (1991) p. 115.
44. C. Dyhouse, *No Distinction of Sex? Women in British Universities, 1870–1939* (London: University College of London, 1995) p. 7.
45. J. Purvis (1991) p. 117.
46. I. Ford, *Women's Wages and the Conditions Under Which They Are Earned* (London: Reeves, 1893) p. 5.
47. This situation is described in B. Drake, *Women in Trade Unions* (London: Labour Research Department, 1920; Virago edition, 1984), Chap. IV.
48. M. Zimmeck, 'Jobs for the Girls: the Expansion of Clerical Work for Women 1850–1914' in A. John (ed.), *Unequal Opportunities, Women's Employment in England 1800–1918* (Oxford: Blackwell, 1986) p. 154.
49. C. Dyhouse (1995) p. 137.
50. D. Thom, 'The Bundle of Sticks: Women, Trade Unionists and Collective Organization before 1918' in A. John (1986) p. 261.
51. E. Mappen (1985) p. 18.
52. S. Boston, *Women Workers and the Trade Unions* (London: Davis-Poynter, 1980, 2nd ed., 1987) p. 68.
53. D. Thom (1986) pp. 273–5.
54. S. Boston (1980), pp. 65–7.
55. *Liverpool Echo*, 23 November 1911. I am grateful to Linda Grant for this reference.
56. S. Boston (1980) p. 80.
57. S. Boston (1980) p. 82. For women teachers see also H. Keen, *Deeds Not Words: The Lives of Suffragette Teachers* (London: Pluto, 1990).
58. J. Liddington, *The Life and Times of a Respectable Rebel, Selina Cooper 1864–1946* (London: Virago, 1984) p. 113.
59. P. Hollis, *Ladies Elect, Women in English Local Government 1865–1914* (Oxford: Oxford University Press, 1987).
60. P. Hollis (1987) p. 463.
61. P. Hollis (1987) pp. 462–3.
62. P. Hollis (1987) p. 57.
63. E. Carpenter, *Love's Coming of Age* (Manchester: Labour Press, 1896) p. 67.
64. O. Schreiner, *Woman and Labour* (London: T. Fisher Unwin, 1911) pp. 166–7.
65. Fabian Tract no. 149, *The Endowment of Motherhood*, 1910.
66. J. Hannam, *Isabella Ford* (Oxford: Blackwell, 1989) p. 101.
67. D. Nield Chew (1982) pp. 230–4.
68. K. Hunt, *Equivocal Feminists, The Social Democratic Federation and the Woman Question 1884–1911* (Cambridge: Cambridge University Press, 1996).

69. E. B. Bax, *The Fraud of Feminism* (London: Grant Richards, 1913).
70. There were 86 active branches in 1914. C. Collette, *For Labour and For Women: The Women's Labour League 1906–1918* (Manchester: Manchester University Press, 1989) p. 140.
71. S. Holton, *Feminism and Democracy: Women's Suffrage and Reform Politics in Britain 1900–1918* (Cambridge: Cambridge University Press, 1986) p. 28.
72. L. Tickner, *The Spectacle of Women: Imagery of the Suffrage Campaign 1907–1914* (London: Chatto and Windus, 1987).
73. L. Garner, *Stepping Stones to Women's Liberty: Feminist Ideas in the Women's Suffrage Movement 1900–1918* (London: Heinemann Educational, 1984) p. 11.
74. J. Liddington (1984) p. 122.
75. J. Liddington (1984) p. 181.
76. S. Holton (1986), Chap. 4.
77. S. Holton (1986) p. 115.
78. Viscountess Rhondda, *This Was My World* (London: Macmillan, 1933) p. 120.
79. V. Rhondda (1933) p. 152.
80. Unpublished memoir, *My Suffragette Experiences*, n.d., in private hands, consult author.
81. G. Mitchell (ed.), *The Hard Way Up: The Autobiography of Hannah Mitchell, Suffragette and Rebel* (London: Virago, 1977) p. 162.
82. P. Hesketh, *My Aunt Edith, the Story of a Preston Suffragette* (London: Peter Davies, 1966) p. 54.
83. E. King, 'The Scottish Women's Suffrage Movement', in E. Breitenbach and E. Gordon (eds), *Women in Scottish Society 1800–1945* (Edinburgh: Edinburgh University Press, 1992) p. 145.
84. M. Fawcett, *Women's Suffrage* (London: T.C. and E.C. Jack, 1911) p. 63.
85. M. Vicinus (1985) p. 271.
86. Lady C. Lytton, *Prisons and Prisoners: The Experiences of a Suffragette* (London: Heinemann, 1914; E.P. Publishing edition, Yorkshire, 1976) p. 269.
87. C. Morrell, *'Black Friday': Violence Against Women in the Suffragette Movement* (London: Women's Research and Resources Centre, 1980) p. 33.
88. ELFS Minute Book, 27.1.1914, Pankhurst Archive, Institute of Social History, Amsterdam.
89. E. King (1992) p. 142.
90. E.S. Pankhurst, *The Suffragette Movement: An Intimate Account of Persons and Ideals* (London: Longman, 1931; Virago edition, 1977) p. 396.
91. ELFS Minute Book, January 1914.
92. J. Marcus (ed.), *Suffrage and the Pankhursts* (London: Routledge and Kegan Paul, 1987) p. 2.
93. J. Marcus (1987) pp. 5–6.
94. M. Vicinus (1985) p. 252.

95. E.S. Pankhurst (1977) p. 4.
96. S. Kingsley Kent (1990) pp. 5–8.
97. J. Wyatt, see above.

Chapter 2: No Time to Weep: The First World War, 1914–1918

1. D. Mitchell, *Women on the Warpath* (London: Jonathan Cape, 1966).
2. A. Marwick, *Women at War 1914–1918* (London: Fontana with the Imperial War Museum [hereafter IWM], 1977).
3. G. Braybon, *Women Workers in the First World War* (London: Croom Helm, 1981).
4. J. Liddington, *The Long Road to Greenham* (London: Virago, 1989). J. Vellacott, 'Feminist Consciousness and the First World War', *History Workshop Journal*, no. 23 (Spring 1987). J. Alberti, *Beyond Suffrage* (London: Macmillan, 1989).
5. M. Pugh, *Women and the Women's Movement in Britain 1914–1959* (London: Macmillan, 1992).
6. S. Kingsley Kent, *Making Peace: The Reconstruction of Gender in Interwar Britain* (Princeton: Princeton University Press, 1993) p. 10.
7. C. Tylee, *The Great War and Women's Consciousness: Images of Militarism and Feminism in Women's Writings, 1914–64* (London: Macmillan, 1989).
8. S. Boston, *Women Workers and the Trade Unions* (London: Davis-Poynter, 1980, 2nd ed., 1987) pp. 96–8.
9. For details see G. Braybon (1981) pp. 67–82.
10. G. Braybon (1981) p. 72.
11. S. Boston (1980) p. 99.
12. P. Hamilton, *Three Years or the Duration: Memoirs of a Munition Worker* (London: Peter Owen, 1978) p. 37.
13. G. Braybon (1981) p. 50.
14. M. Hamilton, *Mary Macarthur, A Biographical Sketch* (London: Leonard Parsons, 1925) p. 148.
15. G. Braybon (1981) p. 46.
16. M. Kozak, *Women Munition Workers During the First World War, with Special Reference to Engineering* (Hull: PhD Thesis, University of Hull 1976), p. 205.
17. D. Thom, *Women Munition Workers at Woolwich Arsenal in the 1914–1918 War* (Warwick: MA Thesis, University of Warwick 1975) p. 62.
18. S. Walby, *Patriarchy at Work* (London: Polity, 1986) p. 156.
19. A. Marwick (1977) p. 74.
20. R. Adam, *A Woman's Place 1910–1975* (London: Chatto and Windus, 1975) p. 46.
21. S. Lewenhak, *Women and Trade Unions* (London: Ernest Benn, 1977) p. 161.

22. S. Boston (1987) p. 127.
23. D. Thom (1975) p. 135.
24. S. Boston (1987) p. 122.
25. S. Hetherington, *Katherine Atholl 1874–1960* (Aberdeen: Aberdeen University Press, 1989) p. 72.
26. M. Stocks, *My Commonplace Book* (London: Peter Davies, 1970) pp. 115–16.
27. R. Strachey, *The Cause: A Short History of the Women's Movement in Great Britain* (London: 1928; Virago, 1978) p. 338.
28. B. McLaren, *Women of the War* (London: Hodder and Stoughton, 1917) p. 21.
29. Mrs D.M. Richards (née Bowcatt), Memoir held by the IWM (Department of Documents).
30. V. Brittain, *Testament of Youth: An Autobiographical Study of the Years 1900–1925* (London: Gollancz, 1933) p. 410.
31. S. Grayzel, '"The Outward and Visible Sign of Her Patriotism": Women, Uniforms and National Service During the First World War', *Twentieth Century British History*, vol. 8, no. 2, 1997.
32. E. Crosthwait, '"The Girl Behind the Man Behind the Gun"', in +L. Davidoff and B. Westover, *Our Work, Our Lives, Our Words* (London: Macmillan, 1976) p. 164.
33. A. Marwick (1977) p. 101.
34. S. Walby (1986) p. 165.
35. F. Nesham (ed.), *Socks, Cigarettes and Shipwrecks: A Family at War* (Gloucester: Sutton, 1987).
36. E.S. Pankhurst, *The Suffragette Movement* (London: Longman, 1931) p. 594.
37. A. Marwick (1977) p. 32.
38. J. De Vries, 'Gendering Patriotism: Emmeline and Christabel Pankhurst and World War One' in S. Oldfield (ed.), *This Working-Day World* (London: Taylor and Francis, 1994).
39. Details can be found in the Pankhurst Archive at the Institute of Social History, Amsterdam.
40. P.W. Romero, *E. Sylvia Pankhurst, Portrait of a Radical* (New Haven: Yale University Press, 1990) p. 120.
41. L. Garner, *Stepping Stones to Women's Liberty* (London: Heinemann Educational, 1984) p. 85.
42. For details see M. Mulvihill, *Charlotte Despard, A Biography* (London: Pandora, 1989).
43. J. Alberti, *Beyond Suffrage: Feminists in War and Peace* (London: Macmillan, 1989) p. 52.
44. L. Garner (1984) p. 23.
45. J. Alberti (1989) p. 59.
46. M. Pugh 'Politicians and the Woman's Vote 1914–1918', *History*, vol. 59, 1974. See also M. Pugh (1992) pp. 34–42.
47. S. Kingsley Kent (1993) Chap. 4, especially pp. 84–6.
48. M. Pugh (1992) pp. 34–42.

49. B. Harrison, *Separate Spheres: The Opposition to Women's Suffrage in Britain* (London: Croom Helm, 1978) p. 215.
50. M. Pugh (1992) p. 34.
51. B. Harrison (1978) p. 204.
52. The net change was 15 MPs or 8 per cent, M. Pugh (1976) p. 369.
53. M. Mulvihill (1989) p. 110.
54. M. Stocks (1970) p. 117.
55. There are numerous accounts, but J. Alberti (1989) seems to be the most thorough.
56. J. Vellacott (1987) p. 86.
57. S. Oldfield, *Women Against The Iron Fist: Alternatives to Militarism* (Oxford: Basil Blackwell, 1989) p. 54.
58. For a detailed account of the British women who applied to attend the Hague Conference see S. Oldfield, 'England's Cassandras in World War One' in S. Oldfield (1994).
59. A. Wiltsher, *Most Dangerous Women, Feminist Peace Campaigners of the Great War* (London: Pandora, 1985) p. 126.
60. J. Alberti (1989) p. 55.
61. A. Wiltsher (1985) p. 124.
62. H. Mitchell, *The Hard Way Up* (London: Virago, 1977) p. 186.
63. J. Liddington, *Selina Cooper, the Life and Times of a Respectable Radical* (London: Virago, 1984) p. 205.
64. S. Rowbotham, *Friends of Alice Wheeldon* (London: Pluto, 1986) pp. 80–1.
65. A. Wiltsher (1985) p. 187.
66. J. Winter, *The Great War and the British People* (London: Macmillan, 1985) p. 240.
67. H. McShane and J. Smith, *No Mean Fighter, Harry McShane* (London: Pluto, 1978) p. 75.
68. J. Winter (1985) p. 216.
69. J. Winter (1985) p. 123.
70. J. Winter (1985) p. 283.
71. G. Braybon (1981) p. 168.
72. Reproduced by permission of the Oral History Archive, Southampton City Council.
73. A. Woollacott, ' "Khaki Fever" and its Control: Gender, Class, Age and Sexual Morality on the British Homefront in the First World War', *Journal of Contemporary History*, vol. 29, 1994, p. 327.
74. M.P. Daggett, *Women Wanted: The Story Written in Blood Red Letters on the Horizon of the Great World War* (London: Hodder and Stoughton, 1918) p. 25.
75. A. Marwick (1977) p. 162.
76. V. Brittain (1933) p. 262.
77. I am grateful to A. Light for her paper on 'Gender and the First World War' which was given to the Women's Seminar at the Institute of Historical Research, May 1991, for her insights into death and mourning.
78. Letters of Gilbert Nash, IWM.

Chapter 3: A New Femininity, 1919–1939

1. S. Kingsley Kent, *Making Peace: The Reconstruction of Gender in Interwar Britain* (Princeton: Princeton University Press, 1993).
2. See, for example: M. Hewins, *After the Queen; Memories of a Working Girl* (Oxford: Oxford Univeristy Press, 1985); E. Chamberlain, *29 Inman Road* (London: Virago, 1990); P. Willmott, *Growing Up in A London Village: Family Life Between the Wars* (London: Peter Owen, 1979); W. Foley, *A Child in the Forest* (London: BBC, 1974); R. Gamble, *Chelsea Child, an Autobiography* (London: BBC, 1979); M. Wade, *To the Miner Born* (Stocksfield, Northumberland: Oriel, 1984); M. Powell, *Below Stairs* (London: Peter Davies, 1968).
3. Published as M. Spring Rice, *Working Class Wives* (Harmondsworth: Penguin, 1939). R. Hall (ed.), *Dear Dr Stopes: Sex in the 1920s* (Harmondsworth: Penguin, 1978). This volume also includes letters from men.
4. For example: E. Roberts, *A Woman's Place: An Oral History of Working Class Women 1890–1940* (Oxford: Blackwell, 1984); D. Gittins, *Fair Sex, Family Size and Structure, 1900–1939* (London: Hutchinson 1982); M. Glucksmann, *Women Assemble: Women Workers and the New Industries in Inter-war Britain* (London: Routledge, 1990); P. Graves, *Labour Women: Women in British Working-Class Politics 1918–1939* (Cambridge: Cambridge University Press, 1994).
5. D. Beddoes, *Back to Home and Duty* (London: Pandora, 1989) p. 48.
6. M. Kozak, *Women Munition Workers during the First World War, with Special Reference to Engineering* (Hull: PhD Thesis, University of Hull, 1976) p. 365.
7. D. Thom, *Women Munition Workers at Woolwich Arsenal in the 1914–1918 War* (MA Thesis: University of Warwick, 1975) pp. 123–7.
8. S. Boston, *Women Workers and the Trade Unions* (London: Davis-Poynter, 1980) p. 137.
9. M. Pugh, *Women and the Women's Movement in Britain 1914–1959* (London: Macmillan, 1992) p. 81.
10. I. Clephane, *Towards Sex Freedom* (London: John Lane, 1935) pp. 200–1.
11. See, for example, D. Beddoes (1989) p. 49.
12. D. Thom (1975) p. 122.
13. *Portsmouth Evening News*, 13.2.19. I am grateful to D. Beddoes for this reference.
14. M. Pugh (1992) p. 83.
15. M. Hewins (1985) p. xiii.
16. M. Wade (1984) p. 37.
17. W. Foley (1974) pp. 148–50.
18. M. Powell (1968) p. 36.
19. W. Foley (1974) p. 159.
20. M. Powell (1968) p. 63.
21. W. Foley (1974) p. 161.

22. M. Powell (1968) p. 136.
23. S. Bruley, *Socialism and Feminism in the Communist Party of Great Britain, 1920–1939* (PhD Thesis: University of London, LSE) pp. 195–7. This thesis was republished as *Leninism, Stalinism and the Women's Movement in Britain 1920–1939* (New York: Garland Press, 1986).
24. S. Bruley, 'Gender, Class and Party, the Communist Party and the Crisis in the Cotton Industry between the Two World Wars', *Women's History Review*, vol. 2, no. 1, 1993, pp. 86–7.
25. *Cotton Factory Times*, 28.8.31.
26. S. Bruley (1993) pp. 84 and 89.
27. The exception is A. Hutt, *The Post-War History of the British Working Class* (London: Gollancz, 1937).
28. Interview with Maggie Nelson in *Socialist Worker*, 18.12.76, and subsequent interview by author 11.3.77.
29. *Daily Worker*, 7.11.36.
30. A. Deacon, *In Search of the Scrounger* (London: Bell, 1976) p. 82.
31. NUWM London 1935. A copy is held at the Marx Memorial Library, London.
32. This topic is explored in more detail in S. Bruley, 'A Woman's Right to Work? The Role of Women in the Unemployed Movement between the Wars' in S. Oldfield (ed.), *This Working-Day World, Women's Lives and Culture(s) in Britain 1914–1945* (London: Taylor and Francis, 1994).
33. M. Glucksmann (1990) p. 95.
34. N. Branson and M. Heinemann, *Britain in the Nineteen Thirties* (London: Collins Panther, 1973, first published 1971), p. 126.
35. Interview, Violet Ryan, Carshalton, 12.12.93 and subsequent interviews.
36. M. Glucksmann (1990) Chap. 5.
37. S. Bruley, 'Sorters, Pressers, Pippers and Packers: Women in Light Industry in South London, 1920–1960.' *Oral History*, Spring 1997, vol. 25, no. 1.
38. S. Walby (1986) p. 168.
39. M. Powell (1968) p. 25.
40. M. Pugh (1992) p. 94.
41. T. Davy '"A Cissy Job for Men; A Nice Job for Girls": Women Shorthand Typists in London, 1900–1939' in L. Davidoff and B. Westover (eds) *Our Work, Our Lives, Our Words: Women's History and Women's Work* (London: Macmillan, 1986) p. 142.
42. Interview, Nan MacMillan, London, 26.11.76 and subsequent correspondence.
43. H. Keane, *Deeds Not Words: The Lives of Suffragette Teachers* (London: Pluto, 1990), see Chap. 7.
44. S. Kingsley Kent (1993) p. 113.
45. D. Gittins (1982) p. 19.
46. D. Gittins (1982) pp. 186–7.
47. R. Hall (1981) p. 42.

48. A. Jackson, *Semi-Detached London* (Allen and Unwin: London, 1973) p. 159.
49. J. Giles, *Women, Identity and Private Life in Britain 1900–1950* (London: Macmillan, 1995) p. 24.
50. J. Giles (1995) pp. 129–30.
51. E. Chamberlain (1990) p. 59.
52. R. Gamble (1979) p. 129.
53. M. Spring Rice (1939).
54. M. Spring Rice (1939) p. 165.
55. M. Spring Rice (1939) p. 179.
56. M. Spring Rice (1939) p. 163.
57. M. Wade (1984) p. 24.
58. M. Hewins (1985) p. 35.
59. S. Taylor, 'Suburban Neurosis', *The Lancet*, 26 March 1938. I am grateful to J. Giles for this reference.
60. J. Giles (1995) p. 81.
61. P. Ayers and J. Lambertz, 'Marriage Relations, Money and Domestic Violence in Working Class Liverpool, 1919–39' in J. Lewis (ed.), *Labour and Love, Women's Experience of Home and Family 1850–1940* (Oxford: Blackwell, 1983).
62. W. Foley (1974) pp. 22 and 150.
63. P. Willmott (1979) p. 18.
64. O. Banks, *Faces of Feminism* (Oxford: Blackwell, 1986) pp. 183–4.
65. M. Stopes, *Married Love* (London: A. Fifield, 1918) p. 50.
66. S. Jeffreys, *The Spinster and Her Enemies: Feminism and Sexuality 1880–1930* (London: Pandora, 1985) p. 120.
67. S. Kingsley Kent (1993) pp. 109–11.
68. J. Giles (1995) pp. 9 and 31.
69. M. Hewins (1985) p. 69.
70. S. Humphries, *A Secret World of Sex* (London: Sidgwick and Jackson, 1988) p. 65.
71. S. Humphries (1988) pp. 67 and 88.
72. J. Weeks, *Coming Out, Homosexual Politics in Britain, from the Nineteenth Century to the Present* (London: Quartet, 1977) p. 109, pp. 107–11 has an account of the trial.
73. For details see S. Cline, *Radclyffe Hall: A Woman Called John* (London: John Murray, 1997).
74. J. Weeks (1977) p. 111.
75. B. Harrison, *Prudent Revolutionaries: Portraits of British Feminists Between the Wars* (Oxford: Clarendon, 1987) p. 7.
76. O. Banks (1986) p. 162.
77. E. Rathbone, *Disinherited Family* (first published 1924, Falling Wall Press edition: Bristol, 1986) p. 147.
78. S. Kingsley Kent (1993) pp. 116–21.
79. V. Bryson, *Feminist Political Theory* (London: Macmillan, 1992) p. 105; also see next reference.
80. J. Lewis, *Women in England 1970–1950* (Brighton: Wheatsheaf, 1984) p. 104.

81. H. Smith, 'British Feminism in the 1920s' in H. Smith (ed.), *British Feminism in the Twentieth Century* (Aldershot: Edward Elgar, 1990) p. 60.
82. Quoted in S. Kingsley Kent (1993) p. 124.
83. W. Holtby, *Women* (London: John Lane, 1934) p. 146.
84. W. Holtby (1934) p. 150.
85. B. Harrison (1987) p. 8.
86. M. Pugh (1992) p. 110.
87. M. Pugh (1992) p. 201.
88. E. Summerskill, *A Woman's World, Her Memoirs* (Heinemann: London, 1967) p. 61.
89. Quoted in J. Alberti, *Eleanor Rathbone* (London: Sage, 1996) p. 96.
90. M. Pugh (1992) p. 65.
91. P. Graves (1994) p. 81.
92. P. Graves (1994) p. 109.
93. For details see M. Durham (1992) 'Gender and the British Union of Fascists', *Journal of Contemporary History*, London, vol. 27.
94. For details see S. Bruley (1980).
95. For details see S. Bruley, 'Women against War and Fascism; Communism, Feminism and the People's Front' in J. Fyrth (ed.), *Britain, Fascism and the Popular Front* (London: Lawrence and Wishart, 1985).
96. P. Hollis, *Ladies Elect, Women in English Local Government 1865–1914* (Oxford: Clarendon, 1987) p. 478.
97. H. Mitchell (1977) p. 240.
98. See *New Generation*, particularly 1922. Also Ben Davies, interview, 25.7.77, Dryffryn Cellwen, South Wales, and subsequent correspondence. Mr Davies attended one of Browne's lectures on birth control in the Rhondda.
99. M. Stopes, *Radiant Motherhood* (New York: Putnam, 1920) p. 7.
100. For details see D. Russell, *The Tamarisk Tree, My Quest for Liberty and Love* (Virago: London, 1977), Chap. 9, and P. Graves (1994), Chap. 3.
101. P. Fryer, *The Birth Controllers* (London: Secker and Warburg, 1965) p. 263.
102. D. Gittins (1982) p. 180.
103. See S. Rowbotham, *A New World for Women: Stella Browne – Socialist Feminist* (London: Pluto, 1977).
104. P. Graves (1994) p. 195.
105. S. Bruley (1980) p. 255.
106. J. Alberti, *Beyond Suffrage: Feminists in War and Peace 1914–1928* (Macmillan: London, 1989) p. 197.
107. M. Joannou, *'Ladies Please Don't Smash These Windows': Women's Writing, Feminist Consciousness and Social Change 1918–1938* (Berg: Oxford, 1995), see Chap. 1.
108. V. Woolf, *Three Guineas* (first published 1938; Oxford: Oxford University Press edition 1992) p. 313.
109. V. Woolf (1992) p. 365.

110. W. Holtby (1934) p. 151.
111. P. Graves (1994) p. 215.
112. S. Bruley (1980) p. 251 and J. Liddington, *Selina Cooper, The Life and Times of a Respectable Rebel* (London: Virago, 1984) pp. 410–11.
113. J. Alberti, 'British Feminists and Anti-Fascism in the 1930s', in S. Oldfield (1994) p. 120.
114. For details see International Brigade Archive at the Marx Memorial Library, London. Also J. Fyrth, *The Signal Was Spain: The Aid Spain Movement in Britain 1936–39* (Lawrence and Wishart: London, 1986).
115. L. Manning, *A Life for Education, An Autobiography* (London: Gollancz, 1970) Chap. X.

Chapter 4: 'We Can Do It!': The Second World War, 1939–1945

1. For a good overall account of the war see A. Calder, *The People's War, Britain 1939–1945* (London: Jonathan Cape, 1969 Pimlico edition, 1992).
2. See, for example, P. Summerfield, The 'Levelling of Class', in H. Smith (ed.), *War and Social Change, British Society in the Second World War* (Manchester: Manchester University Press, 1986).
3. A. Calder, *The Myth of the Blitz* (London: Jonathan Cape, 1991; Pimlico edition, 1992).
4. R. Broad and S. Fleming (eds), *Nella Last's War, A Mother's Diary 1939–1945* (Bristol: Falling Wall Press, 1981). P. Donnelly (ed.), *Mrs Milburn's Diaries, An Englishwoman's Day-to-Day Reflections 1939–1945* (London: Harrap, 1979; Fontana, 1980). C. and E. Townsend, *War Wives, A Second World War Anthology* (London: Grafton, 1989).
5. Mass Observation (MO) was founded in 1937 as a social research organization with the aim of pursuing projects which would illuminate aspects of everyday life in Britain. Its data was collected from observers and volunteer diarists. The MO Archive is housed at the University of Sussex.
6. See for example, A. Marwick, *War and Social Change in the Twentieth Century* (London: Macmillan, 1974) p. 160, 'in general the war meant a new economic and social freedom for women, the experience of which could never be entirely lost'.
7. P. Summerfield, *Women Workers in the Second World War* (London: Croom Helm, 1984).
8. P. Summerfield (1984) p. 5.
9. See for example H. Smith, 'The Effect of the War on the Status of Women', in H. Smith (ed.) (1986).
10. P. Summerfield, 'Women, War and Social Change: Women in Britain in World War II', in A. Marwick (ed.), *Total War and Social Change* (London: Macmillan, 1988) pp. 96–7.

11. S. Carruthers, '"Manning the Factories": Propaganda and Policy on the Employment of Women, 1939–1947', *History*, 1990, vol. 75, no. 244, p. 232.
12. G. Braybon and P. Summerfield, *Out of the Cage: Women's Experiences in Two World Wars* (London: Pandora, 1987) p. 187.
13. G. Braybon and P. Summerfield (1987) p. 155.
14. H. Smith (1986) p. 213.
15. P. Summerfield (1984) p. 5. Although I have used many works for this section I am particularly indebted to Penny Summerfield.
16. P. Summerfield (1984) p. 43.
17. M. Pugh, *Women and the Women's Movement in Britain 1914–1959* (London: Macmillan, 1992) p. 275.
18. G. Braybon and P. Summerfield (1987) p. 278.
19. The Report's findings are dealt with in the following chapter. For a detailed account of the Royal Commission on Equal Pay, see P. Summerfield (1984) pp. 174–8.
20. P. Summerfield (1984) p. 31. Readers should be aware that the 1931 figure is likely to be an underestimate as so much of married women's work was 'unofficial'.
21. T. Harrison (ed.), *War Factory, A Report by Mass Observation* (London: Gollancz, 1943) p. 36.
22. P. Summerfield (1984) p. 145.
23. P. Summerfield (1984) p. 145.
24. D. Riley, *War in the Nursery: Theories of the Child and the Mother* (London: Virago, 1983) p. 122.
25. S. Walby, *Patriarchy at Work* (London: Polity, 1986) p. 189.
26. MO, *People in Production* (London: John Murray, 1942) p. 227.
27. MO (1942) pp. 227–8.
28. M. Stott, *Organisation Woman: The Story of the National Union of Townswomen's Guilds* (London: Heinemann, 1978) p. 67.
29. MO (1942) p. 266.
30. MO (1942) p. 353.
31. MO (1942) pp. 7 and 124.
32. MO (1942) p. 119.
33. T. Harrison (1943) pp. 27–31.
34. MO (1942) pp. 138–9. In general, three-quarters of the women 'expressed varying degrees of satisfaction in their work'. This is reinforced by the oral testimony in S. Bruley, '"A Very Happy Crowd", Women in Industry in South London in World War Two', *History Workshop Journal*, no. 44, Autumn 1997.
35. J. Costello, *Love, Sex and War: Changing Values 1939–1945* (Pan: London, 1985) p. 201.
36. P. Summerfield (1984) p. 157.
37. S. Boston, *Women Workers and the Trade Union Movement* (London: Davis Poynter, 1980) p. 209.
38. A. Exell, 'Morris Motors in the 1940s', *History Workshop Journal*, no. 9, Spring 1980, p. 94.

39. R. Croucher, *Engineers at War* (London: Merlin, 1982) pp. 285–91, provides a lengthy account of the dispute.
40. P. Summerfield (1988) p. 97.
41. G. Braybon and P. Summerfield (1987) p. 180.
42. G. Braybon and P. Summerfield (1987) p. 181.
43. T. Katin, *"Clippie", the Autobiography of a Wartime Conductress* (London: Gifford, 1944) p. 34.
44. D. Sheridan, 'Ambivalent Memories: Women and the 1939–1945 War in Britain', *Oral History*, Spring 1990.
45. Imperial War Museum (Department of Documents), London, Mrs B. Johnson.
46. Held at the IWM.
47. M.R. Higgonet and P.L-R. Higgonet, 'The Double Helix' in M.R. Higgonet *et al.*, *Behind the Lines: Gender and the Two World Wars* (New Haven: Yale University Press, 1987).
48. D. Sheridan, 'Ambivalent Memories' (1990) p. 38.
49. E. Taylor, *Heroines of World War Two* (London: Robert Hale, 1991). See Chap. 1, 'Underground Operator'.
50. E. Taylor (1991) p. 189.
51. R. Minns, *Bombers and Mash: The Domestic Front 1939–1945* (London: Virago, 1980) p. 77.
52. IWM, Miss I. Allen.
53. A. Hall, *Land Girl, Her Story of Six Years in the Women's Land Army, 1940–46* (Trowbridge: Ex Libris, 1993) p. 29.
54. Women's Land Army Timber Corps, *Meet the Members, A Record of the Timber Corps of the Women's Land Army* (no place of publication: Women's Land Army, n.d. *c.* 1945).
55. D. Sheridan (ed.), *Wartime Women, A Mass Observation Anthology* (London: Heinemann, 1990) p. 139.
56. B. McBryde, *A Nurse's War* (London: Chatto and Windus, 1978; Saffron Walden: Cakebread's edition, 1993) p. 85.
57. C. Graves, *Women in Green: The Story of the Women's Voluntary Service* (London: Heinemann, 1948) p. 15.
58. IWM, Mrs H. Appleby.
59. R. Minns (1980) p. 70.
60. C. Graves (1948) p. 128.
61. C. Graves (1948) p. 101.
62. T. Benson, *Sweethearts and Wives, Their Part in War* (London: Faber and Faber, 1942) p. 106.
63. E. Summerskill, *A Woman's World, Her Memoirs* (London: Heinemann, 1967) p. 74.
64. P. Donnelly (ed.) (1980) p. 186.
65. D. Sheridan, *Wartime Women* (1990) p. 152.
66. R. Minns (1980) p. 37.
67. P. Brookes (1967) pp. 138–9.
68. H. Smith (1986) pp. 224–5.
69. R. Minns (1980) p. 32.

70. For example, see V. Brittain, *Seeds of Chaos: What Mass Bombing Really Means* (London: New Vision, 1944).
71. M. Bondfield *et al.*, *Our Towns, A Close Up* (London: Oxford University Press, 1943).
72. D. Sheridan, 'Wartime Women' (1990) p. 64.
73. A. Calder (1992) p. 62.
74. R. Minns (1980) p. 18. A smaller allowance was paid for second and subsequent children.
75. A. Calder (1992) p. 63.
76. A more detailed account of rationing is in P. Summerfield (1984) pp. 104–5.
77. D. Sheridan 'Wartime Women' (1990) p. 142.
78. C. and E. Townsend (1989) pp. 82–5.
79. A. Marwick, *Britain in the Century of Total War* (London: Bodley Head, 1968) p. 257.
80. C. and E. Townsend (1989) p. 106.
81. C. and E. Townsend (1989) p. 118.
82. R. Broad and S. Fleming (1981) p. 138.
83. C. and E. Townsend (1989) p. 291.
84. R. Broad and S. Fleming (1981) p. 168.
85. R. Broad and S. Fleming (1981) p. 229.
86. H. Smith (1986), p. 211. P. Summerfield (1988), p. 96 and p. 109.
87. T. Benson (1942) p. 37.
88. J. Costello, *Love, Sex and War: Changing Values 1939–1945* (London: Pan Books, 1985) p. 319.
89. C. and E. Townsend (1989) p. 278.
90. J. Costello (1986) p. 80.
91. IWM, copyright holder requires anonymity, consult author.
92. M. Pugh (1992) p. 271.
93. J. Costello (1985) p. 82.
94. E. Summerskill (1967) p. 75.
95. S. Neild and R. Pearson (eds), *Women Like Us* (London: Women's Press, 1992) p. 34.
96. *Woman's Own*, 10.12.43, quoted in J. Waller and M. Vaughan-Rees, *Women in Wartime, the Role of Women's Magazines* (London: Macdonald Optima, 1987) p. 76.

Chapter 5: From Austerity to Prosperity and the Pill: The Post-war Years, 1945–c. 1968

1. E. Wilson, *Only Half Way to Paradise, Women in Postwar Britain 1945–1968* (London: Tavistock, 1980). J. Lewis, *Women in Britain since 1945* (Oxford: Blackwell, 1992). E. Roberts, *Women and Families, An Oral History, 1940–1970* (Oxford: Blackwell, 1995). S. Rowbotham, *A Century of Women: The History of Women in Britain and the United States* (London: Viking, 1997).

2. For material on the Equal Pay Commission see P. Summerfield, *Women Workers in the Second World War* (London: Croom Helm, 1984) pp. 174–8, E. Wilson (1980) pp. 45–47, D. Riley, *War in the Nursery, Theories of the Child and the Mother* (London: Virago, 1983) pp. 165–6, S. Lewenhak, *Women and Trade Unions* (London: Benn 1977) pp. 248–9.
3. S. Carruthers, "Manning the Factories': Propaganda and Policy on the Employment of Women 1939–1947' *History*, vol. 75, no. 244, p. 233.
4. Interview Glynis Baker 17.1.94, Morden, Surrey.
5. G. Braybon and P. Summerfield, *Out of the Cage, Women's Experiences in Two World Wars* (London: Pandora, 1987) p. 264.
6. D. Riley (1983).
7. D. Riley (1983) p. 149.
8. M. Pugh, *Women and the Women's Movement in Britain 1914–1959* (London: Macmillan, 1992) p. 287.
9. For details see W. Croft, 'The Attlee Government's Pursuit of Women' *History Today*, August 1986.
10. See, for example, E. Wilson (1980) p. 43.
11. S. Carruthers (1990) p. 252.
12. This point is developed from D. Riley (1983) p. 195 and C. Blackford, 'The Best of Both Worlds?: Women's Employment in Post-War Britain', in J. Fyrth (ed.), *Labour's High Noon: The Government and the Economy 1945–51* (London: Lawrence and Wishart, 1993) pp. 220–1.
13. P. Summerfield, 'Women, War and Social Change: Women in Britain in World War Two', in A. Marwick (ed.), *Total War and Social Change* (London: Macmillan, 1988) p. 100.
14. J. Lewis (1992) pp. 82–91.
15. M. Hobbs, *Born to Struggle* (London: Quartet, 1973) p. 28.
16. E. Wilson (1980) p. 41.
17. J. Lewis (1992) p. 66.
18. E. Roberts (1995) p. 123.
19. J. Bowlby, *Maternal Care and Mental Health* (Geneva: World Health Organization, 1951).
20. V. Klein, *Britain's Married Women Workers* (London: Routledge and Kegan Paul, 1965) p. 119.
21. V. Klein (1965) p. 24.
22. See, for example the testimony from employers in V. Klein (1965), Chap. 3, 'Employing Married Women'.
23. Interview Beryl Sutherland 5.1.94, Carshalton, Surrey.
24. E. Roberts (1995) pp. 136–7.
25. Unfortunately, it has not been possible to obtain a gender breakdown of West Indian immigrants. It is clear, however, that although the early settlers were overwhelmingly male, many women followed. There was also immigration from the Indian sub-continent in these years, which was much more male-dominated. Larger numbers of Asian women came to Britain

198   Notes and References

from the early 1970s, so this is referred to in the following chapter.

26. G. Lewis, 'Black Women's Employment and the British Economy', in W. James and C. Harris (eds), *Inside Babylon, The Caribbean Diaspora in Britain* (London: Verso, 1993).
27. North Kensington Community History, *Life Stories of Senior Citizens from the Caribbean* (London: Hammersmith and Fulham Council, 1991) p. 25.
28. J. Gillot, 'The World of Learning', in Six Point Group, *In Her Own Right* (London: Harrap, 1968) p. 31.
29. 1956, London: Routledge and Kegan Paul.
30. J. Lewis, 'Myrdal, Klein, Women's Two Roles and Postwar Feminism 1945–1960' in H. Smith (ed.), *British Feminism in the Twentieth Century* (Aldershot: Edward Elgar, 1990).
31. M. Laski, 'The Cult of Servility', in The Six Point group (1968) p. 19.
32. S. Lewenhak (1977) p. 252.
33. *Socialist Worker*, 21.9.1968. Reprinted in D. Widgery, *The Left in Britain 1956–1968* (Harmondsworth: Penguin, 1976) pp. 297–9.
34. C. Blackford (1993) p. 217.
35. S. Lewenhak (1977) p. 262.
36. S. Lewenhak (1977) p. 265.
37. See E. Wilson (1980) p. 33 and J. Lewis (1992) p. 23. There were numerous government reports concerning different aspects of girls' education in these years. There is insufficient space here to deal with this degree of detail. A useful summary can be found in J. Finch and P. Summerfield, 'Social Reconstruction and the Emergence of the Companionate Marriage, 1945–59' in D. Clark (ed.), *Marriage, Domestic Life and Social Change* (London: Routledge, 1991) pp. 14–15.
38. M. David, *The State, the Family and Education* (London: Routledge and Kegan Paul, 1980), p. 70.
39. J. Gillot (1968) quotes LEA grammar schools as spending 12s 6d for every boy and 8s for every girl in 1959, p. 32.
40. M. Evans (1991) p. 27.
41. M. Evans (1991) pp. 10–23.
42. M. Evans (1991) p. 23.
43. P. Donnelly (ed.), *Mrs Milburn's Diaries, An Englishwoman's Day-to-Day Reflections 1939–45* (London: Harrap 1979) p. 371.
44. P. Donnelly (1979) p. 372.
45. J. Costello, *Love, Sex and War: Changing Values 1939–1945* (London: Pan, 1985) p. 274. G. Braybon and P. Summerfield (1987) p. 272.
46. E. Wilson, *Women and the Welfare State* (London: Tavistock 1977) p. 150.
47. E. Wilson (1977) Chap. 7.
48. J. Lewis (1992) p. 94.
49. B. Abel-Smith, 'Sex Equality and Social Security' in J. Lewis (ed.), *Women's Welfare, Women's Rights* (London: Croom Helm, 1983) pp. 90–91.

50. J. Stacey, *Star Gazing, Hollywood Cinema and Female Spectatorship* (London: Routledge 1994).
51. E. Wilson (1980) p. 111.
52. J. Stacey (1994) p. 89.
53. M. Young and P. Willmott, *Family and Kinship in East London* (Harmondsworth: Penguin, 1957). It should be noted that these studies referred only to white families. We know little of the family structures of the ethnic minorities at this time. This question is referred to in the following chapter.
54. M. Young and P. Willmott (1957) p. 24.
55. M. Young and P. Willmott (1957) p. 30.
56. R. Fletcher, *The Family and Marriage in Britain* (Harmondsworth: Penguin, 1973).
57. J. Finch and P. Summerfield (1991).
58. J. Finch and Summerfield (1991) p. 12.
59. J. Finch and P. Summerfield (1991) p. 30.
60. N. Dennis, F. Henriques and C. Slaughter, *Coal is Our Life: An Analysis of a Yorkshire Mining Community* (London: Tavistock, 1956).
61. N. Dennis *et al.* (1956) p. 239.
62. N. Dennis *et al.* (1956) p. 194.
63. H. Gavron, *The Captive Wife, Conflicts of Housebound Mothers* (Harmondsworth: Penguin, 1968; first published, London, 1966).
64. H. Gavron (1968) p. 125.
65. H. Gavron (1968) pp. 130–2.
66. E. Roberts (1995) pp. 82–6.
67. E. Roberts (1995) pp. 92–3.
68. E. Roberts (1995) p. 140.
69. E. Wilson (1980) p. 87. See also Birmingham Feminist History Group, 'Feminism as Femininity in the Nineteen-fifties?', *Feminist Review*, no. 3, 1979, p. 59.
70. H. Cook, paper given to the Women's History Seminar, Institute of Historical Research, 21.11.97, p. 11. This paper relates to Hera Cook's work for a PhD Thesis, *The Long Sexual Revolution: British Women, Sex and Contraception in the Twentieth Century* (University of Sussex, 1998) which I hope very much will be published. I am very happy to acknowledge the contribution of Hera Cook to this chapter in this reference and several subsequent references, which has made me look at this topic with new insight.
71. H. Cook (1997) p. 6.
72. J. Weeks (1981) p. 24.
73. E. Roberts (1995) pp. 158–9.
74. A. McRobbie, 'Settling Accounts with Subcultures, A Feminist Critique', *Screen Education*, no. 34, Spring 1980.
75. E. Wilson (1980) p. 141.
76. S. Maitland (ed.), *Very Heaven: Looking Back at the 1960s* (London: Virago 1988) p. 4.
77. J. Weeks (1977) p. 253 and J. Lewis (1992) p. 48.
78. E. Roberts (1995) pp. 63 and 75.

79. H. Cook (1997) p. 10.
80. H. Cook (1997) p. 20.
81. L. Manning, *A Life for Education: An Autobiography* (London: Gollancz 1970) pp. 250–2.
82. H. Cook (1997) p. 24. Details of the National Survey of Health and Development can be found in K. Wellings *et al.*, *Sexual Behaviour in Britain, The National Survey of Sexual Attitudes and Life Styles* (Oxford: Blackwell, 1994). I am grateful to Hera Cook for this reference.
83. C. Dix, *Say Sorry to Mother: Growing up in the Sixties* (London: Pan, 1978) p. 87.
84. J. Lewis (1992) p. 45.
85. J. Weeks (1977) p. 251.
86. S. Neild and R. Pearson (eds), *Women Like Us* (London: Women's Press, 1992) p. 20.
87. E. Wilson, 'Memoirs of an Anti-heroine', in B. Cant and S. Hemmings (eds), *Radical Records* (London: Routledge, 1988) p. 45.
88. P. James in S. Neild and R. Pearson (1992) p. 60.
89. N. Branson (ed.), *London Squatters 1946*, Communist Party History Group, Our History pamphlet no. 80, August 1989, p. 7.
90. N. Branson (1989) p. 23.
91. N. Branson (1989) p. 23.
92. J. Hinton, 'Militant Housewives: the British Housewives' League and the Attlee Government', *History Workshop Journal*, no. 38, Autumn, 1994, p. 131. I am grateful to J. Hinton for information on the League for this paragraph.
93. J. Hinton (1994) p. 141.
94. J. Hinton (1994) p. 144.
95. P. Hornsby-Smith, 'Women in Public Life', In Six Point Group (1968) p. 136.
96. P. Brooks, *Women at Westminster* (London: Peter Davies, 1967) pp. 204–11.
97. M. Pugh (1992) p. 306.
98. For details of women in the Conservative Party, see B. Campbell, *The Iron Ladies, Why Do Women Vote Tory?* (London: Virago, 1987).
99. See M. Whitehouse, *Who Does She Think She Is?* (London: New English Library, 1971) for details.
100. M. Whitehouse (1971) p. 11.
101. For details see T. Davies, 'What Kind of Woman Is She? Women and Communist Party Politics 1941–1955', in R. Brunt and C. Rowan, *Feminism, Culture and Politics* (London: Lawrence and Wishart, 1982).
102. J. Liddington, *The Long Road to Greenham: Feminism and Anti-Militarism in Britain since 1820* (London: Virago, 1989) pp. 178–81. I am grateful to Jill Liddington for this section.
103. J. Eglin, 'Women and Peace: From the Suffragists to the Greenham Women', in R. Taylor and N. Young (eds), *Campaigns for Peace* (Manchester: Manchester University Press, 1987) p. 236.
104. J. Eglin (1987) p. 232.

105. J. Liddington (1989) p. 191.
106. For details, see B. Johnson, ' "*I think of My Mother*": Notes on the Life and Times of Claudia Jones' (London: Karia Press, 1985).
107. B. Johnson (1985) p. 83.
108. B. Johnson (1985) p. 81.
109. B. Bryan, S. Dadzie and S. Scafe, *The Heart of the Race: Black Women's Lives in Britain* (London: Virago, 1985), p. 138.
110. Birmingham Feminist History Group (1979), *Feminist Review*, no. 3, p. 63.
111. E. Wilson (1980) p. 187.
112. Six Point Group (1968) p. 9.
113. Birmingham Feminist History Group (1979), *Feminist Review*, no. 3, p. 64.

Chapter 6: Second-wave Feminism and Beyond; The Personal Is Political, *c.* 1969–1999

1. S. Rowbotham, *Women's Liberation and the New Politics* (Nottingham: Spokesman Pamphlet no. 17, 1971; first published 1969) p. 3.
2. O. Banks, *Faces of Feminism* (Oxford: Blackwell, 1986) p. 226.
3. M. Wandor (ed.), *Once a Feminist: Stories of a Generation* (London: Virago, 1990) p. 113.
4. Audrey Wise in M. Wandor (1990) pp. 201–4.
5. E. Meehan, 'British Feminism from the 1960s to the 1980s' in H. Smith (ed.), *British Feminism in the Twentieth Century* (London: Edward Elgar, 1990), p. 193.
6. Anna Davin in M. Wandor (1990) pp. 55–6. See also the contributions in this volume by Sheila Rowbotham and several others who attended the conference.
7. S. Rowbotham in M. Wandor (1990) p. 36.
8. 'Women and the Family' by J. Williams *et al.*, reproduced in M. Wandor (ed.), *The Body Politic: Writings from the Women's Liberation Movement in Britain 1969–1972* (London: Stage 1, 1972) pp. 31–5.
9. G. Philpot, 'Consciousness-Raising: Back to Basics', *Spare Rib*, no. 92, March 1980. Reproduced in M. Rowe (ed.), *Spare Rib Reader* (Harmondsworth: Penguin, 1982) pp. 585–7. See also S. Bruley 'Women Awake: The Experience of Consciousness-Raising', in Feminist Anthology Collective (eds), *No Turning Back: Writings from the Women's Liberation Movement 1975–80* (London: Women's Press, 1981) pp. 60–7.
10. J. Weeks, *Coming Out: Homosexual Politics in Britain from the Nineteenth Century to the Present* (London: Quartet, 1977) pp. 199–200.
11. For the seven demands see B. Campbell and A. Coote, *Sweet Freedom: The Struggle for Women's Liberation* (Oxford: Blackwell, 1987; first published 1982) pp. 16–18. Also L. Segal, *Is the Future Female? Troubled Thoughts on Contemporary Feminism* (London:

Virago, 1987) p. 57. There was a final socialist-feminist conference in London in 1979.

12. For some details see E. Meehan (1990) pp. 198–9.

13. B. Bryan, S. Dadzie and S. Scafe, *The Heart of the Race: Black Women's Lives in Britain* (London: Virago, 1985) p. 149.

14. S. Rowbotham. *The Past Is Before Us: Feminism in Action since the 1960s* (London: Pandora, 1989) p. 66.

15. E. Pizzey, *Scream Quietly or the Neighbours Will Hear* (Harmondsworth: Penguin, 1974) p. 145.

16. For details of the marches in November 1977 see *Spare Rib*, no. 66, January 1978, pp. 22–3.

17. J. Liddington, *The Long Road to Greenham: Feminism and Anti-Militarism since 1820* (London: Virago, 1989) p. 212.

18. See C. Blackwood, *On the Perimeter* (London: Fontana, 1984).

19. B. Harford and S. Hopkins (eds), *Greenham Common: Women at the Wire* (London: Women's Press, 1984), has a chronology of events at Greenham. The activities described in the next paragraph are listed in this chronology.

20. L. Jones, 'Perceptions of "Peace Women" at Greenham Common 1981–5: A Participant's View' in S. MacDonald, P. Holden and S. Ardener (eds), *Images of Women in Peace and War* (London: Macmillan, 1987) p. 201.

21. Report of the Court Proceedings, reproduced in L. Jones (1987) p. 195.

22. B. Campbell, *The Iron Ladies: Why Do Women Vote Tory?* (London: Virago, 1987) pp. 125–6.

23. For details see B. Whisker, J. Bishop, L. Mohin and T. Longdon, *Breaching the Peace: A Collection of Radical Feminist Papers* (London: Onlywomen Press, 1983).

24. J. Liddington (1989) p. 215. L. Segal (1987) provides an in-depth analysis of the feminist peace movement.

25. See L. Segal (1987) Chap. 3 and J. Weeks, *Sexuality and its Discontents: Meanings, Myths and Modern Sexualities* (London: Routledge and Kegan Paul, 1985) pp. 231–6. S. Rowbotham (1989) Chap. 14, has many useful references to this topic.

26. B. Bryan *et al.* (1985) pp. 214 and 217.

27. L. Segal (1987) pp. 61–5.

28. Pearl in J. Miller (1986) p. 23.

29. Pearl in J. Miller (1986) p. 21.

30. Nita in J. Miller (1986) p. 42.

31. L. Segal (1987) pp. 231–3.

32. B. Campbell and A. Coote (1987) p. 181.

33. J. Miller (1986) p. 40.

34. For example, J. Mitchell, *Feminism and Psychoanalysis* (London: Allen Lane, 1974).

35. S. Walby, *Patriarchy at Work: Patriarchal and Capitalist Relations in Employment* (London: Polity, 1986), Chap. 1 summarizes these attempts.

36. For a summary of feminism and post-modernism see V. Bryson (1992) Chap. 12.
37. E. Meehan (1990) p. 196.
38. E. Meehan (1990) p. 196.
39. For details see B. Campbell and A. Coote (1987) pp. 122–3.
40. B. Campbell and A. Coote (1987) p. 134. The EOC budget for 1998/9 was £5.8 million. It has 170 employees. This information was kindly supplied by the EOC.
41. This legislation is outlined in B. Campbell (1987) pp. 103–5.
42. For details see *Equal Pay for Work of Equal Value: A Guide to the Amended Equal Pay Act* (Manchester: Equal Opportunities Commission, n.d, c. 1984).
43. *Fairness at Work, Consultation Paper* (London: Department of Trade and Industry, 1998) pp. 32–5.
44. See the leaflet *The Parental Leave Directive, What WILL It Mean to You?* (Manchester: Equal Opportunities Commission, October 1997).
45. For details see B. Campbell and A. Coote (1987) pp. 105–8.
46. B. Campbell and A. Coote (1987) p. 35.
47. P. Norris and J. Lovenduski, *Political Recruitment, Gender, Race and Class in the British Parliament* (Cambridge: Cambridge University Press, 1995) p. 103.
48. D. Butler and D. Kavanagh, *The British General Election of 1997* (London: Macmillan, 1997) p. 199. I am grateful to Helena Cole for help with the political statistics.
49. *Roots of the Future: Ethnic Diversity in the Making of Britain* (London: Commission for Racial Equality (CRE), 1997; first published 1996) p. 116.
50. J. Green (ed.), *Them, Voices from the Immigrant Community in Contemporary Britain* (London: Secker and Warburg, 1990) pp. 318–9.
51. J. Green (1990) p. 334 and Commission for Racial Equality (1997) p. 116.
52. J. Purvis, Editorial, *Women's History Review*, vol. 6, no. 3, 1997, p. 315.
53. For details see B. Campbell, *Diana, Princess of Wales, How Sexual Politics Shook the Monarchy* (London: Women's Press, 1998).
54. For details see the saturation press coverage from her death on 31 August 1997 until the funeral a week later.
55. Briefing Paper, *The Labour Market* (Manchester: Equal Opportunities Commission, 1997).
56. S. Walby, *Gender Transformations* (London: Routledge, 1997) p. 55.
57. M. Benn, 'The Future is Female', *The Guardian* (Saturday section) 8 August 1998, pp. 1–2.
58. B. Toner, *Double Shift, A Practical Guide for Working Mothers* (London: Arrow, 1975) p. 16.
59. B. Toner (1975) p. 26.

60. Briefing Paper, *Work and Parenting* (Manchester: Equal Opportunities Commission, 1997).
61. See *Challenging Inequalities between Women and Men: Twenty Years of Progress 1976–1996* (Manchester: Equal Opportunities Commission, 1996).
62. S. Walby (1997) p. 35.
63. S. Walby (1997) pp. 34–5.
64. R. Crompton, *Women and Work in Modern Britain* (Oxford: Oxford University Press, 1997) p. 119.
65. R. Crompton (1997) p. 120.
66. R. Crompton (1997) p. 119.
67. S. Dex, S. Lissenburgh and M. Taylor, *Women and Low Pay: Identifying the Issues* (Manchester: Equal Opportunities Commission, 1994) p. 31.
68. Briefing paper, *Pay,* (Manchester: Equal Opportunities Commission, 1996).
69. R. Crompton (1997) p. 82.
70. B. Campbell and A. Coote (1987) p. 72.
71. S. Dex *et al.* (1994) p. ix.
72. R. Crompton (1997) p. 87.
73. Reported in M. Benn, 'The New Motherhood', *The Guardian*, 2, 31 December 1997, p. 5, from an interview with L.L. Potter.
74. R. Crompton (1997) p. 72.
75. M. Freely (1998) p. 5.
76. R. Crompton (1997) p. 113.
77. S. Alexander, *Becoming a Woman* (London: Virago, 1994) p. 261. This is reproduced from *Red Rag*, no. 6, date given as '1973?'.
78. S. Rowbotham (1989) p. 221.
79. S. Rowbotham (1989) p. 227.
80. There is an interview with J. Desai in *Spare Rib*, January 1977, issue no. 54, p. 18.
81. S. Westwood, *All Day Every Day: Factory and Family in the Making of Women's Lives* (London: Pluto, 1984) Chap. 4.
82. S. Westwood (1984) p. 74.
83. S. Westwood (1984) p. 58. This applies to the bulk of the women. There was a small minority of very fast women workers who earned more under the system of 'Measured Day Work'.
84. S. Westwood (1984) p. 90.
85. B. Campbell and A. Coote (1987) p. 177.
86. S. Dex *et al.* (1994) p. 25.
87. S. Milne, 'After the Brothers Here's Sister', *The Guardian*, 2, 14 March 1998, pp. 2–3.
88. S. Milne (1988) p. 3.
89. D. Spender, *Invisible Women: The Schooling Scandal* (London: Women's Press, 1989; first published 1982) p. 54.
90. D. Spender (1989) p. 60.
91. S. Sharpe, *'Just Like a Girl': How Girls Learn to Be Women* (London: Penguin, 1976), gives evidence for this.

92. B. Dixon, *Catching Them Young Vol. 1: Sex, Race and Class in Children's Fiction* (London: Pluto, 1977) pp. 1–2.
93. B. Dixon (1977) p. 7.
94. A. Turnbull, J. Pollock and S. Bruley, 'History' in J. Whyld (ed.), *Sexism in the Secondary Curriculum* (London: Harper and Row, 1983).
95. A. Turnbull *et al.* (1983) p. 152.
96. A. Oakley, *Housewife* (London: Penguin, 1976; first published 1974) preface. A. Oakley has a more developed critique of sexism in sociology in *The Sociology of Housework* (Oxford: Blackwell, 1985; first published 1974) Chap. 1.
97. B. Bryan *et al.* (1985) pp. 85–6.
98. *Statistics of Education, Public Examinations GCSE/GNVQ in England 1997* (London: Department for Education and Employment, 1998) p. 9. Thanks to the EOC for supplying this information.
99. D. MacKinnon, J. Statham and M. Hales, *Education in the UK, Facts and Figures* (London: Hodder and Stoughton in association with the Open University, 1995) pp. 174–5.
100. S. Walby (1997) pp. 47–8.
101. S. Walby (1997) p. 46.
102. *Black and Ethnic Minority Women and Men in Britain 1994* (Manchester: Equal Opportunities Commission, 1994) p. 14.
103. A. Halsey (ed.), *British Social Trends since 1900* (London: Macmillan, 1988, 2nd edition) p. 278.
104. S. Walby (1997) p. 48.
105. A. Oakley (1976) p. 233.
106. A. Oakley (1976) p. 109.
107. Briefing paper, *Work and Parenting* (Manchester: Equal Opportunities Commission, 1997).
108. For the situation in 1976 see E. Stephen 'Out of the Closet into the Courts', *Spare Rib*, no. 50, 1976, reproduced in M. Rowe (1982) pp. 91–8.
109. As reported in C. Milhill, 'New Man Still Shunning Equal Share of Chores', *The Guardian*, 8 September 1997, p. 4.
110. C. Milhill, 'Women's Lot is Still Less Pay, More Work', *The Guardian*, 9 August 1995, p. 4, using data taken from *Social Focus on Women* (London: HMSO, 1995).
111. R. Crompton (1997), reporting work from R. Pahl (1984) p. 87.
112. C. Milhill (1995).
113. R. Scase and J. Scales, 'Single, Bright Female', *The Guardian*, 22 July 1998, pp. 6–7.
114. C. Mil hill (1995).
115. S. Sharpe (1976) p. 233. This book has a lengthy chapter on black girls in Britain in the 1970s.
116. EOC (1994) p. 10.
117. A. Wilson, *Finding a Voice: Asian Women in Britain* (London: Virago, 1978), Chap. II forms the basis for information on Asian family life

in this paragraph. There is also good coverage of this topic in
S. Westwood (1984).
118. S. Begum Mossabir, 'Making My Own Culture', in N. Kassam
(ed.), *Telling It Like It Is, Young Asian Women Talk* (London:
Women's Press, 1997) pp. 32–3.

Conclusion: Transforming Femininity, Transforming Masculinity

1. V. Bryson, *Feminist Political Theory* (London: Macmillan, 1992)
p. 261.
2. G. Bock and S. James, *Beyond Equality and Difference: Citizenship,
Feminist Politics and Female Subjectivity* (London: Routledge, 1992)
p. 196.
3. M. Benn, *Madonna and Child: Towards a New Politics of Motherhood*
(London: Cape, 1998); K. Figes, *Life after Birth – What Even Your
Friends Won't Tell You About Motherhood* (London: Viking 1998).
4. This point came from a discussion with Brenda Kirsch.
5. V. Bryson (1992) p. 231.
6. C. Ramazanoglu, 'Feminism and Liberation' in L. McDowell and
R. Pringle (eds), *Defining Women, Social Institutions and Gender
Divisions* (Cambridge: Polity Press in association with Blackwell and
The Open University, 1992) p. 288.
7. C. Bacchi, *Same Difference: Feminism and Sexual Difference* (London:
Unwin Hyman, 1990) p. 264.
8. J. Lewis, *Women in Britain since 1945* (Oxford: Blackwell, 1992)
p. 90.
9. C. Ramazanoglu (1992) p. 292.

FURTHER READING

This is a guide to basic texts for the reader new to the subject. For a complete list of all works used, including primary sources, readers are referred to the notes for each chapter.

J. Alberti *Beyond Suffrage: Feminists in War and Peace* (London, Macmillan, 1989).
What happened to feminism in the First World War and the 1920s.

J. Alberti *Eleanor Rathbone* (London: Sage, 1996).
Biography of the foremost inter-war feminist.

O. Banks *Faces of Feminism: A Study of Feminism as a Social Movement* (Oxford: Blackwell, 1981).
Survey of feminist movements in Britain and the USA.

D. Beddoes *Back to Home and Duty: Women Between the Wars* (London: Pandora, 1989).
Survey text.

L. Bland *Banishing the Beast: English Feminism and Sexual Morality 1885–1914* (Harmondsworth: Penguin, 1995).
Essential text for this period.

S. Boston *Women Workers and the Trade Unions* (London: Davis-Poynter, 1980).
Uses a lot of TUC archives, useful on strikes and the equal pay struggle.

G. Braybon and P. Summerfield *Out of the Cage: Women's Experiences in Two World Wars* (London: Pandora, 1987).
Focuses on women's consciousness rather than state policies, which is the focus for the authors' separate books.

G. Braybon *Women Workers in the First World War* (London: Croom Helm, 1981).
The basic text for this topic.

E. Breitenbach and E. Gordon (eds) *Out of Bounds, Women in Scottish Society 1800–1945* (Edinburgh: Edinburgh University Press, 1992).
Interesting collection, especially article on Scottish women's suffrage movement.

V. Brittain *Testament of Youth* (London: Gollancz, 1933; Virago edition 1978).
Classic account of the impact of the First World War on a young woman.

R. Broad and S. Fleming (eds) *Nella Last's War, a Mother's Diary* (Bristol: Falling Wall, 1981).
War diary, with some revealing insights.

P. Brookes *Women at Westminster* (London: Peter Davies, 1967).
Survey of women MPs from 1918 to the 1960s.

S. Bruley 'Gender, Class and Party: The Communist Party and the Crisis in the Cotton Industry between the Two World Wars in England', *Women's History Review*, Vol. 2, no. 1, 1993.
Analysis of the Communist Party's approach to women through its involvement with women weavers in a period of crisis.

B. Bryan, S. Dadzie and S. Scafe *The Heart of the Race: Black Women's Lives in Britain* (London: Virago, 1985).
A moving account of how racism has shaped the lives of black women in Britain.

V. Bryson *Feminist Political Theory, An Introduction* (London: Macmillan, 1992).
Very readable, makes even post-modernism comprehensible.

B. Campbell and A. Coote *Sweet Freedom, The Struggle for Women's Liberation* (Oxford: Blackwell, 1987).
Broad-ranging analysis of 'second-wave' feminism and its impact.

B. Campbell *The Iron Ladies: Why do Women Vote Tory?* (London: Virago, 1987).
Feminist analysis of Thatcherism and its appeal to women.

D. Chew (ed.) *The Life and Writings of Ada Nield Chew* (London: Virago, 1982).
The life of a remarkable working woman who became a socialist-feminist activist in the suffrage period.

J. Costello *Love, Sex and War, Changing Values 1939–1945* (London: Pan, 1985).
A racy account, using American as well as British material.

R. Crompton *Women and Work in Modern Britain* (Oxford: Oxford University Press, 1997).
Theoretical and empirical account which summarizes recent sociological work.

A. Davin 'Imperialism and Motherhood', *History Workshop Journal*, no. 5, Spring 1978.
Seminal essay on 'social imperialism'.

M. Llewelyn Davies (ed.) *Maternity: Letters from Working Women* (London: Virago edition, 1978).
Vivid accounts of the conditions of maternity before 1914 by members of the Women's Co-operative Guild.

W. Foley *A Child in the Forest* (London: BBC, 1979).
Lovely autobiography from the Forest of Dean between the wars.

R. Gamble *Chelsea Child, An Autobiography* (London: BBC, 1979).
Graphic account of growing up in one room in Chelsea between the wars.

L. Garner *Stepping Stones to Women's Liberty: Feminist Ideas in the Women's Suffrage Movement 1900–1918* (London: Heinemann Educational, 1984).
Devotes a chapter to each of the suffrage organizations.

H. Gavron *The Captive Wife, Conflicts of Housebound Mothers* (Harmondsworth: Penguin, 1966).
Path-breaking text breaking the mould of postwar liberal optimistic sociology of the family.

J. Giles *Women, Identity and Private Life in Britain, 1900–1950* (London: Macmillan, 1995).
Focuses on domesticity, especially inter-war period.

D. Gittins *Fair Sex, Family Size and Structure, 1900–1939* (London: Hutchinson, 1982).
Detailed analysis of working-class declining fertility.

M. Glucksmann *Women Assemble: Women Workers and the New Industries in Inter-war Britain* (London: Routledge, 1990).
The growth of the 'new industries' from a socialist-feminist perspective.

P. Graves *Labour Women, Women in British Working Class Politics 1918–1939* (Cambridge: Cambridge University Press, 1994).
Analysis of women in the Labour Party between the wars.

A. Hall *Land Girl, Her Story of Six Years in the Women's Land Army, 1940–1946* (Trowbridge: Ex Libris, 1993).
Biographical account.

Hall Carpenter Archives/Lesbian Oral History Group *Inventing Ourselves, Lesbian Life Stories* (London: Routledge, 1989).
Lesbian testimony from 1930s, but mainly contemporary.

R. Hall *The Well of Loneliness* (London: Cape, 1928; Virago edition, 1982).
Lesbian novel which created a furore resulting in a famous trial.

B. Harford and S. Hopkins (eds) *Greenham Common: Women at the Wire* (London: Women's Press, 1984).
One of the many books on Greenham Common; contains useful chronology.

B. Harrison *Prudent Revolutionaries, Portraits of British Feminists between the Wars* (Oxford: Clarendon, 1987).
Biographical accounts of well-connected inter-war feminists.

L. Heron (ed.) *Truth, Dare or Promise: Girls growing Up in the 50s* (London: Virago, 1985).
Personal testimony on girls in the 1950s.

J. Hinton 'Militant Housewives: The British Housewives' League and the Attlee Government', *History Workshop Journal*, no. 38, Autumn 1994.
Detailed account of a little-known grass-roots movement.

S. Holton *Feminism and Democracy: Women's Suffrage and Reform Politics in Britain 1900–1918* (Cambridge: Cambridge University Press, 1986).
The basic text for the non-militant suffrage movement.

S. Kingsley Kent *Making Peace: The Reconstruction of Gender in Interwar Britain* (Princeton: Princeton University Press, 1993).
Places gender at the heart of a new perspective on the impact of the First World War on British society.

V. Klein *Britain's Married Women Workers* (London: Routledge and Kegan Paul, 1965).
Empirical study of women workers in the 1950s and early 1960s.

S. Lewenhak *Women and Trade Unions: An Outline of the History of Women in the British Trade Union Movement* (London: E. Benn, 1977).
(Comments as for Boston.)

J. Lewis *The Politics of Motherhood, Child and Maternal Welfare in England 1900–1939* (London: Croom Helm 1980).
The basic text for this topic.

J. Lewis *Women in Britain since 1945* (Oxford: Blackwell 1992).
Useful analysis of changes in work, family and state.

J. Liddington *The Life and Times of a Respectable Rebel, Selina Cooper 1864–1946* (London: Virago, 1984).
Biography of a leading activist in the radical suffrage movement who later fought fascism.

J. Liddington *The Long Road to Greenham: Feminism and Anti-militarism in Britain since 1820* (London Virago, 1989).
Broad survey of pacifism and feminism.

A. Light *Forever England: Femininity, Literature and Conservatism between the Wars* (London: Routledge, 1991).
A new view of conservatism in the inter-war years.

S. Maitland (ed.) *Very Heaven: Looking Back at the 1960s* (London: Virago 1988).
Personal testimony from a wide range of women.

J. Marcus *Suffrage and the Pankhursts* (London: Routledge and Kegan Paul, 1987).
Original sources from the militant suffrage movement, combined with a revisionist introduction.

B. McBryde *A Nurse's War* (Saffron Walden: Cakebreads, 1993).
Biographical account, World War Two.

R. Minns *Bombers and Mash: The Domestic Front 1939–1945* (London: Virago 1980).
Detailed account of the 'home front' in World War Two.

H. Mitchell *The Hard Way Up* (London: Virago, 1977).
Autobiography of a working-class socialist suffragette.

S. Neild and R. Pearson *Women Like Us* (London: Women's Press, 1992).
Lesbian testimony from the 1950s to the 1980s.

A. Oakley *Housewife* (Harmondsworth: Pelican, 1976, first published Allen Lane, 1974).
Feminist sociological analysis of domesticity in the 1970s.

S. Oldfield *This Working Day World, Women's Lives and Cultures 1914–45* (London: Taylor and Francis, 1994).
Useful collection of short articles on a wide variety of topics, including women artists.

E.S. Pankhurst *The Suffragette Movement, An Intimate Account of Persons and Ideals* (London: Virago edition, 1977).
Very long narrative account which should be read in conjunction with J. Marcus.

M. Powell *Below Stairs* (London: Peter Davies, 1968).
Lively biography of a domestic servant.

M. Pugh *Women and the Women's Movement in Britain 1914–1959* (London: Macmillan, 1992).
Very detailed treatment of inter-war politics.

J. Purvis *A History of Women's Education in England* (Milton Keynes: Open University, 1991).
Useful account of the development of women's education.

M.P. Reeves *Round About a Pound a Week* (London: Virago edition, 1979).
Classic primary source on household budgets before the First World War.

D. Riley *War in the Nursery: Theories of the Child and Mother* (London: Virago, 1983).
Definitive account of Second World War nursery provision and after.

E. Roberts *A Woman's Place: An Oral History of Working Class Women 1890–1940*, (Oxford: Blackwell, 1984).
Oral history from three northern towns, focusing on daily life and work.

E. Roberts *Women and Families: An Oral History, 1940–1970* (Oxford: Blackwell, 1995).
Similar to the above, but for the post-war period.

P. Romero E. *Sylvia Pankhurst, Portrait of a Radical* (New Haven: Yale University Press, 1990).
Biography of one of the century's most formidable socialist-feminists.

S. Rowbotham *A New World for Women: Stella Browne – Socialist Feminist* (London: Pluto, 1977).
Biography of a pioneering socialist-feminist and sexual radical.

S. Rowbotham *The Past Is before Us, Feminism in Action since the 1960s* (London: Pandora, 1989).
In-depth account of 'second-wave' feminism.

D. Russell *The Tamarisk Tree: My Quest for Liberty and Love* (London: Virago, 1977).
Biography of a birth-control activist and socialist-feminist intellectual.

L. Segal *Is the Future Female? Troubled Thoughts on Contemporary Feminism* (London: Virago, 1987).
Controversial and challenging analysis of 1980s feminism.

D. Sheridan (ed.) *Wartime Women: A Mass Observation Anthology* (London: Heinemann, 1990).
Useful collection from the Mass Observation archives.

J. Stacey *Star Gazing: Hollywood Cinema and Female Spectatorship* (London: Routledge, 1994).
A cultural history of the impact of Hollywood stars and glamour.

E. Summerskill, *A Woman's World, Her Memoirs* (London: Heinemann, 1967).
Autobiography of a feminist MP and Minister.

P. Summerfield *Women Workers in the Second World War* (London: Croom Helm, 1984) .
The basic text for this topic.

E. Taylor *Heroines of World War Two* (London: Robert Hale, 1991).
Includes material on women secret agents.

D. Thom 'The Bundle of Sticks: Women Trade Unionists and Collective Organisation before 1918', in A. John (ed.) *Unequal Opportunities: Women's Employment in England 1800–1918* (1986).
A break from the traditional labour history perspective.

L. Tickner *The Spectacle of Women: Imagery of the Suffrage Campaign* (London; Chatto and Windus, 1987).
A cultural analysis of the visual imagery of the women's movement.

C. and E. Townsend *War Wives: A Second World War Anthology* (London: Grafton, 1990).
Testimony, using short extracts from a large number of women, including German women's experience of war.

C. Tylee *The Great War and Women's Consciousness: Images of Militarism and Feminism in Women's Writings, 1914–1964* (London: Macmillan, 1989).
Comprehensive account, both pacifist and pro-war.

B. Vernon *Ellen Wilkinson 1891–1947* (London: Croom Helm, 1982).
Biography of the fiery Labour MP and Minister.

S. Walby *Gender Transformations* (London: Routledge, 1997).
Analysis of women's position in the 1990s.

S. Walby *Patriarchy at Work* (London: Polity Press, 1986).
Feminist analysis of women and work from the late nineteenth century.

M. Wandor (ed.) *Once a Feminist: Stories of a Generation* (London: Virago, 1990).
Firsthand accounts of 'women's liberation movement' activists of the 1970s.

J. Weeks *Sex, Politics and Society: The Regulation of Sexuality since 1800* (Harlow: Longman, 1981).
Survey which puts social movements into a broad contextual and analytical frame.

S. Westwood *All Day, Every Day: Factory and Family in the Making of Women's Lives* (London: Pluto, 1984).
Lively and analytical account, including material on Asian women.

A. Wilson *Finding a Voice: Asian Women in Britain* (London: Virago, 1978).
Detailed and moving account.

E. Wilson *Only Halfway to Paradise: Women in Postwar Britain, 1945–1968* (London: Tavistock, 1980).
Broad-ranging, includes cultural history.

B. Winslow *Sylvia Pankhurst: Sexual Politics and Political Activism* (London: University College of London, 1996).
Concentrates on Pankhurst's involvement with London's East End.

Index

feminists/feminism (*continued*)
  education groups, 171
  internal differences, 180
  theory, 157–8
Ferguson, Mrs (Partick), 55
Figes, Kate, 179
Finch, Janet, 132–3
Finding a Voice, Asian Women in Britain (1978), 176
Firestone, Shulamith, 148
First Aid Nursing Yeomanry (FANY), 102
First World War, 37–58
  casualties in, 53
  conscription in, 53
  gendered patriotism in, 47
  strikes outlawed in, 39
  women workers in, 38–43, 55
  working conditions in, 41
Fishwick, Gertrude, 143
Flather, Shreela, 161–2
Fletcher, Ronald, 132
Foley, Winifred, 63, 75
Food, Ministry of, 111
football teams, women's, 56
force-feeding, 32–3
Ford, Isabella, 18, 26, 27, 49, 52
Ford equal pay strike (1968), 126–7
Freewoman, The (journal), 14
Freud, Sigmund, 76
Friedan, Betty, 145–6
fundamentalism, 181

Gallagher, Claire, 175
Gamble, Rose, 73
Garner, Les, 35
Gavron, Hannah, 133–4
Gay Liberation, 151
gender
  backlash, 70
  divisions, 171, 180
  gendered patriotism in First World War, 47
  segregation in employment, 164, 165, 167
General Election of 1966, 142

General, Municipal, Boilermakers and Allied Trades Union (GMBATU), 169
General and Municipal Workers Union (GMWU), 61
Giles, Judy, 72, 76–7
Girl Guides, 106
girls
  absence from school, 16
  curriculum, 16–17
  education, 15–18, 68, 127–8, 169–72, 198 n.37, 198 n.39
  grammar schools, 128
  higher education, 17–18, 128
  under-performance at school, 169–70, 172
GIs, 114, 115
  black, 115
Glucksmann, Miriam, 67
grammar schools, girls', 128
Graves, Pamela, 83, 89
Great Scourge and How To End It, The (1913), 14
Great War and Women's Consciousness, The (1989), 38
Greater London Council (GLC), 160
Greenham Common, 154–5
Greer, Germaine, 150
Grieg, Teresa Billington, 34
Grigg, Sir James, 107
Grunwick strike (1976–7), 168
Guardian, The (newspaper), 144, 175

Hague Congress, 52–3, 88, 188 n.58
Hall, Anne, 104
Hall, Catherine, 13
Hall, Radclyffe, 15, 78
Hamilton, Cecily, 13
Hamilton, Peggy, 40
Hannam, June, 26
Hannington, Wal, 65
Hargraves, Amy, 65
Haskins, Ada, 77
Hawkes, Jacquetta, 144
Health, Ministry of, 96–7